W9-DER-783

The Library
INTERNATIONAL CHRISTIAN
GRADUATE UNIVERSITY

The Leadership Passion
A Psychology of Ideology

David Loye

The Leadership Passion

Jossey-Bass Publishers
San Francisco · Washington · London · 1977

THE LEADERSHIP PASSION
A Psychology of Ideology
        by David Loye

Copyright © 1977 by: Jossey-Bass, Inc., Publishers
                    615 Montgomery Street
                    San Francisco, California 94111
                            &
                    Jossey-Bass Limited
                    44 Hatton Garden
                    London EC1N 8ER

Copyright under International, Pan American, and
Universal Copyright Conventions. All rights
reserved. No part of this book may be reproduced
in any form—except for brief quotation (not to
exceed 1,000 words) in a review or professional
work—without permission in writing from the publishers.

Library of Congress Catalogue Card Number LC 76-45481

International Standard Book Number ISBN 0-87589-302-3

Manufactured in the United States of America

JACKET DESIGN BY WILLI BAUM

FIRST EDITION

Code 7618

The Library
INTERNATIONAL CHRISTIAN
GRADUATE UNIVERSITY

BF
637
L434
L923
1977

The Jossey-Bass
Behavioral Science Series

30211

ABOUT THE AUTHOR

David Loye, a graduate of Dartmouth College, received his M.A. in the psychology of personality and his Ph.D. in social psychology from The New School for Social Research. Formerly with the psychology department at Princeton University, he is presently research director of the Program on Psycho-social Adaptation and the Future, Department of Psychiatry, School of Medicine, University of California at Los Angeles. He is the author of *The Healing of a Nation* (Norton, 1971; Delta, 1972), which received the Anisfield-Wolf Award in 1971.

Preface

Our stability and happiness as individuals and as nations seem heavily dependent on the extent to which both social science and social leadership can find answers to two increasingly pressing questions. The first is a question of ideological (or systematically predictable) social directions: Where are we headed? The second is a question of individual psychology and leadership styles: Can we shape the future to desirable ends, or are we helplessly adrift?

For many years the study of the psychology of ideology has been greatly neglected while all about us mounts evidence of its social relevance (for example, the ideological disparities of humanistic leadership policies and the factual deceit, corruption, and inhumanism of Vietnam and Watergate). Why then this neglect? One reason is that psychology as a field has been going through a prolonged disassembly of the "parts" of human nature for ever closer and finer inspection, but the psychology of ideology requires a major effort in the other direction—that is, reassembly of the parts into larger, and more socially useful, wholes, a task this book attempts.

Our major purpose in *The Leadership Passion* is to try to

regain a lost sense of ideological bearings during a time of great psychological and sociological change. To this end we have surveyed 180 years of thought and research bearing on the relationships between ideology in the individual and social leadership and management styles. We reexamine theoretical views of Hegel, Nietzsche, Pareto, Weber, Freud and Pavlov; the "classic" psychological studies of Adorno, Rokeach, Eysenck, and Tomkins; and a widely diversified new range of studies. Variables receiving major attention include liberalism-conservatism, risk taking, alienation, anomie, extremism, activism, Machiavellianism, locus of control, as well as leader-follower, parent-child, and age generational relationships. Results are then used to shape recent original studies of campus leadership elites in training at Princeton University and older West Coast men and women during the 1976 presidential primaries.

Our findings support important new models of ideological functioning, including the framework for a new dialectical theory of personality and social change based on norm changing versus norm maintaining; a new perspective on alienation and anomie, relating the first to Marx and norm changing and the second to Durkheim and norm maintaining; ideological functions of risk taking; clarification of the muddled concept of locus of control; and relation of Rokeach, Osgood, and Winter theoretical models to the structure of ideology. To make these complex findings meaningful in terms of "real life," we show how they emerge in the development of personality through parent-child relationships, and how they apply in fully active adult life to problems of major concern to social science and social leadership.

In Part One we examine left-right goals in historical leadership and the "end to ideology" debate (Chapter One), and reexamine theoretical views of Hegel, Nietzsche, Marx, Pareto, Weber, Freud, Pavlov, and the early development of a psychology of ideology (Chapter Two).

Part Two explores the pioneering Adorno, Rokeach, and Eysenck studies, factor analysis, and the neglected major theory of Silvan Tomkins (Chapter Three). We then outline the potential of new work by Greenstein, Wilson, Comrey, the "Tomkinsonians," Rokeach's new equality-freedom model of political ideology, the "new holism" of Hampden-Turner and Knutson, studies of activism and extremism, and especially Maslow's self-actualizing theory (Chapter Four).

Part Three describes the training of leadership elites at Princeton University, with portraits of liberals and conservatives (Chapter Five), and examines extreme and moderate liberal and conservative groups (Chapter Six).

Part Four outlines hypotheses for empirical exploration. These include our norm-changing versus norm-maintaining theoretical framework; a "core" to ideology composed of liberalism-conservatism, activism-inactivism, and extremism-moderation; and a "periphery" including risk taking, Machiavellianism, alienation, anomie, locus of control, and parent-child developmental variables (Chapter Seven). We describe study measure developed by Adorno, Tomkins, Kogan and Wallach, Stouffer and Toby, Christie, Rotter, and Loye (Chapter Eight); detail correlational, factor, and item analytic findings and use analysis of variance to identify personality dynamics (Chapter Nine); and explore meanings for theorists of "core" and "periphery" findings and outline needs for further research (Chapter Ten). This section concludes with our replication of key findings through a West Coast follow-up study conducted during the heat of the 1976 presidential primary—a study which also extends our findings into age, sex, occupational, regional, and leader-follower differences (Chapter Eleven).

Part Five relates findings to major "real life" problems for educators, therapists, personality and social psychologists, sociologists, economists, political scientists, political leaders, welfare and defense analysts, futurists, and business and governmental managers (Chapter Twelve). We next develop the case for new three- and four-dimensional models of ideological functioning relating to models of Osgood, Winter, and the Rokeach equality-freedom model (Chapter Thirteen). For the consideration of social scientists, philosophers, historians, and concerned leadership, our final chapter (Fourteen) then speculatively probes the question we raise of social direction.

It is our hope that this examination of the "leadership

passion" may lead to a better understanding of the flow of history and thereby to a better reading and shaping of the future. In Chapter Fourteen, we seek beneath the manifest surface of the "end-of-ideology" debate for latent meanings. We find a suggestive gap between psychological and sociological man, wherein ideology persists relatively unchanged in the former, but in the other is fluid, searching, and uncertain. This split in ideological functioning suggests we are undergoing a fundamental shift in ideological and leadership styles with profound implications for our future. Indeed, it may be the third major shift in basic ideological style in the history of humanity. It is our belief, based in part on this study, that following a first stage of thousands of years of the traditional dominance of conservatism, and a second stage of a few hundred years of the liberal release of the individual, we are moving into a new dominating "middle" style of ideology. In our last chapter, we attempt to define the nature of this style and the future it portends.

The reference to "psychological and sociological *man*" above is not intended to be sex explicit. For understandable reasons many readers are sensitive to the use of the word *man*, as well as to the traditional use of the masculine pronouns *he* and *his*. In this book I have substituted *person, individual,* or *human* for *man* and have tried to avoid masculine pronouns, unless doing so would falsify thought or be self-defeating. When *man* is used, it is because *man* is the species, and no other word adequately conveys this concept in certain contexts.

I am indebted to many for help with this book. Above all are Silvan Tomkins and Milton Rokeach. Without the inspiration of their work and their encouragement, I doubt whether I could have sustained the obsession producing this volume and others in progress.

I want to thank Nathan Kogan, chairman of my dissertation committee at the New School for Social Research, and members Shirley Weitz and Nathan Brody, for prolonged guidance in tracking through the main Princeton study reported here; Klaus Riegel for key emotional and philosophical support and Robert Kraut for helpful suggestions; Educational Testing Service of Princeton, N.J., for dissertation and data processing support—in particular Donald Rock, Ernest Anastasio, Donald Rubin, John Barone, and John Narducci; Richard Whittle, Nathaniel Hartshorne, and Elizabeth Dolmat for editorial and morale support; Jocelyn Jacks and Trudy Krohn for their fine typing; Tracy Gildmeister for aid in indexing.

For their aid in conducting the Princeton study I am indebted beyond expression to literally hundreds of young volunteers and my own students there. Unfortunately, the full lists are buried in an attic far away as I write, so I must rely on memory only (but still plan to list all participants in a future volume). Thanks especially to John Adams, Arthur Bergeron, Thomas Montebell, Paul Wilson, T. Harding Jones, David Versfelt, Gerald Raymond, Ronald Levine, and Henry Furst. Thanks also to Robert Van de Velde, old friend, and to Woodrow Wilson School; to Michael Shepherd and Whig-Clio, for providing test facilities and personnel; and to Princeton University for providing a home for this research during my all-too-brief teaching association with a remarkable psychology department faculty.

Lastly, my thanks for many kinds of support to my wife, Billy, and to my cohorts on The Program for Psychosocial Adaptation and the Future, Department of Psychiatry, UCLA School of Medicine—Roderic Gorney, director, Gary Steele, Katherine Baum, John Long, Charles Swagman, and in particular Lawrence Landers who, with the UCLA Campus Computing Network and advisory facilities, carried out the data processing for Chapter Ten.

Los Angeles, California   David Loye
November 1976

Contents

Part Four   The Ideological Personality in Theory

Part Five   Implications for Social Scientists, Therapists, Leaders, and Managers

Figures
and Tables

Figures

xvii

Tables

The Leadership Passion
A Psychology of Ideology

1

Of Ideology and the "Leadership Passion"

ᵉᵉ**S**omething there is that doesn't love a wall," Robert Frost once wrote. The same nameless adversity seems to work against the study of the psychology of ideology. Its "father," Machiavelli, is today damned everywhere for a knave, yet in reality he was a humane and sensitive artist hard put to survive among Renaissance cutthroats. Karl Marx, who established the term ideology, was hounded by the police from country to country while at times his high-born wife and children nearly starved. The first great psychologist of ideology, Frederich Nietzsche, went mad. Its great systems engineer, the proud Vilfredo Pareto, was chiefly remembered by the neighbors as the man whose wife ran away with his chauffeur. Max Weber was tortured for years by the charismatic appeal of ideological involvement in conflict with his scientific need for noninvolvement. Sigmund Freud was denounced by fervent

1

admirers for a majestic pronouncement, which he felt laid bare
the core of ideological meaning. This thought has overtones of
the old tale of the mummy's curse, but it is as though there is
something deep within us which must cut off pursuit of a
psychology of ideology by the unintimidated mind. It is as
though we sense the search could lead to a violation of the tem-
ple wherein are kept the ultimate secrets of self and society.
And so in this book we ask, what is this subject that generates
strange passions and has clouded so many well-known lives?

On the surface, the study of the psychology of ideology
hardly seems earth shaking. In fact, what we know of it today
suggests beginnings for a rather idyllic tale. From earliest times
it appears we have puzzled over the sides of our nature we call
liberal and conservative. On bad days for primitive man, when
beasts or enemies threatened, a conservative side concerned
with defending himself and his belongings had to prevail. On
good days, however, when the sun shone brightly and the forest
beckoned, he was impelled from the safety of his own territory
not solely by the need for food, but by a more general need to
search for new visual, auditory, tactile, and conceptual stimuli.
Within the group life of the tribe, these motivations were mir-
rored in a pattern of "conservative" elders, whose function was
to defend the traditional ways, in conflict with more venturesome, youthful power seekers. Over time then, as civilizations
rose and fell, these sides to human nature seem to have become
the basis for the complex permutations of left and right that
underlie political, economic, and social processes, and provide a
subject for the psychological study of ideology.

While left-right ideology within us was of relatively quiet
interest to observers of personality and small-group differences,
its large-scale social counterparts aroused passionate hopes and
fears. There was, for example, a disquieting pattern to the flow
of political, economic, and social life; exciting but disruptive
periods of advancement alternated with restful but often boring
periods of little change—or with alarming periods of brutal regression. Although baffling to the masses, who had to take
whatever the life of their times offered, this patterning was of
great interest to leaders and managerial elites because of their

unique relation to ideology and social change. Rather than having to take whatever life offered, they had both the opportunity and the obligation to try to shape life to our advantage. That is, it is leadership's function to intervene in the social flow to direct change toward ends that are favorable to the leader and his organization or group. Depending on the nature of the flow, this means the good leader can activate ideology and mobilize a cohort to maintain the prevailing order against its enemies, or reimpose order out of chaos, or shatter the prevailing order to create a new order. The heretic pharoah Akhenaton, who for a brief time (1375-1358 B.C.) forced radical change upon Egypt, was a "liberal" order shatterer. Charlemagne, who bound up the tatters of fallen Rome into the Frankish empire, was a "conservative" order reimposer.

Over history then, we may see the growth of this ambivalent interest—part fascination, part fear—in ideology as a forceful composite of our being. Within individuals it emerges as ideas and behavior expressing right-versus-left motivation and values. Within groups it appears in leadership styles, tactics, and goals. And bridging individual and group is the concern about power—how to use it to advance ourselves or our fellow beings. Hence our view of ideology as "the leadership passion." "We speak of 'embracing an idea,' " Bertrand de Jouvenel writes of this power-oriented eroticism of intellect. "The embraced idea becomes the mistress of our inner life; we value other ideas in relation to it, and feel in the wrong if our behavior should betray it. We are in love with the idea, and this is a most important point. This emotional attitude of ours governs our political ideas, and even applies to scientific ideas" (de Jouvenel, 1967, p. 257).

Our concern in this book is not with sex, but with motivational stability and change. Freud's insight into sex as both a pervasive drive and a forceful analogy for "nonsexual" motivation, however, is meaningful here. Thus we may note a revealing range of expression for "the leadership passion." Love of country is not only considered patriotism at its best, but is a basis for political union. We cluster to what is familiar like chicks to the hen. However, it is no accident that this love becomes savage when pressured by events. History fairly staggers beneath the weight of atrocities committed in the name of patriotism—generally accompanied by erotic butchery and invasion. Thus, rape of the enemy's women routinely accompanies conquest; the Nazis performed their unspeakable perversions on the alien Jews; and in the United States the castration of blacks and black sympathizers, with or without lynching, was into recent times standard treatment by southern patriots for invaders. It is between these extremes that the passion of interest to us prevails. This passion is best stated as a matter of *caring* and *valuing*. It is further characterized by its consistency; it does not erratically come and go, but is sustained in direction. It is also notably holistic in vision, that is, it is a caring for *wholes*, transcending the boundaries between person and person, self and other. It is also shaped by tender- as well as toughmindedness.

Until fairly recently this "leadership passion" operated as a unity within the living personality, as a force whose meaning as a whole was considerably greater than its parceling into the psychological versus the sociological, or the scientific versus managerial perspectives. In modern times this holism of caring began with Hegel in Europe, Jefferson, Franklin, and Hamilton in America, thereafter working forward into our time through Marx, Pareto, Weber, and Freud. With the splitting of psychology, sociology, political science, philosophy, and history into increasingly self-contained disciplines, however, this earlier holistic, and passionate, concern with public affairs fell apart.

While this passion disintegrated among scholars, it also dissolved in political leaders and managers of businesses, schools, cities, churches, charities, and all other contemporary institutions. As numerous studies attest, specialization and bureaucracy, by limiting the purview of the individual, have made it increasingly difficult for leaders and managers to have any comprehensive grasp of, or to personally care for, the organizations for which they are responsible. As a consequence, leadership now often consists of a posturing of decision, optimism, and caring in order to gain or hold power, while in fact the ostensible leader has secretly abandoned both himself and us to the flow of potentially disastrous events.

In short, we have reached a juncture in the history of man-kind where both social science and social leadership is frag-mented, with a minimal sense of direction, while all about us mount huge problems bearing on our survival that can be solved only by the arousal of thoughtful people and great leadership. When confronted with such large-scale social dilemmas in the past, leadership mobilized itself, a cohort, and at times the masses to regain holism and passion by appropriating or encour-aging the development of these belief and value systems we call ideologies (Loye and Rokeach, 1976). One purpose of this expedient was to create some useful order out of a conceptual and motivational drift that failed to come to grips with social reality. Other purposes were to provide social guidance through a new articulation of goals and a firm sense of direction, and to provide a social "head of steam" or motivational thrust.

Leadership responses of these types brought us religious and political ideologies that still govern loosely today, such as Christianity, democracy, communism. However, we appear to be going through one of those vast transitional times for human-ity distinguished by a sense of the inadequacy of established ideologies and a search for new ones—a time of fishing for either radical departures or the transformation of earlier forms. This is the surface to the matter that endless headlines force upon our consciousness. At a deeper, symbolic level, it is as though this leadership passion in man and in woman, like our sex drives and all other intense emotions, must fasten itself to love objects, as though it cannot wander for long unfulfilled, but must achieve holism. Today—and we return to this theme in our last chapter—mankind seems adrift seeking new love objects. As with the sexual forays of adolescence and middle age, where this search may lead is cause for both hope and concern.

It is a time when, through the shattering of earlier unities, disintegration threatens to outrun integration. Hence the pur-pose of this book is to help provide a crucial integration for the scholar and serious student of psychology, sociology, political science, economics, or history, and of educational, governmen-tal, and business management or leadership. In keeping with Kurt Lewin's vision, it seems to us *a central task for the social scientist in this transitional time is to help train leadership and to help leaders and organizational managers solve the horrendous problems of passage which they and we face.* At the heart of these problems lie not only all the highly-publicized external facts of pollution, corruption, famine, the dangers of atomic annihilation and economic disaster, but also the grossly neglected internal facts of this leadership passion and its needs. In this book we hope to clarify the relation of ideology to our survival by beginning to reintegrate the study of left-right motivation and values with the study of political, economic, social, and educational leadership and management.

No doubt some will feel that by trying to span the diverse worlds of thought and action, we bring too much that is extraneous or peripheral into a psychology of ideology. But contrary to our need to chop reality into ever more minute portions, the psychology of ideology is not limited, as some would have it, solely to politics or religion. It operates in literally all lines of work, all types of social activities—in our schools, businesses, clubs, in our marriages and families, and if the predispositions of childhood be rightfully viewed, in all ages. Moreover, its study cannot be confined to the established psychological arena in the same way its components of motivation, attitudes, beliefs, values, and behavior can. As both the pattern to history and the needs of the time suggest, an adequate psychology of ideology must also examine the psychology of leadership styles and management philosophies. Ultimately, it must also deal with the pros and cons of that crucial interface between psychology, sociology, and society represented by the concepts of social management, social engineering, or *directed* social change (Coleman, 1971).

This book records, then, the beginning of a recent search for new answers to both old and new questions about ideology. One new question to which we will devote special attention is why during the 1950s and 1960s, the idea of "the end of ideology" became such a heated issue for world scholarly debate (Bell, 1960; Waxman, 1968). The general thrust to "end-of" views was that ideology is disappearing from mankind's affairs because it is no longer an adequate social-promotional or governing mechanism. In other words, it was contended that right ideologies of fascism and conservatism, and left ideologies of liberalism and communism—both laden with counter-directional motivations and values—are being replaced by a nonideological pragmatism forced on all leaders by the nature of our political, economic, and social tasks. These tasks, it was claimed, have been narrowed by historical and technological development to those that can only be successfully solved by an emotion- and value-free rationality, or in other words, by technocrats.

The fact that during the 1960s and 1970s this philosophy underlay both the economic and social disaster of the U.S. war effort in Indo-China and the political disaster of the Nixon administration indicates a problem with this view. Large social tasks still seem to be best solved by large men rather than by small men masquerading as large machines. However, the question remains, Why did the idea of an "end of ideology" generate so much controversy among social philosophers? What might the answer be, not in terms of a verbal tangle of sociological definitions (Mannheim versus Marx, and so on), but in terms of a rigorously quantified *psychology* of ideology? This book reports the search for such a psychology through studies of the development of personality, motivation, attitudes, values, and leadership styles. It also seeks, through such a search, to resolve a portentous contradiction within scholarship, to which we will return in our closing chapter—the ideological gap between psychological and sociological man, or the problem of free-floating passion and the future.

It is this gap, and our placement at a watershed time historically, which indicates we may be undergoing the third major shift in basic ideological and leadership styles in the multi-thousand year history of our species. It is a prospect that long ago Hegel and others foresaw, yet in a clouded way. Today it seems at last within the power and grasp of modern social science to clarify.

2

Left and Right

$\mathcal{S}$ociety may be usefully viewed
as both a surface and underlying mechanisms. As a "surface" of
people and their activities it presents to us a baffling complexity. Science's liberating purpose is to seek beneath this surface
for the structure and dynamics of variables that make it intelligible. Modern social science, however, is so laden with problems of perception and communication that the probe often
obfuscates more than it liberates. To cut through these difficulties to reach the structure and dynamics of ideology, three simple questions may be asked: What is this social thing we ride?
Where is it headed? Is there anything we can do about it?

The automobile is a useful analogy for a social predica-
ment that is frightening because so few can rise above these surfaces which enmesh us, scholar and layman alike, to view it with
clear eyes. If you bring a certain kind of knowledge to the automobile, it will serve you well. However, if you only bring to it
ignorance, it may kill you. You may know that it will start by
turning an ignition key and by stepping on the accelerator, but
what if you lack knowledge of how to operate the steering

wheel? Or the brakes? Or the gears? And can you ever hope to *drive* the car if all you know is how to be a passenger?

Each of these familiar auto parts and operations has its analogue in the functioning of ideology and the responsibilities of leadership. To gain an understanding of their interactions—or of the *mechanics* of ideology and social change—was the purpose of a few great early thinkers. Their motivation came from their recognition that at stake was not simply a matter of scholarship, *but of social life or death.* As the clarity of their perspectives is generally lost today through overspecialization, let us reground ourselves in what they perceived.

In philosophy, Hegel sought the dynamics of change in the dialectic and Nietzsche in the opposition of the Appollonian and the Dionysian man. In sociology, Karl Marx added a brilliant psychology and the class-struggle view to the dialectic; Vilfredo Pareto investigated the circulation of the "conservative" Lion and the "liberal" Fox elites; and Max Weber probed the impact of personal charisma on history. In psychology, Sigmund Freud projected outward into society the mighty struggle of Eros and Thanatos, and Ivan Pavlov dug inward into physiology to posit excitatory and inhibitory impulses within our nerves.

These sanctified names and concepts have been viewed from many perspectives and raise many overtones, so let us be specific as to exactly what in their thought is of interest here. It is, first, that we may glimpse within their writings a perception of three kinds of "forces" operating within human personality: a left or liberal orientation, a right or conservative orientation, and a nonaligned "middleness"—or the lack of a consistently right or left orientation. It is, secondly, the dynamics these forces embody within and through men and groups that operate to shape social behavior and create the record of this behavior we know as history. These thinkers were concerned with the psychology, sociology, and political science of "the social machine" not as separate entities, or through the separate disciplines, but in holistic, rounded, systems terms reflecting social reality rather than separatist abstractions.

Hegel: A Holistic Systems View

In modern times, following the American and French revolutions, Hegel was the first to make use of this holistic perception in shaping his famous philosophy of history. It is particularly important to understand Hegel's relationship to modern history because of the powerful interaction between the man, his thought, and the times. "Hegel experienced three great political events," Karl Löewith noted. "In his youth, the French Revolution; as a grown man, Napoleon's world rule; and finally, the Prussian wars of liberation. These events also determine the transformations of his political thought: from a radical criticism of the existing order, through the recognition of Napoleon, to justification of the Prussian bureaucratic State" (Löewith, 1967, p. 237). We see, then, this key philosopher for modern times coming into manhood after the triumph of liberal and left forces in the American and French revolutions.

These triumphs were of the liberal belief ("Give me liberty or give me death") in equality of opportunity and justice. Over many centuries, those with this kind of belief had struggled upward against the entrenched conservatism of inequalities, as represented by the traditional pyramid of the social hierarchy with the few at the top and the many below. Hegel felt, however, that the leftward swing in France had gone too far, bringing on the bloody licentiousness and social chaos that prompted the rightist backlash and brought in Napoleon to reimpose order. It was Hegel's desire, then, to define the historical mechanism powered by the interaction of these forces, one ancient and well entrenched, the other newly come to strength. It was also his desire to define the goal of historical movement. It was his conclusion that the historical mechanism was the dialectic—an oppositional movement of these forces whereby each caused change within the other, or brought on a new synthesis of forces. As for the goal of history, it was clear to the young Hegel—as it was for Karl Marx, who followed him historically and was so strongly influenced by him—that it was liberal in direction. The goal rising out of man and his situation and shaping history was the freedom to realize the human potential, to reach the state of social development where "man as man is free" (Kaufman, 1965, p. 9).

As Hegel aged, his views became more conservative; in *The Philosophy of the Right* he embraced the counternotion that the control of freedom represented by the modern state was the supreme good. Thus we may see in this first great thinker to wrestle with the central political problems for modern times the elements that succeeding thought has had to confront: the polarities, interactions, sequences, and social products of right versus left.

"In the course of history, the preservation of a people, a state, and the preservation of the ordered spheres of its life, is one essential moment," Hegel noted of those times when the values of the conservative, or of the right, must prevail. "The other moment, however, is that the stable persistence of the spirit of a people . . . is broken because it is exhausted and over-worked . . . the world spirit proceeds . . . tied to a demotion, demolition, destruction of the preceding mode of actuality. . . . It is precisely here that the great collisions occur between the prevalent, recognized duties, laws, and rights and, on the other hand, possibilities which are opposed to this system" (Kaufman, 1965, p. 269).

Nietzsche: The Psychology of Left Versus Right

Whereas Hegel was absorbed with vast social dynamics within which small psychological insights lay buried, his successor, Friedrich Nietzsche, was for a time absorbed in mining the psychology. His findings lie fallow today within a seldom read book, *The Birth of Tragedy*. Here, seemingly far removed from the realm of politics in a study of aesthetics, Nietzsche accomplished an important early abstraction of the right-left personality base. He perceived what he identified as the Apollonian and Dionysian psychological states.

"The word 'Apollonian' stands for that state of rapt repose in the presence of a visionary world, in the presence of the world of *beautiful appearance* designed as a deliverance from *becoming*: the word *Dionysos,* on the other hand, stands for

strenuous becoming, grown self-conscious, in the form of the
rampant voluptuousness of the Creator, who is also perfectly
conscious of the violent anger of the destroyer. . . . The antago-
nism of these two attitudes and the *desires* that underlie them.
The first-named would have the vision it conjures up *eternal*: in
its light man must be quiescent, apathetic, peaceful, healed, and
on friendly terms with himself and all existence; the second
strives after creation, after the voluptuousness of willful creation, i.e., construction and destroying" (Nietzsche, 1964, pp.
xxv-xxvi).

Here we see posed the psychological polarities between the
Apollonian "right," as the orientation toward stability and
order, and the Dionysian "left," as the orientation toward
change and disorder. It is also notable that Nietzsche is sym-
pathetic to both sides in man—that rather than taking one side
or the other, he sees them as functionally interrelated. Many
years of social polarization and the efforts of social science to
"define variables" lay ahead of this gentle, early statement. For
sensitivity and holism of insight, it is still unrivaled.

In this early book Nietzsche also projected, in a playful
way, a vision of linkages modern social science has yet to adequately define. For example, in the following swift—and admittedly difficult—passage he links the psychology of ideology to
its sociological superstructure and historical direction. "An
'idea'—the antithesis of 'Dionysian *versus* Apollonian'—trans-
lated into metaphysics; history itself as the evolution of this
'idea'; the antithesis dissolved into oneness in Tragedy; through
this optics things that had never yet looked into one another's
face, confronted of a sudden, and illumined and *comprehended*
through one another: for instance, Opera and Revolution"
(Nietzsche, 1964, p. 190).

We might also consider the power of an insight that perceived that "when the Dionysian powers rise with such vehe-
mence as we experience at present, there can be no doubt that,
veiled as in a cloud, Apollo has already descended to us; whose
grandest beautifying influences a coming generation will perhaps behold" (Nietzsche, 1964, p. 186). Here Nietzsche notes
an aspect of something we have lived through ourselves—the

surge of liberalism in the 1950s and early 1960s, followed by the conservative "backlash" of the late 1960s, which set the tone for the 1970s. Yet even today the reasons for this alternation of liberal and conservative social dominance—obviously highly meaningful—is still practically unexplored.

Marx: The Viewpoint of the Left

The relating of holistic and ideological thinking to the problems of society is best exemplified by Karl Marx, who wrenched social thought from the sheltered harbor of philosophy and thrust it into the turbulence of the real world. "In direct contrast to German philosophy which descends from heaven to earth, here we ascend from earth to heaven," he said to emphasize the crucial difference between the new, social scientific and the older philosophical method of social analysis. "That is to say, we do not set out from what men say, imagine, conceive, nor from men as narrated, thought of, imagined, conceived, in order to arrive at men in the flesh. We set out from real, active men, and on the basis of their real life-process we demonstrate the development of the ideological reflexes and echoes of this life-process. . . . Its premises are men, not in any fantastic isolation or abstract definition, but in their actual, empirically perceptible process of development under definite conditions. . . . Where speculation ends—in real life—there real, positive science begins: the representation of the practical activity, of the practical processes of development of men" (Fromm, 1961, p. 198).

For the amorphous right-left social dynamics discerned by Hegel, Marx substituted the powerful structure that since his time has literally moved men and nations by its memorable simplicity. The right-left interaction was seen in terms of social classes caught within a rigid and inevitable dialectical movement of thesis, antithesis, and synthesis. Before modern times the power-possessing, excluding, conservative feudal aristocracy (the thesis), was pressed by the power-deprived, excluded, new liberal bourgeoisie (the antithesis). This historical conflict resulted in the bourgeoisie-triumphant society of Marx's time (the synthesis). From the perspective of his own time, however, Marx was heralding the next inevitable stage. The bourgeoisie—now bloated with success and transformed into power-posses-sive conservatives—were the thesis against which the antithesis of the new liberal power-desiring proletariat was acting. Ahead in Marx's dreams, shimmering with rainbow colors, was the communist society to provide the new synthesis.

To Marx this pattern was so fundamental that he ascribed "the history of all hitherto existing society" to it as embodied in "the history of class struggles." "Freeman and slave, patrician and plebian, lord and serf, guildmaster and journeyman, in a word: oppressor and oppressed, stood in constant opposition to one another, carried on an uninterrupted, now hidden, now open fight" (Marx and Engels, 1972, p. 8).

Of Marx's contributions, four are of special interest in the context of this study: (1) The left-right psychological insights of a Nietzsche are not to be found in Marx, whose thought called for viewing man in more general terms. The differences of interest to Marx were mainly a function of class situation. (2) Gone is much of the admiration of Hegel and Nietzsche for the function and nature of both parties to the old conflict. Marx makes an unflinching alignment with the left, and his interpre-tive scheme is then one in which the liberals and the left are the "good guys" fighting for liberty against the villains of the right. (3) Marx has been criticized for over-simplifying Hegel's dialec-tical thought; however, it was this very simplicity that made Marx's analysis such a powerful tool for producing social change. It was a pattern that could enlist the minds of both savant and layman, leader and follower. (4) This pattern became the first major theory of the important type to which we called attention in Chapter One—the theory of *directed* social change, or of how we may intervene to shape our social destiny.

What an incredible influence he was! To the scholar, Marx appealed with his eleventh thesis on Feuerbach: "The philos-ophers have only interpreted the world. Our business is to change it" (Marx, 1972, p. 109). To the man in the streets, it was: "Working men of all countries, unite! . . . The proletarians have nothing to lose but their chains" (Marx and Engels, 1972, p. 362).

Pareto: The Viewpoint of the Right

Marx's great right-wing counterpart was Vilfredo Pareto (1848-1923), whose work was used by Mussolini to legitimize fascism in Italy as Marx's work was used by Lenin and Stalin to legitimize communism in Russia. Again we encounter a major theorist whose social analysis is based on the old right-left opposition, only now there is an important change of emphasis. For Marx the leftists were the heroes, the liberal goal of freedom was the social ideal, and the right was the realm of villainy; for Pareto all this was reversed. The rightists who would "apply force on a far-reaching scale" (Parsons and others, 1965, p. 595) are the heroes; the conservative goal of order and stability is the social ideal; and the leftward social trend is seen as leading either to the corruption and chicanery of democracy, or to the social fallacies of communism.

Though this rightist emphasis prevails in Pareto, it is also true that, like Hegel, his views swung from left to right as he grew older. In making this rightward swing over a lifetime, Pareto achieved what remains to this day the most comprehensive and searching examination of the psychology and sociology of ideology and social change. Although he is generally recognized today as one of the formative giants in political science, economics, and sociology, admittedly few would accord him the accolade given here—particularly in regard to the psychology of ideology and social change. For Pareto's psychological insights are buried within one of the most cumbersome, bizarre, and arbitrary thickets of terms ever evolved by a major social scientist. Yet if one approaches Pareto with the advantage of fifty years of psychological study and a modern sense of motivational structure, it is surprising how much psychological insight he was trying to convey at the turn of the century.

The grim outline of the well-known authoritarian personality investigated by T. W. Adorno and associates in the 1940s is clearly evident in Pareto's much earlier characterization of the Lion leadership type. Hans Eysenck's great work of the mid-1950s, *The Psychology of Politics*, is also foreshadowed in the "toughminded" characteristics of Pareto's Lion versus the more "tenderminded" characteristics of his Fox leadership type.

These types—Lions and Foxes—were the leadership elites whose interaction determined the course of political history. Pareto's term for this interaction was the *circulation of elites*. The Lions, he felt, were predominantly motivated by "Class II residues" of "a persistence of aggregates"—or the conservative feeling for the accumulations of the past, for what exists, for the status quo. The Foxes, by contrast, were motivated by "Class I residues" of "the instinct for combining"—or the social venturesomeness we associate today with liberalism.

Pareto also radically advanced the study of right-left phenomena into the shaping of personality by social role, and into social dynamics as seen from the useful viewpoint of social functional analysis. All these levels of insight are evident in the following bit of characteristic insight expressed in terms of his Lion and Fox economic counterparts, the speculators (S) and rentiers (R): "The two groups perform functions of differing utility in society. The S group is primarily responsible for change, for economic and social progress. The R group, instead, is a powerful element in stability, and in many cases counteracts the dangers attending the adventurous capers of the Ss. A society in which Rs almost exclusively predominate remains stationary and, as it were, crystallized. A society in which Ss predominate lacks stability, lives in a state of shaky equilibrium that may be upset by a slight accident from within or from without" (Parsons and others, 1965, pp. 556-557).

In a particularly bold leap into the future, Pareto reduced his thoughts regarding the interaction of those motivated by Class I versus Class II "residues" to mathematics. To him the formula $q = B/A$ was as meaningful as Einstein's well-known $E = mc^2$. In this case, B equals the force or social weight of the Class II residues supporting the Lion elite; A equals the force or social weight of the Class I residues supporting the Fox elite; q equals a particular historical event whose outcome is determined by this ratio of the Lion to the Fox power (Finer, 1966, pp. 74, 75).

Pareto was trained as an engineer and was a sucessful business manager and entrepreneur before he became a social scientist. This may account for why, flawed though it may be, his work still remains the most wholly advanced in this area of investigation. For Pareto probed the dimensions of our subject both with the old feeling for the holism of philosophy and history and with the new feeling for disciplinary particularism tempered with the modern systems view. Though the disciplines of social science have all advanced separately since his time, no one mind has again attempted to grasp so much that is pertinent to this investigation. No one since his time, for example, has been able to conceive of the right-left alternation in the following way, or to express it so beautifully—while also seeking beneath this shimmering verbal surface for the psychology and mathematics that might explain it. "In virtue of class circulation," he noted, "the governing *elite* is always in a state of slow and continuous transformation. It flows on like a river, never being today what it was yesterday. From time to time sudden and violent disturbances occur. There is a flood—the river overflows its banks. Afterwards, the new governing *elite* again resumes its slow transformation. The flood has subsided, the river is again flowing normally in its wonted bed" (Parsons and others, 1965, p. 555).

Weber, Freud, and Pavlov

An even greater influence than Pareto on the formation of modern sociology, political science, and economics was exercised by Max Weber (1864-1920). To the study of political personality in history he contributed the key perception of how much of history (and, indeed, all social movement) requires the transformation of a liberal into a conservative leadership style. At the beginning is a leadership of charisma, which breaks "with continuity . . . overturns institutions . . . challenges the established order and customary restraints and appeals to a new concept of human relations" (Freund, 1969, p. 233). But over time there is a shift from the early excitement of the charismatic leader and leadership styles. The need for routinizing charisma —or for establishing the operational routines for an expanding organization—require the staid and sober approach of more conservative leaders and leadership styles.

Freud's most compelling observation relating to ideology almost lost him a portion of his hard-won following. Struck by the "conservative character of instinctual life" he concluded that "beside the instinct preserving the organic substance and binding it into ever larger units, there must exist another in antithesis to this, which would seek to dissolve these units and reinstate their antecedent inorganic state" (Freud, 1946, p. 97). Thus Freud was led to posit the death instinct, Thanatos, along with the life instinct, Eros, and "the phenomena of life would then be explicable from the interplay of the two and their counteracting effects on each other." Indeed, Freud felt that in the interplay of these forces "the meaning of the evolution of culture is no longer a riddle," but may be described as the "struggle of the human species for existence" (Freud, 1946, p. 103).

Freud's positing of the "struggle of the Titans," between Thanatos and Eros, was decried by many of his followers as unscientific and a dangerous regression to the days of large and loose philosophical concepts from which social science had labored so long to emerge. Yet at the core of Freud's discernments lay something that also fascinated the father of ostensibly the most scientific and "hardnosed" school of psychology. For at the heart of Ivan Pavlov's theory of conditioning lie the concepts of excitation and inhibition of neural response. That is, Pavlov saw human behavior as an assembly of learned or conditioned responses established by an increase in the conductivity of connecting links in the central nervous system between the stimulus and the response forming each behavioral unit. This increase in neural conductivity was excitation. This excitation, however, was limited in several ways by inhibition, which could lead to extinction of the response (Eysenck, 1957).

The Rebirth of Psychology

Many other examples of suggestive early insights into the left and the right could be added. However, we can afford to dwell in the past only long enough to revive the insights and large originating visions of some of the precursors and founders of modern social science. Our purpose is also, quite frankly, to try to revive the sizeable visions of these earlier prophets as an inspiration to research today on the organizational leadership and political front. For, after a time in the grand pursuit of these matters in the nineteenth and early twentieth centuries, interest dwindled, until today the social science of this area is a scattering of intellectual nomads roaming the academic plains with little sense of shared directions. Meanwhile, in the real life that affects the destinies of each of us, we are threatened, for lack of understanding, both by organizational suffocation and political chaos.

Following the times of Hegel, Nietzsche, Marx, Pareto, Freud, and Pavlov—and following the crucial trends to bureaucracy, specialization and the division of labor predicted by Weber and Durkheim—the social sciences split apart into narrow compartments, and fewer and fewer thinkers felt equipped to attempt the synthesis. In sociology Parsons (1965), Sorokin (1966), Gurvitch (1972), Myrdal (1962), Boulding (1970), Etzioni (1968), and in management theory Simon (1960a), McGregor (1960), and others persisted. For a variety of reasons, however, the components and dynamics of our concern tend to disappear or become difficult to track in these important works. There were courageous attempts by Harold Lasswell (1948), Wilhelm Reich (1970), and the thinkers of the Frankfort school (Jay, 1973) to maintain the old cross-disciplinary perspective on this subject area. But the atomization of social science was working against them, and, with the exception of Adorno, Marcuse, and Fromm, they largely served only to keep alive the flame of this particular investigation without appreciably extending its glow.

Within modern psychology, Erich Fromm, formerly of the Frankfort school, and the political scientist Lasswell developed suggestive typologies within useful frameworks. The politically sophisticated psychologist Kurt Lewin made an attempt cut short by his death. Founder of leadership studies and much of modern social psychology, in the last year of his life Lewin began an analysis in terms of liberative versus repressive forces (Lewin, 1951). Among historians, Arthur Schlesinger, Sr., produced his controversial short masterwork "The Tides of Politics" (Schlesinger, 1964). Written in the 1930s, this still remains one of the most provocative views of the interaction of left and right that over time seems to shape history. But again these were all small and isolated efforts in comparison with the size of the challenge laid down by history and the works of earlier thinkers.

While the drive to gain some large comprehension of the dynamics of ideology and social change waned, there were highly significant advancements in another direction. Within psychology a number of brilliant experimentalists and theoreticians have sporadically investigated what appears to be the main cluster of grounding elements within the social dynamo—individuals and groups of right, left, or no marked ideology. Here the core works are the investigations of T. W. Adorno, Else Frenkel-Brunswik, Daniel Levinson, Nevitt Sanford, and associates into the nature of the right; of Milton Rokeach into the dogmatism and core values of both right and left; of Hans Eysenck into gradations from right to left, as well as into William James' closely related dimension of the tough- versus the tenderminded; of Silvan Tomkins into a basic division across all knowledge and affective functioning of right, left, or middle orientations; and of Abraham Maslow into a motivational scheme in man that moves from rightist "defense" to leftist "growth" needs and values. Moreover, out of the ground prepared by these pioneering works there now flowers an important new range of modern psychological studies.

We shall examine this heritage of modern psychology in the terms that make it scientifically meaningful in Part Two, The Measurement of Ideology. That is, the great contribution of psychologists to this area has been to bring down from their verbal "heaven" all these befuddling abstractions and subject them to the most earthly of the tools of science, that of measurement. As a chemist will break down water into its component parts of hydrogen and oxygen, so the psychologists have begun to reduce these abstractions of ideology to their component variables for counting, weighing, and analyzing relationships.

Summary and Historical Perspective

In Chapter One we examined the purpose of this book—to reassess the historic connection between ideology and social and organizational change in philosophical, empirical, and experimental terms. We do this to help advance social science and an embattled and often overwhelmed social and organizational leadership. In Chapter Two we examined the views of right versus left of Hegel, Nietzsche, Marx, Pareto, Weber, Freud and Pavlov. We also noted the rise of a new psychology of ideology from the ashes of a magnificent earlier social science.

Whether this new psychology rising from the old is to prove a phoenix or a firefly depends on specifics we deal with in chapters ahead. Beyond the specifics, however, there is a matter of aspiration and scope that must be recaptured. It is hard to forecast the future, but it seems to us that whether psychology attains this scope will depend on the extent to which it confronts the questions underlying the cogent analysis of historian Arthur Schlesinger, Sr.

"If neither presidential administrations nor masterful personalities nor parties are the prime movers in political life, whence comes the motive power? Is some influence at work less obvious to the eye?" Schlesinger inquires. He has raised the central question for our investigation: how ideological motivations and values operate within the psychology of leadership to shape our economic, social, and educational, as well as political, futures. He cites the observations of our first great American leadership psychologist (Schlesinger, 1964, p. 92).

> *Jefferson hinted at the answer when he observed, "Men, according to their constitutions, and the circumstances in which they are placed, differ honestly in opinion." Some, he said, "fear the people, and wish to transfer all power to the higher classes of society"; the others "consider the people as the safest depository of power in the last resort; they cherish them, therefore, and wish to leave in them all the*

powers to the exercise of which they are competent."
He called these contrasting conceptions Tory and
Whig, aristocratic and democratic, Federalist and
Republican. Historians have called them Hamiltonian
and Jeffersonian. Today we would call them conser-
vative and liberal. A Gallup poll taken in 1939, when
conservatism was on the upgrade, revealed that the
voters were about equally divided between the two
schools, 52 percent describing themselves as conserva-
tives and 48 as liberals. Probably the balance has al-
ways been much the same, a small shift from one side
to the other determining the dominant mood.

Any scrutiny of American history discloses the
alternation of these attitudes. A period of concern for
the rights of the few has been followed by one of
concern for the wrongs of the many. Emphasis on the
welfare of property has given way to emphasis on
human welfare in the belief, as Theodore Roosevelt
put it, that "every man holds his property subject to
the general right of the community to regulate its use
to whatever degree the public welfare may require
it." An era of quietude has been succeeded by one of
rapid movement.

This alternating process of conservatism and liberalism
"casts a significant light on the workings of American democracy," Schlesinger concludes. Then he adds observations from
the heart that over much of a decade helped sustain the enticing
but most difficult investigation which this book represents. For
his views are the warp and woof of our approach. "Not precon-
ceived theory but empiricism has been the guiding star," Schlesinger observed.

The ship of state has moved forward by fits and
starts, choosing its course in obedience to the prevail-
ing winds of opinion. . . . If this method of progress
seems haphazard and wasteful, it has the merit of its
defects, for it has enabled both groups to make their

distinctive contributions to the public good. . . . This two-way process has been born of the inner necessities of a political order which deems competition between opposing attitudes a positive virtue. . . . With democracy on trial throughout the world today, every citizen should mount guard to see that nothing is done to impair this balance wheel of orderly evolution. Neither conservatism nor liberalism, but a fair field for both, is the American ideal [Schlesinger, 1964, pp. 102, 103].

3

The "Golden Age" of Theory and Measurement

To the nonscientist measurement may seem like a mundane, grubby, even suspicious concern. As William Blake once expressed a basic reservation of the humanist: "He who would bind to himself a joy doth the winged life destroy." To the scientist, however, the "binding" of reality that measurement represents is the core of his method, for unless a concept, affect, or percept can be defined precisely, it cannot be investigated in terms upon which others may agree. This is a matter of particular concern in the study of ideology, for even with the measurement efforts of a horde of psychologists, remarkably little agreement exists as yet on basic concepts.

That such an agreement would prove difficult to reach might seem inconceivable to those with an interest in politics or an acquaintance with the classical perspective outlined previously. For apparently few things could be more obvious than "facts" such as: (1) there are liberals and conservatives in this world, of varying intensities of belief; (2) political activities of all types (intrahousehold, intraclassroom, as well as party matters) involve conflict and interaction among types; and (3) this is a gamelike activity that often involves a tug-of-war between the two extremes for possession of people in the "middle."

The strange truth is that modern psychology has hardly begun to investigate "facts" two and three because it has yet to reach agreement on "fact" one, the definition of liberals versus conservatives. Thus we must adopt a strategy in this section designed to swiftly clear the psychological shrubbery of four decades in order to free some seedlings for growth. To do this we will try to give the reader a clear sense of the leading investigators, their most important measures, and the developmental history of recent studies. A theme of underlying interest will be how the "scientific mind," in the sense of a questing, abstracting entity, seems to be seeking "truth" through the conflict of empiricists, enmeshed in measurement, and theorists, who try to fling their minds free of the web of measurement to perceive underlying structures.

Set and Field Theoretical Perspectives

One great difficulty in understanding the psychology of ideology is the deadly weight of research procedures, statistics, and prestigious references one must ingest before any bold and informed step may be taken in this area. To radically lighten this weight we will make use of a simple visual methodology suggested by two powerful analytic tools, which are based on the ancient Chinese adage that one picture is worth a thousand words. One such tool is set theory, which has been used to radically clarify mathematical and statistical relationships (Hays, 1963). The other is Lewinian field theory, which was used during the heyday of modern psychological theorizing to simplify social-psychological relationships (Lewin, 1951). From both sources we will make use of concepts of meaning expressed in terms of the relation of parts to wholes.

For example, the historical, philosophical, and sociological considerations of Part One have left us at this point with an ideological universe consisting of three "meaning spaces" that look somewhat like Figure 1.

Figure 1

A Basic Ideological Meaning Space

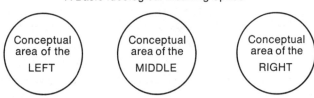

This left, right, middle pattern, simple though it may appear in this form, is not a prevailing conceptualization of ideological relationships in modern psychology. The three major patterns that underlie most work in psychology and in sociology are as follows. First, there is the stark dichotomy (Figure 2) of left versus right. As we shall see, this assumption underlies practically all formal scales purporting to measure liberalism-conservatism.

Figure 2

Ideology as a Dichotomy of Left versus Right

The first major differentiation of these two basic meaning spaces into something more closely approximating reality is the pattern shown in Figure 3 of left, liberal, conservative, and right as a continuum from the extreme at one end, through two positions of moderation, to the extreme at the other end. Every abstraction presents difficulties, of course, to those who spend

Figure 3

Ideology as a Left, Liberal, Conservative, Right Continuum

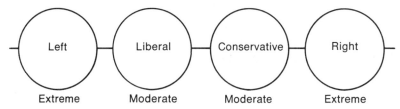

time pondering the extent to which it actually fits reality. Within the continuum view, the chief inconsistency that has been explored by psychologists (for example, the Adorno, Rokeach, Eysenck "debate" to be examined shortly) follows the observation that there are similarities between the extremes that the continuum view, by placing them at polar opposites, obscures and in fact falsifies. So we then have a meaning space of the type shown in Figure 4 to consider.

Figure 4

Ideology as Circular,
or the Question of the Proximity of the Extremes

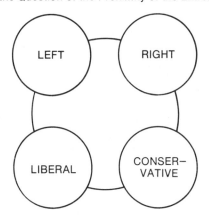

To proceed from these largely sociological visualizations into the psychological perspective, we must employ increasingly finer analytic tools. We will now move in on one of the left or right circles shown in Figure 4, as in the old science fiction plot where a spaceship and its occupants are miniaturized to enter the worlds within the shiny circle of a Lincoln head penny. For grounding purposes in this miniaturized world of the person we may take from the field theory developed by Kurt Lewin the visual concept of a person within his "life space." This is represented by an ellipse in which the person is symbolized as a circle (Figure 5).

Figure 5

Person in Lewinian Life Space

The inner circle encloses the person, whom we will call Frank to give life to this abstraction, and the outer circle encloses everything that is psychologically meaningful to Frank—whether it be his girlfriend, a steak for dinner, or a ski trip he is planning. Within these two circles, then, there conceptually exist all the variables both within Frank and within his environment that may interact, or co-vary, at any one given time. Now let us introduce a second visual concept, from set theory. This is the visualization of the concept of covariance. It is, for example, well established that the degree of one's liberalism or conservatism may shift with a change of setting. Let us assume, for example, that Frank was originally a somewhat conservative youth in his home, a small farm community, who became considerably more liberal under campus influence when he went to college. But after graduation, he shifted again toward conservatism, under the influence of a business milieu. In these instances, certain aspects of Frank as a person and certain aspects of his original home, his college, and his later occupational situation all co-vary. We observe a shifting in the variable of (1) his ideology, as change occurs in the variable of (2) his *exposure to* a new setting. The two sets of variables thereby co-vary.

A conceptual twist of equal importance, which all too often is overlooked, is that at the same time this covariance of interest to us is taking place, there is a much larger area of involvement for both Frank and his setting in which no such covariance is occurring. His love for hominy and red beans, for example, may persist unchanged throughout the shifts from home, to college, to occupational setting. This seemingly complex array of relationships can actually be reduced to the simplicity of Figure 6.

Figure 6

Covariance of Ideology and Exposure to Setting

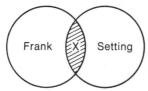

This kind of relationship is formalized in psychology and all social science, in more familiar terms, as correlation. For example, in this instance there is a correlation between ideology and exposure to setting that might be represented as r = .70, which might be highly significant, or r = .15, which might be marginally significant. Such correlations are what we repeatedly seek and find in psychology, but the most important point of the Figure 6 visualization to keep in mind as we proceed is the significance of the area of the non-X, or those portions of Frank and his setting wherein everything else is occurring beyond the narrow beam of our probe. As the story of the search for the meaning of ideology repeatedly demonstrates, the situation of all social science is like the movement of a hardy little band of men and women equipped only with flashlights through a very dark forest. We will see how again and again they report what their flashlights find, and in the process do manage some agreement on what is really out there in the forest. But at the same time, what the flashlight of research reveals varies greatly according to the differences of the paths we take through the forest of man. Repeatedly, through becoming fixated on the X, we overlook co-variation in the non-X. And so we face great difficulty in reconstructing from such limited reports the truth of the whole. Let us now examine what such "flashlights" in the hands of a few of the most intrepid of modern investigators have revealed.

The Adorno, Rokeach, Eysenck Debate

Prior to 1950 there were many studies of left-right ideology by psychologists. Much of this work is summarized in Stagner (1936) and Robinson, Rusk, and Head (1968). This early work, however, was wholly eclipsed by the publication in 1950 of one of the most influential books in modern psychology, *The Authoritarian Personality* (Adorno, Frenkel-Brunswik, Levinson, and Sanford, 1950). Here in 990 pages was drawn together six years of work by a research team composed of seven principal investigators, with over thirty research associates and the counsel of many other leading investigators. To the task of piercing the darkness they applied the major "flashlights" of the time—Freudian personality theory and a wide array of measurement and experimental social-psychological techniques perfected during the 1930s by Rensis Likert and others. Nothing bearing on ideology comparable to the size of this effort has been attempted since then. It rapidly set in motion a proliferation of studies, the majority of which clustered about the central debate in the journals of the time, between what are known—after the names of the three chief investigators—as the Adorno, Rokeach, and Eysenck positions.

Adorno and the Authoritarian Personality. The Adorno study was a melding of two great contemporary social concerns. One was the desire to understand how Hitler and fascism could arise, in order to prevent the reemergence of such grave threats to civilization. This concern shaped the ultimate focus on "the authoritarian personality." A second major purpose was to understand how prejudice against Jews and other minorities arose. This concern provided a practical thrust, which encouraged the American Jewish Committee to grant the sizeable funding required to hold together a sufficiently large body of investigators over a sufficiently long time to produce a study of large impact. This point of economics is of major importance because one reason for relatively little progress in this area is that no comparable sums have since been directed by American funding agencies to support ideological research.

These two underlying major objectives then shaped the operational emphasis of the Adorno group upon four primary sets of psychological variables: (1) anti-Semitism, for which an anti-Semitism scale (A-S) was developed; (2) ethnocentrism, for which the E scale was developed; (3) political-economic conservatism, for which the PEC scale was developed; and (4) the authoritarian personality, for which the famous F scale (F for fascism) was developed.

Likert Questionnaire Methodology. The basic measurement approach taken by the Adorno group is the Likert technique of questionnaire construction and data analysis. (A good description of this technique may be found in Adorno, 1950, pp. 57-205, or Selltiz, Jahoda, and Cook, 1959.) This was also the primary measurement approach for Rokeach and Eysenck and remains the prevailing technique for liberalism-conservatism scales today. To articulate the purpose and findings of the Adorno study and to establish an understanding basic to most psychological investigations of ideology we will briefly describe the technique here in terms of the Adorno probe.

The first step in constructing such a scale is to collect statements of opinion from interviews, books, or other measures which seem to express some aspect of the attitude one wants to measure. For example, in developing the PEC scale for this study, Adorno's co-principal investigator Daniel Levinson felt that statements of opinion of the type shown in Table 1 were characteristic of people with politically or economically liberal or conservative attitudes.

After several hundred statements of the type shown in Table 1 are collected, they are assembled in questionnaire form. This questionnaire asks the respondent to rate each statement for the degree to which he or she agrees or disagrees with the item on a 5, 6, 7, or 9 point scale. In the case of the Adorno

Table 1

Sample Items for the Adorno PEC Scale

1. America may not be perfect, but the American Way has brought us about as close as human beings can get to a perfect society. (Conservatives tend to agree with this statement, liberals to disagree.)

2. It is the responsibility of the entire society, through its government, to guarantee everyone adequate housing, income, and leisure. (Liberals tend to agree, conservatives to disagree.)

3. In general, full economic security is harmful; most men wouldn't work if they didn't need the money for eating and living. (Conservatives agree, liberals disagree.)

measures, the instructions were for a six-point scaling as illustrated in Table 2.

This Adorno format has been greatly streamlined since its original appearance, but the basic approach remains the same; we include it as a table here to focus on exactly what we're confronting operationally in LC measurement. By adding the scores for each item (ranging from +3 to −3), one may obtain a single number total score that hypothetically represents the subject's degree of liberalism or conservatism. In the case of the Adorno PEC scale, high scores indicated liberal and low scores indicated conservative beliefs.

Such scales are refined and validated by a variety of ingenious methods. The Adorno measures, for example, were in part refined and validated by a sequence of the following type. Following administration of the first questionnaires, composed of "gross" assemblies of possibly useful items, the resulting data were statistically analyzed to determine the discriminatory

Table 2

A Portion of the Instructions for the Original Adorno PEC Questionnaire

The following are statements with which some people agree and others disagree. Please mark each one in the left margin, according to the amount of your agreement or disagreement, by using the following scale:

+1: slight support, agreement	−1: slight opposition, disagreement
+2: moderate support, agreement	−2: moderate opposition, disagreement
+3: strong support, agreement	−3: strong opposition, disagreement

power of each item—or the degree to which each item separated those who made high total scores from those who made low scores on the attitude being measured. Items with low discriminatory power were eliminated. The remaining items were then subjected to what is known as split-half analysis to obtain a measure of their reliability, or the consistency with which they measured liberalism-conservatism. The tests so perfected were then validated by administering them to people who belonged to groups known to be dominantly conservative or dominantly liberal—Republicans or Democrats, businessmen or teachers of social science. It was thereby shown that the performance means for liberal-conservative groups did differ significantly from one another in the directions one might hypothesize—that Republicans would score markedly more conservative than Democrats, for example.

The preceding summary covers only the surface of an operation involving the processing of thousands of forms and millions of numbers, but it is offered to help make two points of basic importance to our investigation. The first is that the Adorno measures did work and they were a tremendous accomplishment; rather than being mere transitory "busy-work" this type of activity represents the most fundamental of contributions by psychology to the study of ideology. By succeeding in producing tests that reduce something so seemingly amorphous as a person's ideology to something as exact as numbers, psychologists have made it possible to subject the data of investigation to rigorous methods of statistical analysis. Instead of an endlessly open-ended debate on ideology, we may begin to establish the "truth" through the objective power of numbers and mathematical calculation.

However, there is a second point of equal importance: numbers and statistics in social science represent a power that must be closely monitored by minds that are as much attuned to social reality as to sanctified wisdom. For repeatedly in social science we use numbers to sanctify what are only portions of reality. One of the great contributions of the Adorno study was that it also made this methodological pitfall apparent.

The Adorno Study's Debatable Findings. The findings in

the four, key variable areas for the Adorno study, and the questions raised by others about these findings, now occupy thousands of printed pages. However, by again resorting to the visualization of part-whole relationships we can reduce many years into a tiny patch of space. In terms of the Adorno-Rokeach-Eysenck debate, which provides the major grounding point for the psychological study of ideology, the central findings of the Adorno study can be represented as shown in Figure 7.

Figure 7

Right Personality Relationships for the Adorno Study

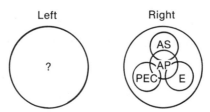

Figure 7 visually summarizes the following "operational facts" for the debate that ensued. (By "operational facts" we mean not what any of these studies revealed as a whole, but that limited portion of the findings that became the subject for debate). A first operational fact was that the primary focus for the Adorno group was on the personality variables of far-rightists and conservatives, but the left was much less precisely defined. Within the right conceptual area, then, we may see in Figure 7 the findings of continuing interest to investigators. Anti-Semitism (A-S), ethnocentrism or lack of empathy for any but one's own group (E), and politico-economic conservatism (PEC) were studied as independent entities and as they related to the group's central interest in the authoritarian personality (AP).

Through the testing of groups and intercorrelations of the study's measures, it was found that the authoritarian personality was indeed prejudiced, ethnocentric, and politically and economically conservative. But as the overlapping circles in Figure 7 make apparent, this did not mean that all prejudiced, ethnocentric or conservative people were authoritarian. It only meant that a *portion* of the total variance was shared. This is an important distinction because in the study's popularization among liberals, the conservative was equated with the authoritarian, but the study's data revealed a web of more subtle relationships.

Rokeach and the Left Authoritarian. Misinterpretations of Adorno's findings motivated Rokeach and Eysenck to undertake major attempts to clarify the picture. The work of Rokeach and his associates is chiefly summarized in *The Open and Closed Mind* (Rokeach, 1960). What struck Rokeach was the seemingly obvious imbalance in equating the authoritarian personality with Hitler's fascism, or with the danger from the right. What about the danger of left authoritarianism represented by Stalinist communism? It further seemed to Rokeach that, for all its great pioneering social value, the Adorno study was being used by its investigators, interpreters, and popularizers for some dangerous overgeneralizing. In his estimation, a study was needed that would confine itself mainly to conscious mind and belief and cognitive processing. He further felt that at this level one should seek to establish the truth about psychological functioning in terms of generalities that might then be applied to the specifics of right versus left, rather than risk bias by trying to move toward general truths from the specific.

To operationalize his thinking Rokeach devised two new measures. It struck him, first, that a quality shared by both right and left authoritarians was dogmatism. They seemed to be alike in having closed belief systems, to which they held rigidly, while rejecting the possibility of modification. To measure this possible cognitive processing difference he developed the Dogmatism or D scale. This measured to what extent one's mind was "open" or "closed," hence the title of the book and the study's focus. To examine the effects of right or left bias on dogmatism, he also devised the Opinionation, or O scale, composed of items with which one could agree only if one held extreme right or extreme left beliefs.

Rokeach's main "operational fact" finding was that to the extent that dogmatism, or the closed mind, is a characteristic of authoritarians, there are left as well as right authoritarians. This, of course, substantiated what one might easily observe in the social context. However, Rokeach found something else, which injects a note of dissonance between popular observance and social-scientific finding and also provides us with a classic instance of the difficulties in this area of investigation when one scratches beneath a deceptively simple surface. For Rokeach also found no significant relationship between dogmatism, as measured by his D scale, and ideology, as measured by the O scale. In other words, he found that rightists and leftists were essentially no more subject to the "closed mind" than anyone else of extreme beliefs. This kind of finding, like the fabled will-o-the-wisp, led investigators into such difficulties that they dropped the subject and thereby helped ring the death knell for ideology as a major pursuit of psychology.

Eysenck and Tough- and Tenderminded. In contrast to Rokeach's strategy to radically limit the scope of investigation to the cognitive level, Eysenck's approach was ubiquitous. His foray into ideology was an offshoot of a major attempt to use factor analysis to integrate Pavlovian-Hullian conditioning theory, Jungian personality theory, physiology, and sociology (Eysenck, 1957). He, too, was attracted by the need to explain the nature of left as well as of right authoritarianism. Eysenck's prime motivation, however, was to find structural laws governing the relation of ideology, as a complex of personality variables, to social attitudes and behavior.

Thus far we have been concerned with perspectives viewing ideology in one-dimensional or single-factor terms. In other words, ideology is viewed as a continuum between left and right, either straight line (Figure 3) or circular (Figure 4), but the perspective remains one-dimensional because a person is identified as liberal or conservative depending on a high or low score on a single scale. Eysenck decided to try to seek the "truth" of the matter with a staggering factor analysis. From British, American, German, Swedish, and other sources, he compiled 22,000 statements of attitude bearing on left-right ideology, and through analysis he found that two factors seemed to account for a major portion of the variance.

A first factor of the heaviest loadings (or correlational cumulations on a factor) was the liberalism-conservatism complex, which Eysenck renamed R for radicalism. Sixteen items high loading on this factor became the Eysenck R scale. The new second factor of fewer loadings, but distinct as a factor and seemingly of major importance, reminded Eysenck of an idea from William James. James had observed that an important differentiation between people was whether they were toughminded or tenderminded. To James, the toughminded were materialistic, pessimistic, "practical"; the tenderminded were idealistic, optimistic, and "theoretical." "The tough think of the tender as sentimentalists and soft-heads. The tender feel the tough to be unrefined, callous, or brutal" (Eysenck, 1954, p. 131). It struck Eysenck that if one were trying to account for a similarity between right and left authoritarianism, a toughmindedness held in common could be the answer, for both extremes notably condoned violence. This toughmindedness of the extremes further seemed to differentiate them from the milder, or more tenderminded, politics of liberals and conservatives. Thirty-two items high loading on this factor became his T scale.

Figure 8 shows what an important advancement Eysenck's work represented in extending the realm of debate in psychology, for he posited a perspective that might reconcile the continuum and circular views of ideology. Far left gradated to liberal, to conservative, and to far right on the continuum measured by the R scale (and the Adorno PEC and F scales as well). The circularity problem was then resolved by finding extreme right and left close to one another in toughmindedness and liberals and conservatives similar in tendermindedness.

Figure 8

Eysenck T and R Factors as a Resolution
to the Dilemma of Ideology

Tough	Tender		Tender	Tough
Leftist	Liberal		Conservative	Rightist

It all would have been delightful, except for the persistence of the obdurate and slippery reality of ideology. For just
as the Rokeach pursuit appeared to lead out of the field of
debate, the Eysenck work seemed to lead to a dead end.
Though Eysenck interpreted his data as supporting the toughversus tenderminded hypothesis, other investigators—chiefly
Rokeach and Hanley (1956) and Richard Christie (1956)—felt
that he was stretching the data far beyond scientific acceptabil-
ity to fit an elegant hypothesis. And so, as often happens in
psychological investigation, this controversy at first attracted,
and then, as the novelty wore off, repelled further investigation.

Adorno, Rokeach, and Eysenck Revisited. By reducing the
debate to its essentials we hope to have brought the reader to a
juncture where he now holds two conflicting impressions. The
first would be some impression of the size of the effort that
went into the study of ideology by psychologists during what
must be viewed as the golden age for this line of investigation.
During this period, the findings of the three investigators we
have centered on were greatly multiplied in studies by others.
But in comparison to the richness of the area, and to the size of
the challenge posed by social philosophers, we hope to have
raised a disquieting sense of what it has taken to gain only the
first footholds, and of how unstable these footholds appear to
be. For to this point, little beyond tooling up for a major task
that still lies ahead seems to have been accomplished by modern
psychology. Still unanswered, and in fact barely investigated,
were innumerable questions that both the classics and the
urgent pressures of social reality raised. What, for example, is
the nature of moderate versus extreme ideology? What of activism versus inactivism? What of the function of role and typology? What of both interpersonal and intrapersonal dynamics?
What of the nature and function of the middle?

The customary approach would relegate Adorno, Rokeach,
and Eysenck to the past and hurry on to a heady present for
further research. However, with the important exceptions noted
in succeeding pages, there has been so little basic advance beyond their work in the psychology of ideology that it will benefit us to briefly look again to see what lay in the shadows

beyond the narrow flashlight beams of the central debate. The Adorno study, in particular, looms ever larger in retrospect.

Its true lineage is, first, of enduring interest. Its investigators made much of the fact at the time that it was a wedding of psychoanalytic theory with empirical research technology, with the reduction of prejudice as the practical offspring. Behind this facade, however, lay the old drive of the Hegelian and Marxian interest in the psychology and sociology of ideology. Behind Adorno lay his membership in that rare bastion of multidisciplinary social research, the so-called Frankfort school of brilliant neo-Marxian scholars, which included Max Horkeimer, Erich Fromm, and Herbert Marcuse. Also, behind this study carried out in America lay many previous grounding studies carried out by the Frankfort group in Europe prior to its departure for America, which was forced by Hitler's rise in Germany (Jay, 1973). Thus, in ways that unfortunately we cannot take time to detail, the search of the Adorno group for the meanings of ideology was guided by a far better foundation in the relevant philosophy than anything before or since its time in psychology. (The one exception is the work of Tomkins, who was trained as a philosopher before he became a clinician and psychological theorist).

A second fact in "the shadows" was that the most important findings of this study, which has come to be almost wholly associated with the name of Adorno as senior investigator, were actually the work of his associates. Chief among them was Else Frenkel-Brunswik, who, among many contributions, made at least two of enduring centrality to the study of ideology. One was her identification of intolerance of ambiguity as a key variable differentiating conservatives from liberals. She did this with a perceptual measure that presented subjects with an ambiguous sequence of pictures: what was obviously a cat in the first picture became, through subtle changes of detail in succeeding picture cards, a dog. To a significant degree, conservatives remained fixated on the cat image, but liberals made the transition to perceiving the dog. This was a truly striking finding at the basic perceptual level of cognitive functioning. Within the context of Frenkel-Brunswik's interviews and the work of others in the study (including Nevitt Sanford and Daniel Levinson, whose chapters on liberalism and conservatism remain a landmark), it became evident that social science had at last begun to rigorously substantiate everyday observation. Conservatives had been shown to be resistant and liberals open to change.

Frenkel-Brunswik's other major contribution was her study of the difference between liberal and conservative styles of child raising. Only part of this work was reported in *The Authoritarian Personality*, and unfortunately she died before completing a full report. We mention it because this has so often been the fate of investigations in this neglected area of psychological studies—to be deflected from completion by death, neglect, or economic needs. Through interviews with high and low scorers on a scale of prejudice, Frenkel-Brunswik found that in general the low-scoring "liberals" had parents from whom "less obedience is expected of the children." These parents were "less status-ridden and thus show less anxiety with respect to conformity and are less intolerant toward manifestations of socially unaccepted behavior" (Adorno, 1950, p. 387). By contrast, high-scoring "conservatives" had parents who employed "a relatively harsh and more threatening type of home discipline." She noted that in the "conservative" family "what is socially accepted and what is helpful in climbing the social ladder is considered 'good,' and what deviates, what is different, and what is socially inferior is considered 'bad' " (Adorno, 1950, p. 385).

A complication that masked the significance of her findings for a time was that these original interviews were not of liberals and conservatives per se, but of the prejudiced versus the unprejudiced. One had to infer the relevance of her findings to liberalism versus conservatism from the whole context of the study. As we shall see, although liberals may be prejudiced and conservatives unprejudiced, this essential thrust for the concept of liberal versus conservative differences in parental style was later confirmed by Tomkins and by our own studies.

Another complication was that Frenkel-Brunswik also found evidence of Eysenck's T dimension in those she interviewed. Her "conservatives" showed toughminded "orientation toward power and contempt for the allegedly inferior and weak," which she felt was gained from parental attitudes. By contrast, her "liberal" seemed to "absorb a measure of passivity in his ideal of masculinity. No compensation through pseudo-toughness and antiweakness attitudes is thus necessary" (Adorno, 1950, p. 388). We will shortly encounter more about this masculinity-femininity aspect of the T dimension in the work of Comrey, but the implications of these early perceptions still remain to be untangled.

These findings of Frenkel-Brunswik and other "forgotten" relationships that the Adorno study revealed are shown in Figure 9. Contrasting tendencies are shown for the left to be low and the right high in authoritarianism (A), ethnocentrism (E), and prejudice (P). Tolerance of ambiguity is depicted as tolerance (Tol) for left, or liberal, and intolerance (Int) for conservative, or right. Findings for liberals, we should note, were chiefly those of Levinson's. Particularly fascinating were Adorno's own insights into liberal and conservative subtypologies, which we note in the figure as "Sub" chiefly to record a complexity for examining further in another book. Speculations about the nature of the middle in the study's last pages were, to be frank, rather ludicrous, and are noted in this figure only as a matter of historical interest.

Figure 9

Adorno and Associates Revisited

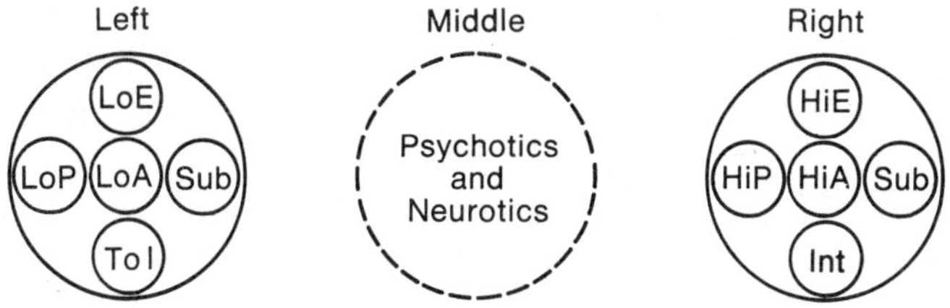

Where, on reexamination, the Adorno study proves to be more richly suggestive regarding ideology, the early Rokeach work is a surprise in that it offers little more than its original contribution to the debate. The problem seems to be that in narrowing the focus of his study to general cognitive mechanisms of belief, Rokeach eliminated aspects of specific personality and interpersonal action that are the warp and woof of actual ideological behavior. In the process he also tried (unsuccessfully, we feel) to eliminate intolerance of ambiguity as a differentiator between left and right. However, of the main pioneers of the "golden age" he was the first to raise the major question of the activist dimension, soon to provide the thrust to the ideological revival of the 1970s. Moreover, he was the only major figure to persist with unabated productivity, which led to his important new two-value theory that we will examine in the next chapter. Figure 10 summarizes one additional relevance of his early work to our concern with ideology: an equating of closemindedness with both left and right, viewed as belief extremes, and an equating of some form of openmindedness with the middle, an area of exceptional structural importance which Rokeach was among the first to empirically explore.

Figure 10

Rokeach Revisited

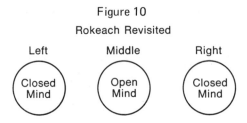

Despite persisting doubts about his data, in some ways Eysenck's theoretical work remains the most interesting of the three modern psychological classics. One reason for this assessment is the unusually powerful synthesis of physiological and sociological theory he brought to bear on the developmental psychology of ideology. Liberalism (or radicalism) and conservatism, he hypothesized, were to some appreciable extent determined by a coupling of social class position with the conditioning principles of reward. The lower classes and the poor were more liberal or radical because they had little to lose and much to gain through social change. By contrast, the higher, wealthier classes were conservative because they had much to lose through change and more to gain by maintaining the status quo. As for the etiology of tough- versus tendermindedness, Eysenck saw these differences as being to some appreciable extent determined by genetics. Those born with nervous systems that readily accepted conditioning, the introverts, were socially *over-*conditioned to suppress hostility, to be sensitive to the rights of others, and became tenderminded. Those born with nervous systems that resisted conditioning, however, the extroverts, were socially *under*conditioned, more prone to violence and to trampling on the rights of others, and became toughminded.

Tomkins: The Hidden Mountain

The psychological study of ideology proceeded during its "golden age," we have suggested, as a poking of flashlights into the darkness, followed by a comparing of notes and agreements and disagreements over the academic campfire. While this search was proceeding, another major investigator was probing the darkness with a lamp of so different a quality of light that others were aware only of a dim, possibly elfin presence along the periphery of their search. This was the psychologist Silvan Tomkins, whose remarkable advancement came in no single memorable book, but in the form of journal articles sandwiched into books on other subjects (Tomkins, 1963a, 1965), and included the development of one new measure for substantiating his theories.

Despite a complexity which some found to be baffling and alien, Tomkins' basic structural advancement can be easily visualized in the spacial terms we have been developing. Where others posited a single-dimensional view of left versus right, or a two-dimensional theory as in the case of Eysenck, Tomkins was the first to handle left and right as both one-dimensional *and* two-dimensional, to add a clear articulation of middleness as a third major dimension, and to further add a fourth dimension of the nonideological. This theoretical patterning was expressed in the first radically new measure for the field, the Tomkins' Polarity Scale (Tomkins, 1966).

As we have seen, for Adorno's, Eysenck's, and all other measures of the prevailing Likert type, the actual richness and variety of a person's ideology was reduced to the relative sterility of a single score located on a continuum from far left to far right. Tomkins' measure, however, presented the subject with a left-versus-right-oriented statement, and then the extremely important option of four choices. One might select the right option, or the left option—or both, or neither. The totaled score then became not a single number on a continuum, but a summary of choices among the four options and a ratio of their opposing or complementary relationships. The complexities of this measure discouraged many psychologists from using it. It was greeted with much more interest by political scientists (Hamden-Turner, 1970). But even if the Tomkins' Polarity Scale had never been used, it would still have served its purpose, for its basic contribution was to operationalize, for the first time, dialectical complexities that lie at the core of ideology, which we will briefly examine. Table 3 is a selection of representative items from this measure.

Table 3

Representative Items from the Tomkins' Polarity Scale

When people are in trouble, they should help themselves and not depend on others. (R)	vs.	When people are in trouble, they need help and should be helped. (L)
Little white lies in the long run lead to big black lies. (R)	vs.	Little white lies are justified when the truth might hurt the feelings of a close friend. (L)
Human nature being what it is, one day there will be no need of prisons. (L)	vs.	Human nature being what it is, prisons will always be with us. (R)
The most important thing in the world is to know yourself and be yourself. (L)	vs.	The most important thing in the world is to try to live up to the highest standards. (R)
The most important thing in science is to be right and make as few errors as possible. (R)	vs.	The most important thing in science is to strike out into the unknown—right or wrong. (L)
Great achievements require first of all great imagination. (L)	vs.	Great achievements require first of all severe self-discipline. (R)
The trouble with democracy is that it too often represents the will of the people. (R)	vs.	The trouble with democracy is that it too seldom represents the will of the people. (L)

In relation to his predecessors, Tomkins' contribution is perhaps best understood as the first adequate flowering of the Hegel-Marx dialectical strain in philosophy that in part guided the Adorno probe. Ironically, the dynamics of ideology to which Adorno was particularly sensitive were lost in his own study within forms of one-dimensional measurement alien to this perspective. The Tomkins measure, however, was a direct expression of multidimensional dialectical thought, and at last made it possible to begin to rigorously examine much that was previously hidden.

At the base of his view—and measure—lay the age-old right versus left polarity. However, Tomkins visualized this polarity, in terms considerably larger than the customary view of liberal versus conservative, as the conflict between the *normative* versus the *humanistic* sides to man (Tomkins and Izard, 1965, p. 79).

> *The issues constitute a polarity extending from the extreme left through a middle of the road position to the extreme right wing position. The issues are simple enough. Is man the measure, an end in himself, an active, creative, thinking, desiring, loving force in nature? Or must man realize himself, attain his full stature only through struggle toward, participation in, conformity to a norm, a measure, an ideal essence basically prior to and independent of man.*

As this quote illustrates, Tomkins considered the questions of the nature of the middle and the development of ideology to be of special importance. This interest is pursued in the following passage, which extends the earlier interest of Frenkel-Brunswik and Eysenck in societal and parental effects.

> *What might be the origins of such a duality in man's view of himself? Consider the basic alternatives open to parents interacting with their children. At one pole is a return of the parent to his own golden age through identification with the child in play and shared delight. The child's zest for life and obvious*

joy in simple human interaction and in elementary curiosity and attempted control over his own body, and the world in general, can revitalize the adult personality. Such a parent bestows on the child the feeling that he is an end in himself and that shared human interaction is a deeply satisfying experience. Further, such a parent will not puncture the child's conception of his ability to control his parent. Eventually such a child must come to the awareness that the world presents endless opportunities for the experience of varied positive affects—joy, excitement, love of people, of places, of activities, and of things. He becomes addicted to creating satisfaction for himself and for others.

There is another possibility open to any parent. This is the conjoint opportunity and obligation to mold the child to some norm. The norm may be a moral norm, a norm of "manners," a norm of competence, a norm of independence. In any case, the parent sets himself in opposition to the child and bestows on the child the sense that positive satisfaction is necessarily an epiphenomenon, consequent to effort, to struggle, to renunciation of his own immediate wishes. The child's feelings and wishes are devalued in favor of some kind of behavior which is demanded of him. When the child wishes to do one thing and the parent wishes him to do another, the normative parent must set himself in opposition to the child's wishes. He must convey to the child that what he wants to do is of no consequence when it is in opposition to the norm. What is expected of him, in opposition to his own wishes, may be presented with all possible attractiveness and positive sanctions, but the fundamental necessity of renunciation and devaluation of his own wishes, thereby of his self, cannot in a normative socialization be sidestepped [Tomkins and Izard, 1965, p. 87].

We may now begin to visualize new levels of relationships. One of the great difficulties in this area of investigation is the bridging of psychological and sociological views of man. It is here that Tomkins' concept of middleness—represented by a choice of *both* the left and the right statements on his measure —proves so useful as a meeting place for many concerns. For we may now see exactly why the simple labeling of a person as either liberal or conservative is a falsification of dialectical reality. On the social level all groups contain people who resonate in both left and right directions, according to circumstance. And on the personal level, within each of us there lie both left and right tendencies. As supported by both psychotherapeutic observation and theory, we are all mixtures of what Maslow termed growth needs vying with defense needs. The point of importance, then, is that both personal and social reality is shaped by a ratio of right to left, as well as an interaction between these polarities, which becomes either "middle" or "extreme" thought and behavior. Tomkins, as both a philosopher and a clinical theorist, was the first to define and investigate ideology in such terms.

Figure 11 depicts some implications of Tomkins' work on three levels of analysis: (1) the intrapersonal, or the left versus right conflict within each of us as individuals; (2) the interpersonal, or conflict between persons and groups; and (3) the developmental sequences involving different kinds of parents and child-raising styles.

Factor Analysis and the Puncturing of the Dream

It is a truism worth remarking that social science advances through the conflict between theorists and empiricists—and between these two sides within the same investigator. The pattern in the psychological study of ideology from 1940 to 1970 was of the projection of large structural views by the theorists, which were then so riddled by the guerilla tactics of the empiricists that one is reminded of the ruins of old fortresses. This attrition led to an abandonment of the field as not one in which

Figure 11

Tomkins' Views of Ideology

I. Intrapersonal: the Left-Right Conflict Within Us

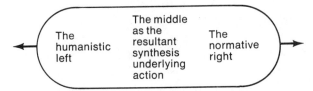

II. Interpersonal and intergroup: the Left-Right Conflict in
    Relations Between People and Groups

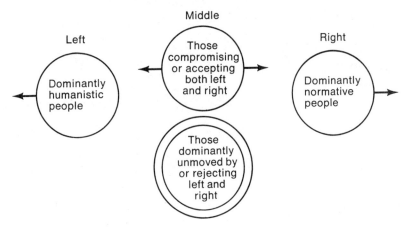

III. Developmental

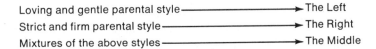

a young investigator might hope to gain funding and make a
name for himself. An early leader of the guerrilla warfare was
Richard Christie, who attacked the Adorno and Eysenck studies
with masterful critical studies and developed two excellent measures bearing on ideology—the Machiavellianism and New Left

scales (Christie, 1969, 1970). Significantly, these new measures backed away from the earlier attempts at comprehensive assessment to concentrate on more specific and limited measurement objectives.

Particularly ironic was the operation of factor analysis within the pattern of crescendo and denouement for ideological studies. Eysenck, the factor analyst par excellence, arrived on the scene heralding the superiority of this powerful statistical tool as a method of finding the structure of "truth" beneath the gloss of theory and scattered empiricism. Earlier we noted how the covariance of two variables can be represented visually as an overlapping of two circles, with the shared portion representing the covariance and the nonshared portion representing variables that are interacting with something else (see Figure 6). In such terms, factor analysis operates approximately as shown in Figure 12.

Figure 12

Factor Analysis of Ideological Variables

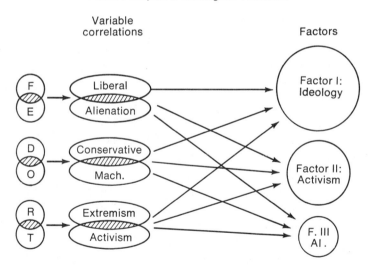

The left side of Figure 12 shows hypothetical test results for some familiar variables in the study of ideology—tests of such variables as the Adorno F and E, the Rokeach D and O, the Eysenck R and T, and other tests measuring liberalism, alienation, conservatism, Machiavellianism, extremism, and activism. The correlations of these variables are represented by the shaded overlaps—the F and E scales correlate, for example, as do liberalism and alienation. If we then take the scores of all these measures and process them according to factor analytic formulae, we will obtain the composites of correlations—or the extraction of basic similarities—known as factors. The figure illustrates how each pair of variables contributes a portion of covariance—some more, some less—to the three factors that are extracted. We see further that these three factors differ in the amount of covariance they account for. Thus, the size of Factor I, Ideology, tells us that whatever underlies liberalism and conservatism is causing the greatest amount of covariance on these tests. Factor II, Activism, and Factor III, Alienation, then account for progressively less covariance.

It appeared to others as well as Eysenck that here indeed was the ideal method for unraveling the mystery of ideology amid the proliferation of test items and ever more slippery and bewildering pairs and matrices of correlations. However, with the exception of the work of Comrey, to be examined in the next chapter, this effort generally led to more rather than less confusion. Through the intimidation of methodology—that is, the apparent requirement of this level of sophistication to advance work in this area—it is also likely that factor analysis helped to further discourage serious work in ideology. The developer of one of the most sensible and sensitive, newer liberalism-conservatism measures, Kerlinger, used his measure as the basis for some mind-boggling factor analyses to prove that liberalism-conservatism was not one but two dimensions (Kerlinger, 1958). As we have begun to see, through a glimpse at Tomkins' work, liberalism-conservatism can be usefully viewed either way. *We are dealing with a phenomenon that repeatedly is not simply a case of the either-or but of the both-and interpretive perspective. We are dealing here with multi- rather than single-faceted truth.* In such situations factor analysis can be exceptionally productive in revealing useful data, but the problem lies in the lack of adequate interpretive frameworks. All too often the net result is destructive because of the confusion that results when the straight jacket of the either-or interpretation must be applied to multifaceted both-and findings.

An excellent factor-analytic study by Hicks and Wright (1970) is prototypical. After examining a majority of the liberalism-conservatism (LC) measures in use during the 1960s, they selected five they considered to be the most carefully constructed. This included a five-item version of the Adorno PEC, a seven-item derivation from Eysenck's work by Centers, a massive seventy-six-item scale developed by a leading factor-analytic investigator, Kerr, and other measures by Hicks and Wright, and Campbell. They also included the Adorno F scale, but nothing from Rokeach or Tomkins. After an extensive factor analysis, and further discriminant function analysis, they concluded that LC is "comprised of at least four independent dimensions: Economic, Political, Religious, and Esthetic LC." However, echoing mounting dissatisfaction with both the concept and its measurement, they also concluded that "none of the scales investigated is fully adequate either as a comprehensive measure of LC or as a measure of the specific LC dimension" (Hicks and Wright, 1970, p. 119).

Moreover, a survey of a majority of LC measures by the University of Michigan's Institute for Social Research concluded that the hopes for a general usefulness of LC had "faded when encountered with research done on the mass level. Repeated samples of the national electorate by the Survey Research Center . . . have convincingly demonstrated that no such organizing dimension or ideological structure exists for most citizens" (Robinson, Rusk, and Head, 1968).

During the 1960s the idea of the "end of ideology" also grew among sociologists (Waxman, 1968). Advanced by some of the field's most prestigious thinkers was the contention that ideology was outmoded as a social motivational system because ideological differences seemed to be disappearing from politics, and because we had either reached, or were so well on the way to the "good society," that the drive of ideology was no longer needed.

It was Rokeach who administered the apparent *coup de grâce* to liberalism-conservatism in psychology. In a devastating critique of previous research he listed five major difficulties with the concept. He felt that the concept of liberalism-conservatism could not be employed ahistorically or cross-culturally; there was little agreement on its defining attributes; it was an ambiguous mixture of ideological and stylistic attributes; it was often confused with the authoritarian-antiauthoritarian concept; and it could be defined only in relative terms, never precisely. "It is unlikely that the liberalism-conservatism concept can be rescued from all such ambiguities," Rokeach concluded (1973, p. 168).

Mark Twain once remarked of his obituary, which appeared in error, that the reports of his death were somewhat exaggerated. As we found in our survey of the classics, and will next encounter in a survey of more recent investigations, this also appears to be the case with ideology.

4

The Ideological Revival

While a first wave of investigators was falling back from the fortress of ideology, bemused or ringing the death knell, from elsewhere a new onslaught was mounting. Earlier we noted the explosion of the late 1960s, when throughout the world, campuses reverberated with student riots and bombings. One effect of this disruption was that psychologists and sociologists, who might otherwise have quietly accepted the idea of the death of ideology, were forced to study its persisting phenomena as both a matter of curiosity and institutional survival. The result was a vast literature (Lipset, 1959; Flacks, 1967), of which the writings of Kenneth Keniston (1965, 1968), the surveys of Richard Peterson (1968), and the New Left measure developed by Richard Christie (1969) were prototypical.

A second factor accounting for continuing interest in ideology was the mounting economic investment in political campaigns and the proliferation of opinion-polling firms. Whatever the theorists and methodologists might say, those social

scientists who made their living by working with political phenomena continued to find that the age-old terminology of liberal versus conservative best fit the facts as they knew them.
During the 1960s this persistence of ideology as a bread-and-
butter issue for polling continued unabated in the pages of the
Public Opinion Quarterly, and it was reflected in thousands of
pages of newspaper reports of the work of Gallup, Roper, and
the rising new firms of Harris, Yankelovich, and Fields.

A third factor accounting for the endurance of left-right
ideology were the questions raised by the "golden age" investigators. We shall examine this abiding interest in the work of
Greenstein on children's attitudes, Wilson on conservatism,
Comrey on factor analysis, the quiet expansion of Tomkinism,
and the return of Rokeach with a striking new values model. In
addition, we will examine the relevance of new studies of activism and extremism; the perception by Lewis and Kraut and
others of the need for a restoration of balance; the new holism
of Hamden-Turner and Knutson; and the developmental potential of Maslow's humanistic motivational theory.

Children's Attitudes: Greenstein

We have seen how Frenkel-Brunswik and Tomkins fo-
cused on the parent-child relation as a key process in the development of ideology. In political science, Greenstein noted that
to understand how "political patterns maintain themselves over
long periods of time . . . the process of preadult political learning will prove to be an important link in system maintenance
and an important place for the analyst—and the would-be reformer, or defender of the status quo—to interject himself"
(Greenstein and Tarrow, 1970, p. 508). The problem was how
to measure and thereby assess the nature of the generational
link. The psychological measures for exploring children's political attitudes seemed inadequate to this political scientist. Greenstein felt that "people do not walk down the street carrying in
their heads the familiar (agree-disagree) continuum of the Likert
scale." He speculated that "the imperfect fit between inner perceptual experience and its representation in survey data may

help explain some of the puzzling qualities of so much of the questionnaire data that have been so carefully collected over the past several decades" (Greenstein and Tarrow, 1970, p. 504).

Driven by an interest akin to Tomkins' in developing a better way to quantify the true dimensions and richness of the ideological experience, Greenstein developed a semiprojective technique for use in cross-cultural studies with British and French as well as American children. His technique derives from a clinical tradition in psychology which includes the well-known Rorschach, TAT, and sentence-completion projective tests. It is semiprojective in that it furnishes a structured beginning for a story that presents the child with a dilemma to be resolved through the child's own creative imagination.

One incomplete story, for example, is this:

> *Two children are playing in their room. Their parents are out. When the parents return, they notice there is a window broken in the kitchen. Finish the story* in any way you like *[Greenstein and Tarrow, 1970, p. 514].*

Another example:

> *The teacher leaves the classroom for a few minutes. She asks the children to do their lessons quietly. She thinks she has left some money on her desk, but when she returns she cannot find the money there. Finish the story* in any way you like *[Greenstein and Tarrow, 1970, p. 515].*

The children's answers are then analyzed by Greenstein. The advantages of this method are that it provides a way of entering the rich cognitive world of the individual, while at the same time it provides data that can be coded and quantified for group comparisons. Of special interest to us are two aspects of Greenstein's investigation. Note first how the story situations above pose a dilemma for the child in which the choices before him are whether he will *maintain* or *violate* established norms for behavior. We will experimentally explore the implications of this dichotomy in Part Four. We would further note that while the etiology of any kind of "stark" right-left ideology is not of primary interest to Greenstein, his reference to the reformers versus the defenders of the status quo, quoted earlier, is an instance of how the right-left polarity seems to remain inescapable in the context of political studies.

Wilson and the "New" Conservatism

While some relegated ideology to the ash heap and others avoided it as a social outcast within psychology, a group of British investigators headed by Glenn Wilson proved the dominance and persistence of this dimension in a wide range of human affairs. Hypothesizing that conservatism is "a general factor . . . underlying the entire field of social attitudes," Wilson (1973) developed a new measure for it and launched cross-cultural studies in Great Britain, New Zealand, and the Netherlands, which in turn encouraged a smattering of American studies.

Building upon Frenkel-Brunswik's original intolerance-of-ambiguity experiments, information theory, and other findings of conservative personality constants, Wilson theorized that the psychological basis of conservative attitudes "is a generalized susceptibility to feeling threat or anxiety in the face of uncertainty (ambiguity, complexity, change, novelty, deviance, individuality, anomie). In this view, the tendency for the conservative person to subjugate his inner needs and feelings to the social order . . . is interpreted as a means of reducing choice (response uncertainty), thus simplifying the cognitive world" (Wilson, 1973, p. 286). The net effect for Wilson is again, as for Durkheim originally and Tomkins more recently, a concern with norms, as "the extreme conservative perceives the world as 'falling apart,' which leads him to seek and place value upon order, simplicity, and security" (Wilson, 1973, p. 288).

With a boldness of attack reminiscent of Eysenck's original foray, Wilson's new measure for exploring conservatism is a radical departure from earlier techniques. Moreover, in contrast to the necessarily cumbersome methods of Tomkins and Greenstein for probing the complexity of ideology, Wilson's measure is such a simplification of format that the whole test can be taken in less than three minutes and scored in a few seconds. It consists of a list of fifty single words or two-word phrases such as death penalty, evolution theory, school uniforms, striptease shows, sabbath observance, beatniks, patriotism, and modern art. You are asked to scan the list and simply check "Yes" or "No" as to whether you favor or believe in what each word or phrase represents.

The measure has shown significant reliabilities and validities cross-culturally, thereby answering one of Rokeach's five criticisms of LC as earlier measured and visualized. Again we encounter evidence of the possible meaningfulness of ideology in *norming* processes. In Tomkins, Greenstein, and now Wilson we may discern the slim but persisting evidential thread of a conservative concern with establishing, maintaining, or defending norms, in contrast with the more laissez faire attitudes of the liberal. Closely related to this norm-process difference, and of exceptional importance in the empirical grounding of the study of ideology, are the experiments of G. B. Kish reported in the basic Wilson text (Wilson, 1973). Kish clearly established the motivational relationship of stimulus-reducing needs to conservatives and stimulus-seeking needs to liberals. The emphasis of the Wilson work, however, is on conservatism, and we must note that for all his methodological gains there is a certain imbalance in focusing on only one end of the LC continuum. It is also of interest that Wilson considers Eysenck's T factor of questionable significance. To Wilson, tough- versus tendermindedness seems a result of the questions asked rather than of the respondent's personality, or, of item *context* rather than attitude *content* (Wilson, 1973). Others, however, would disagree.

Comrey and the Enduring T

Although Eysenck's own data provided questionable support for his T dimension, other factor analysts have found continuing support for it. For Cattell (1965) it is one of sixteen major dimensions for his well-known system of total personality assessment. It is also one of eight prime factors for a more advanced, new personality measure developed by Comrey (1970).

Comrey's work is of considerable interest in that it can be viewed as an assessment of LC functioning within the context of the whole personality. During the 1960s, Comrey was one of several investigators to develop LC measures with existing items and the Likert technique (Comrey and Newmeyer, 1965). Dissatisfied with the results of these measures, however, he seemingly abandoned the field and moved on to develop a new personality test based on a factor analysis of items from Eysenck, Cattell, Guilford, the MMPI, and other sources.

Comrey's sources for items were *not* LC measures per se. They were all instruments for *general* personality assessment. Moreover, Comrey was not seeking to isolate LC. He was simply following the objective, computerized procedures for isolating factors. Yet of eight personality factors, which he found accounted for a majority of the variance in test scores, *four* have been identified by either Tomkins or the Adorno group as differentiating characteristics of liberals or conservatives. The four factors include trust (L) versus defensiveness (C); orderliness (C) versus lack of compulsion (L); social conformity (C) versus rebelliousness (L); and empathy (L) versus egocentricity (C). Within the context of Comrey's investigation, this seems rather compelling additional evidence that ideology is not "ending" but remains a basic and enduring component of human functioning.

A fifth Comrey factor of interest to us is masculinity versus femininity. This is Comrey's version of the factor that both Eysenck and Cattell identify as tough- versus tenderminded. For Comrey it is the least homogeneous of his eight factors, but its importance here is that *continuing analysis and reanalysis has failed to eliminate it.* It endures as a factor of importance in accounting for the operation of human personality.

Finally, there is again the matter of a relation of LC to norming processes. After completing the study we report in Part Four, we had, as will be seen, good reason for wanting to find or develop a better measure for a hypothesized personality dimension of norm violating versus norm maintaining. On a hunch we examined the 180 items of Comrey's measure. We found that in eighteen of them, or ten percent, the probable operation of such an alignment could be discerned. For example: "The laws governing the people of this country are sound and need only minor changes, if any" (hypothetically norm maintaining). Or: "People who break the law while protesting bad social conditions should get off without punishment" (norm violating). Or: "I have done things of a sexual nature that society does not approve of" (norm violating). As we report in Chapter Eleven we followed up this hunch and using Comrey items did develop, we believe, a greatly improved measure for assessing norm violation versus maintenance.

Tomkins and the Tomkinsonians

Following the initial lack of general interest in his theory of ideology, Tomkins continued to pursue his primary field, the psychology of affect, or how emotion and cognition conjointly act to induce and amplify motivation. One of his recognized major contributions to psychology is the study of positive and negative affects (Tomkins, 1962, 1963a). Two aspects of his affect theory kept the ideological pot simmering on a low back burner during the early years of the ideological revival. One aspect was his observation that positive affects, such as enjoyment, were dominantly associated with liberals, and negative affects, such as disgust, with conservatives. The other aspect was Tomkins' controversial view that the human face both generated and expressed this aspect of motivation (typical of his theorizing, Tomkins' work in affect and facial expression predated by more than a decade the wave of face and body-language studies of the 1970s).

The hypothetical linking of affect and face to ideology led to experimental work with Hadley Cantril and others (Tomkins, 1965) in which subjects were shown a sequence of photographs in such a way that one eye saw a smiling face and the other eye a contemptuous face. To form a single image the subject had to suppress one or the other photograph. To a highly significant degree, liberals reported seeing the smiling face whereas conservatives reported seeing the contemptuous face. Another approach to the same general phenomenon was by Carlson and Levy (1970). Item 57 of Tomkins' Polarity Scale poses the differences as between affects of disgust (conservative) and shame (liberal), measured by the choice of statements: "Life sometimes leaves a bad taste in the mouth" (liberal) or "Life sometimes smells bad" (conservative). Three different experiments by Carlson and Levy demonstrated that seemingly remote characteristics of liberals and conservatives were highly predictable from responses to this *single* Polarity Scale item. Still more recently, Tomkins' graduate student, June Vasquez, experimentally replicated his personal ability to differentiate liberals from conservatives simply by observing their facial expressions. Impartial judges observing and rating subjects' facial expressions significantly confirmed a prediction that liberals would smile and reflect more enjoyment whereas conservatives would reflect more disgust (Vasquez, 1975). Thus, by these unusual experimental means, Tomkins' theory of ideology has shown a powerful consistency in linkages of emotion, cognition, beliefs, behavior, and values (Eckhardt and Alcock, 1970), and also in its capacity for predicting responses.

Investigators have also used the Polarity Scale for other kinds of ideological studies. An incomplete study by Tomkins and Messick of the cognition of affect administered the scale in an eighteen-hour battery of tests to high-school students (Loye, 1970). Eckhardt and Alcock (1970) used the scale in a study of ideology and personality in attitudes toward war and peace; Henry Alker with students at Cornell to differentiate subjects for small group studies (Alker, 1971); and Alker and Poppen (1973) to explore variables of ideological personality including dogmatism, Machiavellianism, and locus of control. In our own work for the studies reported later, we pilot-tested the Polarity Scale in three greatly differing academic settings and conducted its first known-group validation. We also developed two new instruments based on the Polarity Scale: the PS-II, a six-item translation to the Likert format for use in large battery administration, and "Exercises in Decision Making," a more advanced measure for the study of group dynamics. This last measure is a translation of Tomkins' items into the Choice Dilemma Questionnaire format developed by Kogan and Wallach (1964) and was used by us in experimental studies defining a phenomenon we call the "M-Shift." We have also used the Polarity Scale to obtain score profiles for leaders and followers of liberal and conservative leadership elites for transhistorical studies of ideological subtypes, roles and role-functional relationships.

The Return of Rokeach

The most striking new contribution to the study of the left-right ideology has come from the investigator who seemingly tried to "kill" it. Spurred on by dissatisfaction with the LC concept and all previous methods of measuring it, Rokeach returned to the fray in the 1970s with a considerable theoretical and measurement advancement.

Following the investigation of belief systems recorded in *The Open and Closed Mind*, Rokeach's interests centered on the study of values. During the 1960s he made what many psychologists consider to be the most important contribution to this area, in the course of which he developed a new two-value model of politics. His purpose was to see if he might devise a way to cut through the ambiguities of the LC complex and define politics "by identifying the minimum number of variables that will adequately describe all major political variations across historical time and cultural space" (Rokeach, 1973, p. 169).

Noting in *The Nature of Human Values* (1973) that the value of *freedom* and the value of *equality* were of special interest in the political context, Rokeach asked himself why. One answer, it seemed to him, was that in all societies there are inequal distributions of power, that politics exists as a method of handling this inequality, and that the way people perceive their own share of power in relation to the power shares of others is reflected in their advocacy of certain values. Those who possess the greater power "will seek to maintain or even enhance their greater freedom and superior status in society. Conversely, those possessing the lesser power . . . will seek to decrease status differences and to increase freedom" (Rokeach, 1973, p. 169).

This analysis is of much the same social realities that

Eysenck perceived in developing his theories, but Rokeach narrows and intensifies the focus. It led him to hypothesize a pattern for identifying all known political variations throughout the world on a relatively simple two-dimensional scale. He hypothesized that the extreme left—communists and communist societies—place a high value on equality, but a low value on freedom. The moderate or socialist left places high values on both freedom and equality. The moderate or capitalist right highly values freedom, but places a low value on equality. And the extreme fascist right places a low value on both freedom and equality.

Very rarely are social scientists able to project such neat theoretical arrangements; rarer still does the data they gather support them. This pattern of hypotheses, however, was strikingly confirmed by research. Rokeach applied content analysis to 25,000 word samples from basic communist, socialist, capitalist, and fascist writings. These writings were selected from different cultural areas of Europe and America, were written at different times in the twentieth century, and were originally written in three different languages—German, Russian, and English. Yet the pattern was exactly confirmed as Rokeach had projected it. That is, the number of references to the concept of freedom was high in socialist and capitalist writings, low in communist and fascist writings. References to equality were high in socialist and communist writings and low in capitalist and fascist writings.

These results have many possible implications. One of potential major importance derives from the observation of Hegel, who first speculated on the meaning of the interaction of right versus left, that history's goal is increasing *freedom* for man. In the Rokeach pattern, the *moderate* left and *moderate* right *both* place a high value on freedom. This suggests the interesting theoretical possibility of a symbiotic functioning by liberal *and* conservative in advancing freedom. Such a symbiosis would be in keeping with the philosophy of the founding of this nation (Schlesinger, 1964) and in marked contrast to the lack of value placed on freedom by extreme left and extreme right.

Another finding, through administrations of the Rokeach

Value Scale, was the following percentage distributions for five primary ideologies. Of a sample of 1409 adult Americans, 2.4 percent were communist-oriented, 24.2 percent socialist, 54.9 percent "middle American," 14.5 percent capitalist, and 4.0 percent fascist-oriented.

The size of the middle (54.9 percent) is of particular interest. This middleness was defined by Rokeach as a lack of homogeneity in subject ranking of equality and freedom. That is, those assigned to the middle position varied considerably in their value rankings and did not fit any of the high-low patterns for equality and freedom as hypothesized. "It is this majority which is presumably the 'silent majority' that has the most say at election time in determining the composition of national and local legislative bodies in the United States," he comments (Rokeach, 1973, p. 193). These observations convey a sense of an area of considerable fluidity to be examined in our *Psychology of the Middle*.

Rokeach's observations, as related to his earlier interest in activism, now also led him to pose the following "law" of political activism: "A more extreme regard for either one or both of the two political values, *equality* and *freedom*, is a minimum condition for sustained political action and is also a minimum consequence of political action" (Rokeach, 1973, p. 211).

The Need for a Balanced Perspective

As we noted earlier, just as social activism forced issue after issue upon the American consciousness during the 1960s, so it also breached the high walls of academia to entice or goad researchers to venture forth in search of ideological meanings. Studies of the New Left and student protest cast new beams into the darkness of ideology. However, while making much of Marx as a symbol for the new defiance, these studies further intensified the disintegration of the classic holistic perspective that Marx helped father. We have seen how the Adorno research, which dominated the 1940s and 1950s, was distorted by concentrating on the rightist extreme. The new wave of studies was similarly imbalanced by a concentration on the left extreme.

"This concentration has hindered the development of a broader view of the distinctive correlates of political behavior and political beliefs over an entire range of each," Lewis and Kraut (1972, p. 134) concluded. They were both recent graduates of Yale, with fresh Ph.D.s and in their first teaching jobs at the time of this assessment—Lewis at Yale and Kraut at the University of Pennsylvania. We emphasize their youth at the time as a meaningful aspect to the revival of interest in ideology; here was evidence of the young investigator being encouraged to explore the field. While most older investigators were still pursuing the phenomena of ideology and social changes in bits and pieces, these scholars from the new "activist" generation were concerned by the need for a more holistic perspective on ideology and called for a restoration of balance and a new extension of scope. "If this literature is to make a contribution to a general understanding of the antecedents and correlates of student political orientations, it must move from a concern with the characteristics of specific groups at specific times to a concern with the *dimensions* of political belief and political activism," they emphasized (Lewis and Kraut, 1972, p. 134).

Hamden-Turner and Knutson. In answer to this need for integrative studies, two important new attempts were launched by Charles Hamden-Turner in *Radical Man* (1970) and Jeanne Knutson in *The Human Basis of the Polity* (1972). Both works are oriented to the "third-force" psychology of Maslow, which we will examine in closing this section. Other than this similarity, however, it would be difficult to imagine two more radically different approaches to the challenge of attaining the lost holism of Hegel, Marx, and Pareto.

A strength of Hamden-Turner's work was its bold embracing of the ideological polarity we have now identified in so many works over modern times. The old left-right polarity was posed anew by Hamden-Turner as that between Radical Man and Conservative or Anomic Man. The chief thrust of his effort was to marshall a variety of studies to support his descriptions of these monolithic supertypes and to develop a purportedly new, theoretical framework of ideological structure and dynamics. As several reviewers noted, *Radical Man* is undoubtedly brilliant. It is reminiscent of the old master Karl Marx in its compilation of empirical riches from many sources, its poetic passion, and its suggestive insights. Perhaps most notably, it is a courageous work in a neglected area of investigation in which ideas of great social import have been obscured by the caution and reluctance of most scholars to venture beyond their own bailiwicks. At the same time the book is flawed as a work of science. One drawback is that while trying to advance under-standing of the concepts of right versus left, Hamden-Turner's work is also retrogressive; it seeks to reconsolidate left and right into the gross stereotypes from which most social scientists have tried to free themselves to gain a more subtle and generally use-ful understanding of ideology in man. A second flaw is that, despite many insights into the nature of "the opposition," the work is mainly a polemic for Radical Man and only occasionally the balanced consideration of ideology it purports to be. A third flaw, to which we are possibly hypersensitive, is that cer-tain theoretical aspects seem to be insufficiently credited to the richer and more rigorous perspective on ideology developed by Tomkins in his seminal essay in the early 1960s (Tomkins, 1963a).

Knutson's is also, in many ways, a bold and wide-ranging work. With doctorates in both political science and psychology, she came to view political science and "the underdeveloped field of political psychology" as "typified by fragmented and haphazard applications . . . of pseudopsychology . . . Instead of peeking, from time to time, into the Pandora's box provided by Freud, it is suggested that we courageously take the lid off" (Knutson, 1972, pp. 10, 11). As with Hamden-Turner, she sets out to explore the interrelationships of authoritarianism, anomie, alienation, dogmatism, as well as efficacy, misanthropy, mental health, and political participation. She also develops a theory of "psychic evolution," this time based on five basic psychodevelopmental needs posited by Maslow. Particularly excellent are her discussions of Rokeach's work—relating his open-closed minded schema to the Maslow growth-defense needs schema—and of intolerance of ambiguity, anomie, and alienation.

Her relating of political-scientific with psychological concepts is unique, and yet again, as with Hamden-Turner, we must raise caveats. Where Hamden-Turner's poetic boldness at times violates both scholarship and reality, after a similarly bold opening, Knutson gradually seems to become overwhelmed both by scholarship and the complexity of ideology. In the end she withdraws from the fray leaving no sharp sense of the promised integration. In addition, where Hamden-Turner constructs gross supertypes of right versus left, Knutson leans over backwards to avoid the old polarities entirely. The word *liberalism* appears once in the whole book; the words *conservatism, leftist* and *rightist* only a half dozen times; nor is there any mention of Tomkins, Hamden-Turner, or Wilson. This strange avoidance of LC reflects a tendency in contemporary academic political studies, possibly influenced by the "end of ideology" debate, to try to ignore the old polarities as being somehow part of a simplistic and infantile past we should have outgrown.

Whatever their deficiencies in relation to the enormous integrative task, both works will be found invaluable by the serious student of ideology. Moreover, despite a marked difference of approach, both works are similar in one strength. Hamden-Turner presents a vivid portrait of the liberal as the creative personality, Knutson a comprehensive survey of the correlates of the democratic personality, and both works begin the exceptionally important task of relating the developmental theory of Maslow to the question of ideal governmental structures for man.

Activism and Extremism. We have glimpsed the rise of a theoretical interest in activism in our summaries of Rokeach's studies. Tomkins' interest in activism was also for a time quite intense and resulted in a remarkable psychohistorical study of its development through parent-child relationships in the abolitionists prior to the American Civil War (Tomkins, 1965). We have also encountered an interest in extremism, subsumed within the concepts of extreme left and extreme right, as compared with the moderate positions of liberal and conservative. The great problem, which we originally noted (Loye, 1974) in developing a case for the study reported in Part Four, was that although various aspects of liberals and conservatives, activists and inactivists, and extremists and moderates had been investigated, only one study (Lewis and Kraut, 1972) had examined all these types as a complex of three personality dimensions—and this approach seems of potentially central importance in the study of ideology. If a broader and more balanced perspective on ideology is to be regained, we reasoned, the relationships between liberalism-conservatism, activism-inactivism, and extremism-moderation must be determined by rigorous modern techniques of investigation and statistical analysis.

Activism and extremism have long been viewed as closely associated with each other, and with ideology, and even as identical to ideology. The stereotypical liberal is thought to be an activist, who is *for* social change, whereas the stereotypical conservative is considered an inactivist, who is *against* social change. Likewise, the extremes of both ideological wings are seen as simply very much for or against social change, whereas the moderates hold less firm convictions. Lewis and Kraut (1972) noted that these popular perceptions are reflected within psychological studies of LC by a serious confounding of activism and right-left beliefs. Studies by several investigators (Cowdry, Keniston, and Cabin, 1970; Silvern and Nakamura, 1971) indicated that variables, which, during the wave of New Left studies, were found to be attributes of radical left activists, were actually characteristic of all students who act on their political beliefs, regardless of ideology. Also, studies separating moderates from the extremes of ideology (De Fronzo, 1972; Alker, 1971) and studies investigating even more varied ideological subtypes (Adorno, 1950; Lane, 1962; Block, 1971) have found marked behavioral differences among subtypes. Thus, it is increasingly apparent that the balanced investigation of ideology must carefully control for and investigate LC interrelationships with activism and inactivism and with extremism and moderation.

Another theme of major interest in studies of ideology spawned by interest in New Left and student activism is the formation of activism and extremism through the parent-child relationship. For our purposes this concern extends the investigative beam with which Else Frenkel-Brunswik and Tomkins probed parent-child relations, child-raising styles, and developmental factors in general. In the New Left and activism research literature this interest centers about the socialization or "continuity" hypothesis and the generational conflict or "discontinuity" hypothesis. The first hypothesis assumes a modeling of child after parent and a continuity in kind and degree of political belief—that is, liberal parents tend to produce liberal children, conservative parents produce conservatives, activists produce activists, and extremists produce extremists. Studies by Greenstein (1965), Flacks (1967), and Keniston (1968) support this position. In contrast, there is evidence of the type of conflict that racked households and became a major national and worldwide concern during the 1960s. This is the once highly publicized conflict of the "generational gap," which pits the more conservative, moderate, or inactivist parent against the more liberal, extreme, or activist child. In the research literature evidence of these types are cited to support a discontinuity hypothesis. In a longitudinal study to resolve the controversy, Lewis and Kraut (1972) and Kraut, Lewis, and Pepitone (1973) found support for both positions.

The study of activism during the 1960s and early 1970s was carried out in dramatic contexts. A leading investigator, Richard Flacks, gained his insights by storming the ramparts as an active participant-observer, whereas for other investigators insight came from the experience of figuratively being seized and held captive by the subject matter. The most useful studies of extremism, however, came from the seemingly humdrum classroom administration of the same old questionnaires, whose relevance has been generally overlooked. These questionnaires investigated extremism as a response style, or ERS—extreme responding style.

Extreme responders were found to have, as did conservatives, high scores on the Adorno F scale (Mogar, 1960), social distance (Triandis and Triandis, 1962), and intolerance of ambiguity (Brim and Hoff, 1957). But in direct contradiction to the first of these findings, extreme responders were found to have, as did liberals, *low* scores on the F scale (Zuckerman, Norton, and Sprague, 1958). Although enticing for the dedicated psychological researcher, this type of Lilliputian contradiction often discourages other social scientists from the further pursuit of psychology. The effect is similar to encountering cobwebs in a dark attic, with good sense telling one to return to open territory. The ERS findings may become even murkier if one seeks to relate them to the mainstream of ideological investigation. Within the literature, however, two highly suggestive patterns may be discerned—of studies revealing "desirable" versus "undesirable" characteristics for extremism. Here one may sense a matter of the ideological viewpoint of the investigator at work. That is, some perceive the extreme believer as a hero, but to others he is a dangerous troublemaker.

Among "undesirable" characteristics found among extreme responders are abnormality—an "increase in ERS as adjustment becomes poorer" (Hamilton, 1968, p. 196); pathology, rapid closure, and lack of verbal skill (Damarin and Messick, 1965); and a "concrete" versus "abstract" cognitive structure (White and Harvey, 1965). Brengelmann (1960) concludes that the "tendency to respond in an extreme manner is a primary characteristic of the 'rigid personality'" (Brengelmann, 1960, p. 197). On the "desirable" side of extremism, Tajfel and Wilkes (1964) show that as an object of judgment gains importance, the judgment is more extreme. O'Donovan (1965, p. 365) concludes that "response to meaningful stimuli will tend toward the extreme (polarize) while response to meaningless stimuli will tend toward the indifferent (depolarize)." Such findings and the eruption of the student protest movement in France inspired an important cycle of studies on student activists in Paris by Moscovici and associates at the Sorbonne in the late 1960s. The conclusion reached by Moscovici and Zavalloni (1969) was that the customary equation of extremism and polarizing with "badness," and moderation and consensus with "goodness," was obscuring the investigation of an important aspect of social reality. Alker (1971) summarized the findings of the Sorbonne group by stating that "people with more extreme views in ambiguous settings are seen as more able and decisive."

Another pattern in ERS literature on extremism is composed of three theories to account for it: theories of the extremist as deviant; as feeling the need for structure to reduce ambiguity; and as a seeker for and respondent to meaningfulness of stimuli. These theories will be examined later in more detail.

A Summary and the Maslow Perspective

In Chapter Three we examined the "golden age" of psychological studies of ideology—the masterworks of Adorno, Frenkel-Brunswik, Levinson, Rokeach, Eysenck, and Tomkins. We thereby observed the rise and fall of interest in ideology from 1940 to roughly 1966. In Chapter Four we have sketched the revival of interest in this subject that began in the late 1960s and slowly regained momentum in the 1970s. The works of Greenstein, Wilson, Comrey, Tomkins and associates, and Rokeach have been reviewed as well as the integrative studies of Hamden-Turner and Knutson, and a variety of studies on activism and extremism.

During the chapters that lie ahead we will attempt to build upon this grounding in the contemporary study of ideology. The research we have covered so far suggests at least four initial conclusions. One is that ideology, far from being dead or dying, is central to our make-up and influences much of what we do in life, in apolitical as well as political contexts. Therefore our goal will be to forcefully relate our research to real life. A second observation is that while more is known about ideology than one might have thought, this is still new territory for the investigator. We hope the original studies we report will serve to encourage venturing by others. It seems further evident, as a third point, that ideological research offers an opportunity to scholars to confront the challenges not simply of human advancement but, because of its leadership implications, of human existence itself. Fourthly, it seems to us that the great task facing the investigator is to help build a new theoretical framework to embrace the diversity of ideology and relate it to the framing of political and other organizational systems that will meet the vast and alarming needs of the times.

Focusing on this need for larger theoretical structures, we

will move step by step toward such a goal throughout the rest of this book. To foreshadow this larger purpose we end this section with some relevant thoughts of the psychological theorist whose work both Knutson and Hamden-Turner found most productive. Although our perspective on Maslow varies considerably from theirs, we agree with their belief that his work, along with that of Tomkins and Rokeach, will be found most useful by the framers of "the new theory of ideology."

> *When the philosophy of man changes, then everything changes, not only the philosophy of politics, of economics, of ethics and values, of interpersonal relations and of history itself, but also the philosophy of education, the theory of how to help men become what they can and deeply need to become [Maslow, 1968, p. 189].*

Such passages by Maslow helped develop humanistic psychology into both a popular cult and a significant force for social-scientific renewal. As is the way with cults, a portion of the master's original vision became the free-floating zeitgeist wherein the liberal is the hero and the conservative the villain. Maslow the scientist, however, originally drew upon both the right (behavioristic) and the left (Gestalt and psychoanalytic) traditions in psychology and sociology to propose a developmental view with unusually wide-ranging socioeconomic implications for the study of ideology.

Long before the Adorno study made the term well known, Maslow began a study of the authoritarian personality (Maslow, 1943). During this early work he reached some conclusions about the nature of conservatism that were later integrated into his chief historic contribution to the field of psychology, his motivational theory. During the 1940s he also studied sexuality and creativity and thereby came upon a special kind of person who fascinated him for the rest of his life. This was the ideal, or ultimate norm, for human development represented by his conception of the *self-actualizing* personality.

Through interviews with a large number of people of this

type, Maslow identified the following characteristics of self-actualizers. They generally had rewarding sex lives. They were without exception extremely creative. Whatever their social position or occupation, they seemed to be characterized by an unusual freedom, spontaneity, and independence of thought and movement. Although they were mature in terms of responsibility and concern for others, they were playful and had retained a childlike sense of wonder and openness. Their sense of humor also had a different quality. Most humor tends to be frenetic and is based in hostility, but theirs was quieter, philosophic, dependent for effect on the surprise of offbeat insights. They also reported a high ratio of peak experiences without the use of drugs or alcohol, and they expressed this experience in terms of being filled with a sense of the joy and wonder of life, of being at one with the universe—an "oceanic" feeling, using Freud's apt term. They also had a superior perception of reality (they were not blinded by perceptual defense); they were more tolerant of themselves and of others; they had a more democratic (as opposed to authoritarian) character structure; and they notably identified with the human species as a whole, rather than limiting themselves to certain in-groups and excluding out-groups.

Probing more deeply into the matter, Maslow found that these people who fascinated him so much seemed to be leading unusually rich and satisfying lives. Moreover, they seemed to occur among all ages, classes, and within occupations of both high and low prestige.

It is evident that Maslow's self-actualizers have characteristics that research has shown to be associated with liberals, such as high creativity (Barron, 1969), more tolerance for themselves and others, a more democratic character structure, and more species identification (less ethnocentrism, more feeling for brotherhood, for equality, for the out-group as well as the in-group). This characterization by Maslow tempts liberals to equate themselves with self-actualizers. However, many self-actualizing characteristics may also be associated with conservatives: satisfying sex lives, freedom and spontaneity and independence of thought and movement, responsibility and concern for others, playfulness, a sense of humor, a sense of the joy and wonder of life. How are we to reconcile such apparent contradictions?

We would suggest three thoughts to this end. One is that despite the hopes of each of us to qualify as self-actualizers, Maslow concluded that only one percent of the American population presently fits the requirements. The percentages of 24.2 for "liberals," 14.5 for "conservatives," and 54.9 for "middles" found by Rokeach (1973) suggests most of us still have a long way to go to become self-actualizers, whatever our ideology.

Secondly, we would note a capacity of the self-actualizer that puzzled Maslow, which he characterized in this way: "At the level of self-actualizing, many dichotomies become resolved, opposites are seen to be unities and the whole dichotomous way of thinking is recognized to be immature. For self-actualizing people, there is a strong tendency for selfishness and unselfishness to fuse into a higher, superordinate unity. Work tends to be the same as play; vocation and avocation become the same thing. . . . Dichotomizing seems now to be characteristic of a lower level of personality development and of psychological functioning" (Maslow, 1968, p. 207). This suggests that self-actualizing transcends ideology, or that the optimum state is neither liberal nor conservative, but a holistic responsiveness that the committed ideologue may find bewildering or irritating. The capacity may show itself as being liberal sometimes, conservative sometimes.

Most suggestive of Maslow's contributions is his magnificent motivational theory, which weds insights from psychoanalysis, behaviorism, Gestalt theory, field theory, and existential or "third force" traditions in psychology. Within all of us, Maslow sees a striving toward self-actualizing at work. The implications of this view for ideology become evident when self-actualizing is seen in relation to the motivational matrix out of which it rises. That is, Maslow views self-actualizing as rising from a personal, social, and historical struggle that involves two levels of human motivation. He sees us as being motivated by both lower-order *deficiency* and higher-order *being* needs. Another way he has expressed this is as the difference between *defense* and *growth* needs.

On one hand we are motivated by egocentric needs such as

those for food, sex, selfish love, safety (from our fellows or the elements); belongingness (to some group, to some other persons); stimulation (we have basic needs for information, for novelty); by needs for something to work with and to manipulate; and by needs for status and personal power. These kinds of needs are fundamental—they must be met for our basic health. And they are elementary—they emerge earliest in our development, in childhood, and they remain highest in the priorities of most adults. They are also those needs that were studied by the early Freudians and behaviorists, those of the id and the autonomic nervous system. They are also the "fixed" needs in the view of motivation used by the young Marx, by Durkheim, and by other sociologists in the construction of social theories.

Once these lower-order defense or deficiency needs have been satisfied, another kind of more gentle, less urgent but quite persistent need begins to act upon us, to guide our thoughts and shape our actions. These are *being* or *growth* needs—for expressing an unselfish or unneeding love, for growth itself and a fuller realization of one's skills, talents, and other potentials, for the discovery of suitable goals and a worthwhile task or mission in life. These are the needs composing the self-actualizing drive, and though they may be denied and blocked during one's personal and social history, they persist in seeking liberation and fulfillment.

The implications of this motivational structure for comprehending the operation of ideology in human affairs are endless. On the one hand, those dominantly motivated by self-protective defense needs tend to horde for themselves, to fear differences, to be ethnocentric as well as egocentric, and to exclude and denigrate the outsider—to be prejudiced. On the other hand, those dominantly motivated by self-enlarging and self-transcendant growth tend to share, to welcome differences, to value human brotherhood as transcending the usual barriers, and to be relatively unprejudiced.

Coupled with the observations and theories of Tomkins, Maslow's theory suggests that some of us are mostly held to the conservative defense-needs level, whereas others operate mainly according to the more sublime dictates of liberal growth needs.

But for most of us life is a mixture of both levels. We worry about ourselves, our immediate needs, our own position—as we must for survival—and within this perspective we are perfectly willing to let our neighbor (and our own higher self) perish if this will just happen out of sight, without involving us even vicariously. But we are also driven by our being and growth needs—by all the worrisome ideals that tie us to our neighbor, and to the ideal in ourselves, and that now and then force us to open our eyes and our hearts to disturbing but uplifting sights and voices.

It is this tug of caring outward from ourselves toward others that links Maslow's views to the central concern of this book with the leadership task. Whether one recognizes our economic interdependency from a "hardnosed" managerial viewpoint, or our involvement in a common fate from the religious viewpoint, the problem that looms before the potential leader is not simply how to improve one's own mind or situation by understanding how we are put together in Maslowian or any other terms. The problem is how to apply such knowledge to improve the situation of the larger unit one is responsible for, whether it be a household, a classroom, a business, a city, state, nation, or this world itself.

In the next chapter we will examine how ideology shapes an unusual group of young men in training for American and world leadership in business, government, and academic pursuits. In relation to leadership goals, an extremely thought-provoking variable that underlies the Maslow scheme, seeming to tip the scale one way or another, is security—the confidence and security that comes from love and a stable home when one is a child, and from having a decent job, a steady source of income, and the respect of one's neighbors when one is an adult. Such personal securities act to satisfy our defense needs and leave us open to the influence of growth needs. This in turn suggests the relation of the stability of the economy and of government to personal growth. It suggests the importance of a larger sense of security within which the person exists as an island: a sense of security that comes from living within a social system that is reasonably well equipped to satisfy the needs of both defense and growth. This, we would submit, whether it be liberal or conservative or otherwise, is the grand goal for all leadership—to help create or maintain the social harbors for these personal islands.

5

The Campus and the Ideological Personality

$\mathbb{F}$rom the time of Machiavelli, both political and management science have to a large extent been the study of elites. This has made them suspect within a democracy where many have preferred to believe that the opportunity for leadership, like God's grace for some theologians, was granted to all impartially. The real world, however, doesn't work this way. Even in a democracy the leadership system largely is controlled by elites, who are in and out of power (Lasswell, 1948), and the individual leaders we would like to think of as independent are approved by and offered to us by these managing elites.

This observation is not meant to underrate the power of the "masses," or of mass public opinion. We have grown accustomed to broad-scale political polling to tap national and local attitudes on a variety of political questions. Behind these techniques lies much psychology and sociology, and this ingenious tapping of mass public opinion has become a powerful force influencing the national leadership and our governing policies (Gallup, 1966). Polls, such as those of Gallup and Harris, mght be termed the tapping of *horizontal* political reality. By contrast, this study is of a *vertical* reality and focuses not on the mass, but on leadership elites. Within the context of the psychology of ideology and social change discussed in our opening chapters, it is a study of the motivations that drive these elites and the dynamics of their interactions.

We will see how, within the protected culture of the campus, these elites play the national power game before they leave college to play the game "for real." We will also examine the potential of this college generation, and of the individual who characterizes or transcends it, for affecting our future. The studies we conducted were carried out in the spring of 1972 and 1973 in a well-known training establishment for American and world business and political elites, Princeton University. We will try to find meaning generalizable to all college campuses by seeing what motivates those who would follow in the footsteps of James Madison, Woodrow Wilson, John Foster Dulles, Adlai Stevenson, Ralph Nader, and other American and world leadership figures who were for a time Princetonians.

The Training of Leadership Elites

A question that should be considered before we proceed is of the generalizability of findings. How, within the confines of political groups on a single campus, may we hope to identify behavioral patterns that might apply to the vast mystery of American and world political and organizational life? As we report our studies we will note their relation to findings elsewhere. We would also note the pertinence of the work of general systems theorists, who find continuities of organization and processes across level after level of organisms (Miller, 1972).

For those who are most comfortable with the inferential support of their own experience, however, may we suggest a reflection upon their own past or present college days. It is customary to think of college as being a matter of books, football, drinking, and the delights of sex away from supervision. However, the core of this experience, we would submit, is that it offers a small, safe practice world of one's own, within which one may begin to find one's way before being let out to sink or swim in the larger world. In this wondrous play world, few activities offer more practice in leadership, and more direct connections to the external world, than campus politics. This is particularly true of Princeton, where the tradition of faculty and student involvement in politics goes back to the days of colonial America, and today its alumni occupy key leadership positions in governments and multinational corporations.

Before America was officially an independent nation, for example, the original College of New Jersey was considered the hotbed of revolution in the Middle Colonies. Nassau Hall, still standing, was hated by the British leadership as the "egghead" bastion of what was then mid-America, halfway between the northern problem of Boston, John and Samuel Adams, and the Green Mountain boys, and the southern problem of Washington, Jefferson, and Patrick Henry. Nassau Hall was also suspect as hard physical evidence of a subtle, obdurate Scotch Presbyterian resistance to all that was officially British. Both a so-called egghead and a Scotch Presbyterian, Princeton's third president, John Witherspoon, was on the "enemies list" of his day for prodding the timorous to defy the British and sign the Declaration of Independence. Two other early graduates were signers of the Declaration along with Witherspoon. Later nine Princeton alumni helped draft and bless the United States Constitution during the Convention of 1787, among them James Madison of the class of 1771, known as the "Father of the Constitution," and later president of the United States for two terms.

Thus it was that over two centuries after John Adams' day and Madison's graduation, in the winter of 1972, I was haunted by a sense of timelessness. For in the chill mist of a Princeton winter evening I found myself meeting with one John Adams, president of the James Madison Society.

Portrait of a Liberal. It had seemed a good omen for the beginning of this study. I had circulated a questionnaire to obtain ratings by selected students and faculty of the degrees of liberalism or conservatism of various campus organizations. The purpose was to define groups known to be one or the other in order to validate the instruments of our study. I had been struck by the hallowed name combination of Adams and Madison in the student directory listing campus organizations and their presiding officers. I had sent John Adams a questionnaire and received the response in a bold hand using a medium-weight, blue felt-tip pen. We had made an appointment to meet for dinner at a local restaurant, the Annex, and now he stood before me.

I will describe John, as I saw him then and came to know him, for several purposes. First, I want to give the reader a sense of a flesh-and-blood liberal in this setting, at this point in time, so that our later abstracting of liberalism may be rooted in this existential reality. Secondly, this sketch will create the basis for a contrasting portrait of the memorable conservative I encountered as a result of this same questionnaire query. But also at this point, I want to note an important matter of social-scientific technique. In our scientific worship of numbers and so-called objectivity we tend to shy away from the subjective report as "unscientific" and "literary." This is unfortunate, for the search for social truth is so difficult we must use every means at our disposal. Moreover, as we noted in Chapter Four, we are continually being entrapped by only parts of the variance of relationships, or of portional rather than whole realities. Only from a *multiplicity* of approaches may we begin to grasp the multifaceted phenomena of life. The next two chapters will be "literary" then, but not unscientific. Within philosophy the subjective has found its home in existentialism; within sociology, in the techniques of the *participant-observer* (Powdermaker, 1966), which will now be employed.

John Adams was a tall and lean senior at the time, with a look about him not of some august young patriot, but of a more cagey modern version of the great American silent-film comedian Harold Lloyd. He had Lloyd's pale, bland, thin-faced look of midwestern innocence, the same round, gold-rimmed,

old-fashioned glasses, the same American conventional short
and well-combed hair. But where Lloyd's eyes were popping behind his glasses with wonder, delight, or fiendish arousal, Adams'
eyes radiated a cool and restless energy.

He had come from a small town in Michigan, a suburb of
some larger city I would guess, a town noted for producing an
unusual number of leading national figure skaters and hockey
players. (I had exclaimed upon discovering that he almost made
the Olympic skating team. He shrugged it off, saying, "It may
mean something here, but in my hometown I'm one of the lesser
lights." It was of interest to me as an indication of the competitive
milieu from which he came.) His family was Catholic, conservative, fairly well-off, I gathered. I thought it of great interest that
the Middle Ages appealed to him most of any period in history; he
admired, among other things, the orderliness of their social
arrangements.

Politically he had begun his Princeton years—a freshman in
1969—as a member of the radical-left SDS. He was unusual in
being a white member of the leftist Association of Black Collegians. However, by the time I met him, in his senior year, he was
not markedly "political," or at least he was outwardly "neutral-
ized" by what I surmised was a conflict between belief in many of
the standard liberal goals and a strongly conservative desire for
stability and order.

His college achievement seemed to me quite remarkable, but
as he said of his hometown situation, it was not considered unusual in this pressured elite setting. He was not only the president
of the Madison Society, I discovered, but also its cofounder. It
was a new eating club created to fill a need, as he saw it, for a
facility for both freshmen and blacks who felt uneasy and possibly unwanted in the traditional eating clubs. I do not know what
his grades were in Princeton's Woodrow Wilson School of Public
Affairs, but he was one of two Princetonians who was accepted by
and went on to Oxford for graduate school.

As for his long-range ambitions, I must base a guess on some
suggestive scraps. I see him in tandem with my memory of his
good friend, Art Bergeron, a fascinating young operator to whom
politics was mother's milk. Art, from a French Canadian family in

the Boston area, and John from Michigan, had originally met
while they were in high school. Both were leading debaters—
trained to take either side of an issue with equal skill. They had
met while traveling the high-school debating circuit—Art laughed
uproariously recalling it. "We divided up the country, you know.
We knew we were good and what the old U.S. needed. John was
going to be Secretary of State. I would be Attorney General, or at
worst, Secretary of the Interior." What impressed me was that
their mutual laughter was not at the memory of some youthful
foolishness, some inconceivable naïveté; it was the laughter of
those who had by no means ruled out the possibility of attaining
such power.

They met faithfully on Sunday nights to play poker—and in
fact again traveled the circuit together, only this time it was an
occasional circuit of the poker games in the Eastern schools. They
were playing for considerable stakes and successfully, as a means
of supporting themselves through Princeton with its yearly cost
then of over $5,000. I shall never forget the estimate John and Art
made of their own card-playing skills as being second and third on
campus only to the number-one campus player who put his earn-
ings down on a plane ticket to Las Vegas during that spring term
and returned with $4,000. This was won, they explained, "the
hard way," at blackjack. What does this have to do with political
interests and skills? As Gary Wills relates in *Nixon Agonistes*
(Wills, 1969), one of few colorful memories of those who knew
the young Richard Nixon was his phenomenal poker-playing ability while he was in the navy. Nixon also supported himself in
those youthful days by his ability to bluff, to conceal his hand, to
dare great risks when he sensed the odds were worth it—all qualities presaging the triumphs of his elections to the presidency and
the tactics with which he desperately tried to conceal his involvement in the Watergate disaster.

Portrait of a Conservative. The first campus conservative I
chanced to meet through the questionnaire query was T. Harding
Jones, a founder and first executive director* of the Undergradu-

---

*One of the fascinations of liberal-conservative studies is how these
differences are so marked they will reveal themselves in seemingly inconse-
quential details. Note here that in their first key posts of campus power,

ates for a Stable America—which forms, one may note, the brilliantly promotional acronym, U.S.A. My memory of T. Harding must inevitably suffer from only three brief contacts. The first and third times were within the sumptuous Edwardian setting of Princeton's Tower Club. Princeton eating clubs somewhat serve the function of fraternities on other campuses, and during 1972 Tower was the chief gathering point for the campus conservative elite. Picture then this massive Gothic structure in a row of similar imposing old edifices: the black ironwork of the gate with its polished brass knob that creaks upon the hinge, the massive paneled oak door, the baffling loose knob that turns with difficulty, the expanse of the entry festooned with the members' letterboxes, the lost pair of gloves by the lamp upon the entry table, the great hall leading to the giant rooms at either end with their stone-faced fireplaces, the worn Persian carpets underfoot, the gray leaded glass in the deep windows, the inviting sprawl of lush red simulated-leather chairs and divans. Then picture T. Harding Jones in the midst of this setting, moving as naturally within it as the manor's young lord.

I should say, from later observations, that Tower and the other Princeton eating clubs have this effect on many who enjoy them, liberal as well as conservative, old as well as young. It is one of the pleasures of the campus, to dwell within and be enlarged by the romance of a more gracious age. But this was my first view of the Club and what I took to be its prototypical inhabitant. He was of medium height, with a large Romanesque nose that provided the unchanging referent for a mouth and eyes of interesting movements. He had a slightly cruel mouth that moved quickly into an expression of hauteur and some disdain, or into a disarming, easy, and winning smile. His eyes were large, either cold and veiled, with protective lids, like Saudi Arabia's King Faisal, or were suddenly boyishly warm and friendly. He had, in short, that quality for which the actor Basil Rathbone was so memorable, a capacity to play either the "bad" Sir Guy of Gysmond (who was Robin Hood's affliction), or the "good" Sherlock Holmes. His hair was full, well cut, in

---

Adams was the more democratic "President," while Jones was the more authoritarian "Executive Director."

the contemporary Edwardian style, and there was just the slightest touch of a dandy in his clothes, suggested perhaps by an ornate vest.

I ventured some questions about his background that first time we met, but he rapidly passed them by as though such matters were not only private but trivial. Consequently I know little of this aspect of his life.

Politically he was precise in his loyalties, which were all carefully qualified. Historically he saw himself as an admirer of Edmund Burke. Among contemporaries one gathered that William Buckley was among the few who approached enlightenment. His feelings toward Nixon and the Nixonians were mixed (this was a year and a half before the Nixon resignation). On one hand, the difficulty of their task in turning the country back from the liberal excesses enlisted his sympathy, and it was rumored that he had connections in Washington and might work in the White House following graduation. On the other hand, he did not see either Nixon or those close to him as being his kind of conservative, and one sensed he did not trust these so-called pragmatists. For the Birchers and the Far Right generally he had either pity or contempt.

As with John Adams, T. Harding Jones' college achievement was considerable. A history major, he had helped found the Undergraduates for a Stable America in order to provide an articulate, and as he saw it, rational and orderly alternative to the irrational and disorderly excesses of the campus left. To some outsiders, Princeton was stereotyped as one of the more conservative campuses during this time, yet Jones perceived the mission of the group he had helped form as providing strength for the minority voice on campus—and in this perception he was quite correct. The conservatives were not only a minority, but saw themselves as being outnumbered and all too often unfairly overwhelmed by a faculty that was predominantly liberal, and even leftist—a faculty they felt sure was every bit as intolerant of student conservatism as conservatives out in the "real world" ostensibly were of everyone who differed from them. And so, bolstered by a national swing toward the right, with the plaudits of William Buckley and the support of some wealthy and aroused alumni—and with the lodestone of a temporarily captive Washington, D.C. in their rear—T. Harding and a handful of cohorts had taken on the bulk of the faculty of Princeton and the articulate majority of the student body. By his senior year he had seen his brainchild grow to almost 100 members. He had also seen it seize control of the Young Republicans on campus through the efforts of a personable and reliable U.S.A. member, David Versfelt.

T. Harding also conducted his own weekly radio talk show, patterned after William Buckley's, with assorted interviews. Shortly after graduation, he founded and became the first editor of *Prospect* magazine, an impressive voice for the Princeton conservative funded by the same wealthy alumni who helped underwrite the formation of U.S.A. When I originally asked him what he planned to do after graduation, he said that possibly he would go on to medical school and become a doctor. But somehow the combination of politics and journalism seemed to hold him in thrall.

Liberal and Conservative Compared. John Adams and T. Harding Jones were obviously different kinds of people, and these differences will become increasingly apparent as this book progresses. But it is meaningful in relation to the future to note here some of the ways in which the liberal John Adams and the conservative T. Harding Jones were alike.

We raised the question at the beginning of this chapter as to what extent it is valid to extrapolate from the college to the "real" political world. We will pursue this question again in the next chapter, but here we would ask the reader to think of the caliber of governmental leadership the world has enjoyed during recent years and then to contemplate the leadership potential within two such young men. Further consider the fact these two merely happened to be among the first students we met of the hundreds of young liberals, conservatives, and "middles" who participated in our studies. Then we would suggest this fact be pondered: these Princeton hundreds were but a drop in the bucket of the organizational leadership potential at thousands of colleges and universities throughout today's world, and our selection only tapped two springtimes out of the worldwide succession of students entering and leaving these remarkable training establishments year after year.

John and T. Harding were alike, then, in reflecting the leadership potential of modern campus elites. Moreover, at this earlier date, to a surprising degree they apparently reflected something of the political future. For they shared a set of qualities that later proved to be remarkably like those noted by some political observers of the two most interesting "new faces" in the 1976 presidential campaign, Jimmy Carter and Jerry Brown. "They were also remarkably efficient young men, in the telling sense that they were able to accomplish a great deal with a maximum economy of motion," I wrote of John Adams and T. Harding Jones in 1973. "They were both detached, cool, generally superb handlers of themselves and skillful manipulators of others. They both showed organizing abilities of a very high order. They both had an engaging smile, when they wished to smile. They were also both rather courtly young men, exceptionally well-mannered."

This is not to suggest they were paragons of virtue. They were both very ambitious young men, out to make their mark upon the world and filled with no illusions as to efficacy of virtue versus being a smart operator. It is, then, something to consider that the power within them, and within their counterparts, can turn to evil as well as good. But what remains is that this power does exist; not all of it will be diverted from its path; and so, mindful of the future, it behooves us to try to understand it and surmise its course.

6

The Campus and Ideological Groups

$\mathbb{W}$e have seen the liberal, the conservative, and a glimpse of the future as exemplified by two prototypical collegians. In this chapter we will examine left, right, and moderate campus groups in 1972 through 1974. Before we do so, however, let us take another look at the individual's impact on society out of the college setting. We noted earlier the historical influence of John Witherspoon and James Madison, both Princeton graduates, on the formation of America. Time went by and in the early 1800s a young southern gentleman named James Birney came to Princeton from Danville, Kentucky. He was from a slave-holding family, was a hard drinker, a fun lover, his only distinction being that he was expelled three times from Princeton for drunkenness. Yet at this school, Birney encountered teachers who bolstered his own liberal bent and primed him for a radical personality transformation. He returned to the South to defy angry mobs, to free his slaves, to flee to the North, and to grow rapidly in stature into the most politically astute of the great abolitionists. In 1840 and 1844 he was the candidate for the United States presidency of the Liberty Party, the first political party organized to free the slaves—a minority party that within a few years flowed as a purifying freshet into the turbid Republican Party mainstream and became a force that shaped the election of Abraham Lincoln (Fladeland, 1955; Tomkins, 1965).

For contrast, one might contemplate the colorful career of Robert E. "Fighting Bob" Stockton, the grandson of an earlier Princetonian who had signed the Declaration of Independence. He was so gifted a student that he finished Princeton at the age of sixteen. He entered the navy and swiftly gained a reputation as a holy terror in the seizure of slave traders. A seemingly liberal facade, however, covered a conservative basic nature. As a young man, equipped only with a pistol and a timid missionary companion, "Fighting Bob" walked fifty miles into the jungle and seized from a heavily armed black African tribe the 43,000 square miles of West Africa that later became Liberia. He then helped put this land into service as the dumping ground for the unwanted American blacks who had been freed from slavery. Later, as a middle-aged naval hero, he equipped himself with a fleet of dreadnaughts and seized California from the Mexicans (Hageman, 1879). Later still, this remarkable rightist became the nominee for the United States presidency of the racist Know Nothing Party—another minority party whose enduring philosophy even today moves within elements of both our major political parties.

The shaping of left and right personalities and their effect on the world future may also be discerned in the contrasting and much better-known careers of two ex-Princeton students: Adlai Stevenson, mover of hearts and minds as a presidential aspirant and in the United Nations, and John Foster Dulles, the powerful advocate of brinksmanship and a world policy of communist containment; or in the 1970s William Ruckelshaus—a conservative establishment reformer—who resigned from the Nixon Administration rather than fire Watergate Special Prosecutor Cox, or Ralph Nader, a liberal antiestablishment reformer.

This brings us to the boiling pot of our study, the campus political stew of the early 1970s, and the question of recipes for the future that yet stretches out before us. We will examine first the extreme campus political groups, then the moderates, and then the mystery of the middle.

Left Versus Right

The general patterns to left extreme campus activity have been documented for many campuses. As Feuer (1969), Lipset (1971), and many others demonstrated, these patterns were worldwide and very similar, the upheavals of the American campus being linked by cause and by personalities to France, Germany, Japan, China, Russia—indeed wherever through radio, television, and books world aspirations of the 1960s were shared. By and large, the Princeton activity was identical with this larger picture. During the heyday of the radical Students for a Democratic Society in the late 1960s, there was an active SDS chapter on campus. But, as elsewhere, the Princeton SDS chapter soon dissolved into small splinter groups and by the spring of 1972 had disappeared from the campus, leaving as a residue a new local group called the University Action Group, or UAG. The emotional core to its attraction was student and faculty hatred of what the Viet Nam War represented and the student fear of being drafted. The UAG rapidly dissolved into scattered sentiments with the formal ending of the war in 1973; however, in the spring of 1972, when this study began, it was still enjoying its twilight power. Its chief objective was to force the university to end the ROTC program and to sever connections with the Defense Department and the Institute for Defense Analysis, or IDA, a local "think tank" adjacent to the Princeton campus that was filled with quiet mathematicians doing top-secret strategic analysis for extremely good salaries. Its other issue was racism; however, the campus black powerists were already well into the national phase of going it alone, with no complicating whites. Lacking encouragement then from those whom their efforts were supposed to benefit, white radicalism was losing steam in this quarter as well.

The more enduring, extreme-left campus power base that was rising during this time was the black movement. This centered in the Association of Black Collegians, which provided another catchy and promotionally astute acronym, ABC. Another, much smaller portion of the extreme-left thrust went into the formation of the Princeton campus women's and gay-liberation groups.

As we have seen in the vignette of T. Harding Jones, at the other extreme from the leftists were the conservative Undergraduates for a Stable America, or USA. We indicated in the last chapter how they were formed to provide a countering voice to student and faculty leftism, and were financed by disgruntled conservative alumni. Their dominant issues included defense of the war effort, the ROTC, and freedom of speech—in response to UAG heckling and harrassment of conservative speakers on campus. Their members also decried what they termed "reverse discrimination"—or the lowering of admission and academic standards for a radical increase in the number of blacks that were being admitted to Princeton in keeping with civil rights pressures mounted during the 1960s. Still farther to the right was the Young Americans for Freedom group, or YAF. However, in the spring of 1972 YAF had only three members, so they were not a factor to be reckoned with at the time.

The struggle, then, at the extreme end was between the UAG and the USA during the spring of 1972. They fired verbal barrages at one another through the news reports and editorials of the ubiquitous campus newspaper, the *Princeton Daily*. Supporters and amiable mischief makers also staged a few debates through Princeton's Whig-Clio Society. One high point for their clash was the campus visit and UAG heckling of Admiral Moorer, then chairman of the Joint Chiefs of Staff. Another was the announced visit of Harvard psychologist Richard Herrnstein, who had joined psychologist Arthur Jensen in reviving the doctrine that genetic deficiencies were lowering black intelligence. The UAG and black furor prompted Herrnstein to cancel his talk, which in turn prompted drum rolling on the freedom of speech issue by USA which lasted for many weeks.

Liberal Versus Conservative

By various means of opinion tapping we found that conflict between the extremes tended to be over issues of some intellectual content, which fluctuated with national and world events and trends. By contrast, the conflict of the moderates was confined more to matters of habit and emotion, of loyalties to party and personality. Where the extremes were concerned with ends—of what the job was, so to speak—the moderates were concerned with mechanics, with means—or of how to get the job done.

In keeping with this general difference between extreme and moderate conflict was also my discovery that for the extremes the link to national politics tended to be through the mentalistic, transitory, and salient issue, whereas for the moderates the link was through the physicality of the amazing networks that connected the campus to the seemingly humdrum, dog labor, practical mechanics of state, national, and even world political machines.

I was plunged into the realities of these networks within a few days of first making contact with the campus leadership of the moderate Young Republicans and Young Democrats. The spring of 1972 was, of course, the prelude to the presidential election that fall which pitted the ill-fated George McGovern against the ill-fated Richard Nixon—an election, one might note, that through the Watergate disaster and poor management of the economy had far-reaching consequences for all the world. The president of the Young Democrats on campus was a bright, intense young sociology major, Ron Levine. Ron's father was commissioner of labor for the Nelson Rockefeller administration in New York. I took this circumstance to be a reason—the head start of an upbringing in a political household—for Ron's rapid rise to political power. He was only a freshman. He had discovered the Young Democrats in disarray on his arrival fresh from high school, and by doggedly hammering away on organization with a dedicated handful, he had succeeded in building an organization with a letterhead and fifty members. His partner in leadership was Henry Furst, a portly young man with a ready smile and eyes that were continually floating on the alert, rather calculating; one could see him as a young Jim Farley. Henry was president of the Youth Coalition for Muskie when we met.

What brought the existence of the moderate network into

view was the $50 I offered to the treasuries of both the Young
Republicans and the Young Democrats as an incentive to pass
out questionnaires among their memberships. Furst leaped on
the offer as a means of pacifying the telephone company. He
was personally several hundred dollars in the hole from the unforeseen mushrooming of expenses incurred in spinning a state-
wide network of young collegians for Muskie out of Henry's
dormitory, through his personal phone. Within days of making
this arrangement came a disastrous primary in Florida and
Muskie's withdrawal. Did this mean my contribution was for
naught and Henry was to go to jail for an unpaid phone bill?
Hardly. Within three days at most, the "fervent" Muskieites had
become "fervent" McGovernites, and the network, far from
having collapsed, was again expanding throughout the state,
now being spun out of both Ron's and Henry's rooms.

This was the beginning for Henry and Ron of the process
whereby hundreds of thousands of collegians from across the
country abandoned other candidates to cohere to the McGovern
"crusade" and helped win victory for his candidacy in Miami in
July 1972.

Meanwhile, for the Young Republicans, it was an entirely
different story. One hesitated to bring up the money at all because there was so little indication they needed it. Young David
Versfelt was very polite in accepting it on their behalf, as
though not wanting to embarrass me. By now the Committee to
Re-elect the President (soon to be immortalized as CREEP by
Watergate) was a prestigious presence on and off the campus, so
that my small contribution was, no doubt, soon pulsating down
the lines of the money-gathering network from the campuses to
Washington, to serve who knows what ends.

Later, as the summer of 1972 wore into fall and the mood
became a mixture of heady frenzy for the McGovernites and
apathetic confidence for the Nixonites, the networks again significantly expanded. During the summer many of these political
moderates departed, some hitchhiking, first to the nominating
conventions in Miami, and then on to Washington to work in
the offices of congressmen and the campaign headquarters for
both parties. (Ron Levine, for example, was working for

Alaska's Senator Mike Gravell.) But the network of networks, to my observation, was created toward the end of summer and into the fall by John Adams' friend, Art Bergeron, a fast-talking, outgoing psychology major, whom I believe derived the greatest pleasure from politics of anyone I've ever seen. Fired up not by McGovern but by the exhilaration of the movement itself, and not finding enough to do along normal channels, Art took off on his own and built a network to link New Jersey high schools into this national movement. Bicycling for many miles, or driving an old car which was only occasionally functioning, he went from school to school giving brief lectures on the movement and sending fresh converts home to work over their parents, or he went to local headquarters to stamp and mail and answer phones.

Working with both moderate groups, one also soon became aware of the attractions that helped spawn and preserve the campus-to-politico networks. Some part of it was idealism, some part conviction, some part the desire to flow together in a social movement promising fun and fresh sexual and intellectual experiences. But another strong appeal was the old question of futures. They were soon to graduate. There were needs for summer work to think of and careers after law school. So why not gamble a little time on a candidate and hope for the spoils of victory?

Whig-Clio and the Watershed 1970s

In the middle of this liberal and conservative activity—and curiously enough, located at the physical center of the campus —was the intriguing presence of Whig-Clio, "the world's oldest debating society." Formed in 1765, it was housed in two prim and matching white buildings of Grecian style that were flanked by two large bronze tigers standing guard. Here it was that liberal and conservative were encouraged to meet, to listen to noted national speakers from both liberal and conservative and all other possible alignments, and to settle their differences in open debate. Here, too, in this single host facility, were the offices not only for the Young Democrats and the Young

Republicans, but the range of other campus political groups including UAG, USA, and YAF.

Something of the function and spirit of Whig-Clio is conveyed by this brief quote from the fall 1973 report to the membership of the society by its young president, Mike Shepherd. "Gerald Ford's nomination as vice-president provides more evidence of Whig-Clio's Magic Touch," Mike wrote. "Ford, who spoke before the Society last year, becomes another in a series of men who have been thrust into the limelight shortly after their address before the Society. Daniel Ellsberg, who addressed the Society in May 1971, and Tom Eagleton, who accepted a Whig-Clio invitation for February 1972, are other examples."

The Whig-Clio presence, in short, was one that would have given much pleasure to its eighteenth-century founders, who had envisaged government as ideally a process of grace and decorum. It was, remains today, and let us hope may endure there forever, the urbane and quiet eye of the storm.

During the spring of 1972 not only was the political scene heating up for a national election, but the worldwide shock waves from the closing months of the Viet Nam War regularly rocked the campus. President Nixon's mining of the harbor in Haiphong sparked a faculty and student uprising. Joined by an angry mob from Princeton High School, they surrounded the Institute for Defense Analysis to keep the mathematicians from getting to work. Local and state police moved in and there were first 60 arrests, and then at the peak of the protest the arrests of 175 more students and faculty. Later that spring, antiwar protest again swelled with a student strike and an attempt to shut down the university. Dean Neil Rudenstine's office was seized by 400 students and there were 204 arrests this time.

We now also know what we didn't then, that these were the months of the meetings of Mitchell, Dean, Magruder, LaRue, Hunt, Liddy, and others implicated in the Watergate break-in and cover-up, which led to an exposure of political corruption and amorality unparalleled in our history. In retrospect, this hidden, symptomatic event reflects a basic confusion and unsettlement in the national macrocosm relating to the changes that rapidly took place within the Princeton microcosm during

1972 and 1973. There was first the devastating rout of McGovern—the small town of Princeton itself was one of few places he carried in the national election of 1972. The message to many of the Young Democrats who had slaved for him was plain: what's the use? Art Bergeron was unaffected; he simply shifted his energies to the forthcoming New Jersey elections and worked in the early stages of what became the successful gubernatorial campaign of Democrat Brenden Byrne. Ron Levine, however, was so dispirited by the McGovern disaster, and by personal exposure to the high level chicanery of both the Republican and Democratic nominating conventions in Miami, that he dropped the Young Democrats and politics, and became fervently involved with the Young Hebrews on campus. (This shift to religion from politics involved many students besides Ron. It harbingered, we believe, the rise of religion in politics through Carter and Brown in the 1976 presidential campaign). For the Young Republicans the aftermath was just as devastating. Their euphoria over the Nixon landslide lessened and was then punctured by the revelations of Watergate and the spectacle of cabinet-, vice-presidential-, and ultimately presidential-level criminality.

The mood developing on campus was signaled by a bizarre event that received national press coverage in the spring of 1973. The item was taken as a joke at the time, both by those who read of it and by those who participated in the movement. The story in the *New York Times* was headed "Princeton Likes 'Perverto Slate.' "

> *PRINCETON, N.J., April 17—Promising their electorate nothing more than "mindless perversion," four Princeton University students were given solid chances today for victory tomorrow in several races in the election for Undergraduate Assembly officers.*
>
> *The four outdistanced both of the two remaining slates of more orthodox contenders in a recent primary.*
>
> *"We are really all mindless perverts, and I think this campus is ready for what we have to offer," com-*

*mented Richard Goodman, the Perverto candidate for
president. "We don't beat around the bush. We don't
have a bush. We have nothing to offer. I think that's
what people want today.*

*"You can't disagree with nothing. We figured
with all the parties promising the world, we couldn't
go wrong. All we have is a rampant desire to pervert."*

Both student analysts and the papers at the time attributed
the popularity of the Perverto party to student dissatisfaction
with campus politics. But to anyone acquainted with the rise of
the Nazis in Germany or the fascists in Italy this time may bring
a shudder of recognition. It is a whiff of the Weimar, pre-Hitler
days, celebrated not by coincidence during this same year in the
prize-winning American musical and movie "Cabaret." It is a
whiff of that strange, mindless disillusion, the dream of democracy shattered, that did in historical fact go hand in hand with
the moral dissolution and perversion that brought in the Nazis
as "saviors," followed by their own unspeakable perversions
with six million Jews.

It was just a whiff of this gust from hell, fortunately, that
in that springtime of 1973 strayed into the pleasant American
college town of Princeton, New Jersey. The Perverto Party was
defeated, and its candidates were in outward fact only some
prankster campus "jocks" having the usual fun. But with leadership passions and the American and world political future in
mind, we must ask: What led these innocents to role play in this
sinister way? Could forces that gathered in the moral crumbling
of the 1920s be gathering again in our time?

Unfortunately, despite these educations we labor for, and
despite all the newspapers we read, we still remain as babes in
the woods when it comes to reading the message of the winds,
ever so slight at first, that rise out of history; the ruffling of the
leaves, the sudden lift of birds, the change in atmosphere. In
succeeding chapters we will take a progressively closer look at
these young bearers of tomorrow to try to glimpse something of
the future for all of us toward which the winds of history blow.

7

The Ideological Personality

In the preceding chapters we have glimpsed bits of research and insight which present a rich, but rather bewildering, perspective on ideology as it operates in man. Part of the difficulty is that we are trying to understand something rooted both in personality, as a matter of genetically and experientially determined individual differences of some constancy over time, and in society, as a matter of historically and socially determined situational pressures upon man. The confusion comes, then, from trying to understand the past or plot the future assuming that liberals and conservatives are fixed personalities—and we confront socially induced behavior that fails to conform to these static expectations. Or from a leadership perspective, we expect that by simply outlining a desirable project and enticing or forcing people to carry it out, they will dutifully do so. Instead, seemingly out of nowhere emerges the age-old tripartite power problem deriving from ideology in personality. Whatever it is we have proposed, we find that it has raised a fierce opposition on one hand, a body of somewhat less fierce adherents on the other, and less noticed, but very much in the picture, the great mass, who are monumentally indifferent.

If this confusion is to be clarified, we must first gain an empirical grounding in the facts of human personality while keeping social influence in the background. We must, as the title of this chapter indicates, gain a better understanding of the ideological personality. There are many ways of doing this, among them methods, quite frankly, far more appealing than the approach we have taken. It would be, for example, much more appealing to readers and easier to follow if we interviewed a few liberals and conservatives in depth and constructed biographies of their lives. Unfortunately, such an approach would be inefficient and add little to what is already known. Another approach would be to give liberals and conservatives a large battery of the customary personality tests and construct profiles therefrom. This approach would result in more efficient data gathering but would produce only another static list of the characteristics of "the liberal personality" contrasted with "the conservative personality."

Thus, we took a different and perhaps more difficult approach to the study of ideology in personality. It has, however, the advantage of providing immeasurably greater gains in understanding in return for a somewhat greater intellectual effort. Our approach was to gain a *structural* sense of ideological personality through the pursuit of two strategies. The first was to gain a rounded sense of ideology by extending the limits of the liberalism-conservatism (LC) context to include the concepts of activism-inactivism (AI) and extremism-moderation (EM). In Chapter Four we noted works suggesting the potential of such an investigation for revealing the possible "core" to ideological personality. There is also considerable evidence of the need to understand such a "core" within the context of other personality variables, to which social psychologists have devoted numerous studies during recent years. Thus, we concluded that any adequate grounding in the psychology of ideology, in addition to investigating liberals and conservatives, activists and inactivists, and extremists and moderates, requires an examination of risk taking, Machiavellianism, alienation, anomie, locus of control, norm violating, norm maintaining, and parent-child relationships that may affect the development of ideology.

The scope of our investigation presents one large problem. In attempting to clarify relationships that are already too scattered for easy comprehension, we will only add to the confusion unless we relate our findings to a framework that lends itself to retention and examination. Throughout these chapters we will resort to various visualizations to provide such a framework. Again, these will not be only "visual aids" in the usual sense, but in reducing complexity to simplicity, they will serve to articulate our own developing theory of ideology and social change.

The chief aspect of the framework will be a view of ideological behavior as the counterposing of two forces, one norm maintaining, the other norm violating (or norm changing). Such a theoretical polarity allows us to ask, whether in empirical fact liberals are concerned with processes of social change and norm violating. We may ask whether conservatives, by contrast, are concerned with processes of social stability and norm maintaining. Many social observers have assumed this was true, but little confirming research exists. If this can be shown to be true—and then used to develop a sufficiently sophisticated theoretical structure—leadership may be armed to better direct social, economic, political, educational, technological, and organizational change in desired directions.

Picking up from the studies in the psychology of ideological personality outlined earlier, we will examine hypothetical *core* variables, hypothetical *peripheral* variables, and *developmental* variables. Lastly, we will examine the possibilities for developing and substantiating a theoretical framework that will show the interrelationships of these variables.

A Hypothetical Framework

As we have seen, various considerations have prompted study of what loosely coheres as the liberalism-conservatism area of measurement and theory. Customarily, this interest is limited within social psychology to attitude measurement, and

LC is studied only for its relation to elections and political parties (Robinson, Rusk, and Head, 1968). However, the source
works in this area have almost all derived from a much broader
range of interests. Concern about anti-Semitic bias prompted
the Adorno studies (Adorno and others, 1950); disagreement
with Adorno's equating of dogmatism with the rightist
prompted the Rokeach work (Rokeach, 1960); and the New
Left movement and student protest prompted work by Keniston, Hamden-Turner, and others. Whatever the initiating stimulus, this field presents a diversity of surface interests that have
driven investigators to, at some point, confront persisting questions of underlying structures, or of the dimensions of ideology.

As we saw in Chapter Two, interest in the theoretical structure of ideological personality has an ancient lineage. Early
psychological thought emerged from a holistic view of psychological systems within a sociological, philosophical, and historical context, and still remains a basic source of insight into the
dimensions of ideology. The theories of both Marx (Fromm,
1961) and Pareto (Finer, 1966) were centered on a dialectical
interaction of liberal and conservative personalities. For Marx,
the conflict of the liberal bourgeoisie with the conservative
feudal aristocrat during early modern history was followed by
the more familiar conflict of the liberal proletariat with the
newly conservative bourgeoisie. For Pareto undesirable liberal "Fox" personalities contended for power with desirable
conservative "Lion" personalities. Within early modern psychology, Freud (1946) centered *Civilization and Its Discontents*
upon the philosophical interaction of a liberative Eros and a
conservative Thanatos. More recently, experts in fields directly
concerned with ideological phenomena—history, sociology,
psychology, and political science—have added to the roster a
number of compelling conceptual pairings of the right-left personality: authoritarian-equalitarian (Adorno, 1950); creativity
versus idolization (Toynbee, 1947); liberal-conservative (Schlesinger, 1964); right-left (Eysenck, 1954; Sorokin, 1966); pro-
gressive-traditional (Kerlinger, 1958); "unfreezing" versus
"refreezing" forces (Lewin, 1951); defense-growth motivation
(Maslow, 1968); humanistic-normative (Tomkins, 1965); radical

versus conservative man (Hamden-Turner, 1970); love versus power (André, 1976).

As these concept pairings suggest, the polarities of ideological personality have been characterized in a variety of ways. At the core of many of these concepts, however, one view is held in common. It is a view associated with the theory and observation of social stability and change in sociology (Parsons and Shils, 1965), and of norming processes in psychology (Asch, 1952; Sherif, 1970). Thus, one may find a repetition through many contexts of a conservative (rightist, traditional, defense-motivated) concern with the states and processes of social stability and norm preservation, and a liberal (leftist, progressive, growth-motivated) concern with states and processes of social change and norm "shattering" or norm "enlargement." The meaningfulness of this opposition of concepts is made evident by their appearance in certain recurring patterns of social conflict. As Sherif has expressed it, the development of social movement "always implies, sooner or later, the confrontation of partisans committed to conflicting positions. Typically, on one side of the confrontation, there are partisans of an established orthodoxy—stabilized even to the point of rigidity. Such partisans represent the classic problems of conformity to an established group: They are satisfied, even complacent, with the practices, human arrangements, values, or norms of the Establishment. . . . On the other side, there are partisans to a new social movement, questioning and challenging the Establishment. The taproot of their partisanship flourishes in unrest, dissatisfaction, and frustration with things as they are" (Sherif, 1970, p. 144).

Another perspective is provided by experimental study. Alker and Kogan (1968) investigated the effects of norm-oriented group discussion on strategies of risk taking. Their procedures involved fifty-five subjects, in five-person experimental groups, who discussed ethical conflicts in story situations based on the Stouffer-Toby (1952) measure of role conflict. The investigators hypothesized that the Stouffer-Toby situations forced a choice of norm-maintaining versus norm-violating positions. The subjects were pre- and post-tested for risk-taking propensities with the Choice Dilemma Questionnaire (Kogan and Wallach, 1964). It was found that subjects in groups that preferred the norm-violating options shifted toward high risk taking, whereas subjects in groups that preferred the norm-maintaining option shifted toward a more conservative risk taking strategy.

Alker and Kogan speculated that this finding might be related to Tomkins' theory of normative (right) versus humanistic (left) polarities within human personality (Tomkins, 1965). As we saw in Chapter Four, the norm-relational core to Tomkins' theory is made explicit in his statement that the "issues constitute a polarity extending from the extreme left through a middle-of-the-road position to the extreme right-wing position. . . Is man the measure, an end in himself, an active, creative, thinking, desiring, loving force in nature? Or must man realize himself, attain his full stature only through struggle toward, participation in, conformity to a norm, a measure, an ideal essence basically prior to and independent of man" (Tomkins and Izard, 1965, p. 79). This polarity of a conservative conformity to established norms versus a liberal expansion of norms through love and creativity is then extended by Tomkins into a theory to account for these ideological alignments in all forms of Western thought—law, mathematics, science, art, educational theory, child-raising theory, and styles of psychiatry as well as politics.

A much narrower theoretical position which is also relevant to this norm-maintaining versus norm-violating pattern is that of Wilson (1973). As we have seen, Wilson theorizes that the psychological basis of conservative attitudes "is a generalized susceptibility to feeling threat or anxiety in the face of uncertainty (that is, ambiguity, complexity, change, novelty, deviance, individuality, anomie)" (Wilson, 1973, p. 286). The effect of this anxiety is again, as for Tomkins, a concern with norms, as "the extreme conservative perceives the world as 'falling apart,' which leads him to seek and place value upon order, simplicity and security" (Wilson, 1973, p. 288).

Thus, throughout these experiments and theories relating to liberalism and conservatism, a concern with the concepts and patterning of norm maintenance versus norm violation may be discerned. Our hypothetical framework for the structure of ideological personality is thus rooted in this age-old polarity of left versus right seen as a difference in orientation to norms and norming processes. But as discussed earlier, the influence of ideology in human affairs cannot be accounted for solely by left-right personality. Other attributes intimately associated with left versus right in actual social behavior comprise the hypothetical "core" of ideology. We will examine the dimensions of activism-inactivism and extremism-moderation from such a perspective. Moreover, beyond this "core" exists a potentially meaningful complex of "peripheral" variables, which at times are intimately associated with the functioning of the ideological personality—variables such as risk taking, Machiavellianism, alienation, anomie, and locus of control. Finally we must consider how ideological personality is formed by examining *developmental* variables.

Core Variables

Norm Violation or Maintenance. We have developed reasons for interest in norm maintenance or violation as a "frameworking" dimension. There can be a vast gap, however, between the time of stating concepts and their adequate measurement in psychology. For our purposes this concept was meaningless unless it could be successfully measured. Previous research by Alker and Kogan (1968) suggested that although it was developed for another purpose, the Stouffer-Toby measure might serve this purpose.

The Stouffer-Toby measure was originally developed to test Talcott Parsons' theory of the pattern variable, universalism-particularism (Parsons and Shils, 1952). The items in the Stouffer-Toby measure pose ethical-conflict situations. In one item, for example, the hypothetical friend of the subject has been involved in an automobile accident and the subject is asked whether he would conceal or reveal the fact his friend had been speeding. In another item, the friend needs a library book and the subject is asked to put the book aside for the friend or allow it to be checked out by someone else in the normal and fair procedure. In each case, then, the conflict is between adherence to an ethical norm and obligation to a friend. The friend has clearly transgressed against a norm of appropriate behavior, and the subject (who is the protagonist in the situation) is asked by the friend to commit an unethical act that would benefit the friend.

The rationale and format for this measure was compelling, and its use in the Alker-Kogan study along with the Choice Dilemma Questionnaire, mandated its use in this study. By the nature of the ethical-conflict situation upon which this measure is built, however, it forces an implicit equation of conservatism with morality and liberalism with immorality. As everyday observation will hardly support such an equation, this underlying contradiction must be kept in mind when interpreting results.

Activism-Inactivism and Extremism-Moderation. The revival of interest in ideology in the late 1960s and the 1970s centered even more on activism and extremism than on liberalism and conservatism. These variables were viewed as closely associated with ideology, and even as identical to it. The stereotypical liberal was thought to be an activist for social change, whereas the stereotypical conservative was seen as an inactivist opposing social change. Lewis and Kraut (1972) noted how these stereotypes were reflected in psychological studies by a confounding of activism with political belief in LC research. Studies by other investigators (Cowdry, Keniston, and Cabin, 1970; Silvern and Nakamura, 1971) showed that variables thought to be attributes of radical-left activists were actually characteristic of all students who act on their political beliefs, and other studies (De Fronzo, 1972; Lewis and Kraut, 1972; Alker, 1971) found behavioral differences among moderates and extremists of either persuasion. Thus, it was apparent a balanced investigation of ideology should examine LC interrelationships with activism and inactivism and with extremism and moderation. As for relationships to our framework, a logical first working hypothesis would be that activism and extremism relate to the tendency to depart from the norm, while inactivism and moderation relate to norm maintenance.

Three other aspects of previous studies of student activism also seemed worth investigation. The first was the usefulness of viewing one's stated beliefs as separate from one's observed actions. An advantage of the Stouffer-Toby role-conflict measure is that responses for both a belief ("what I *should* do") and an action ("what I *would* do") are required for each of its six items. A testable hypothesis was that activists and extremists would show a greater tendency toward norm violating on the Stouffer-Toby measure than inactivists and moderates. Another testable finding by Lewis and Kraut was the puzzling conclusion that conservative activists seem to "share many of the personal and interpersonal values of a left, or humanistic, ideology" (Lewis and Kraut, 1972, p. 147). Still another surprising finding for Lewis and Kraut was that both conservative and liberal activists are less Machiavellian than inactivists. This finding, along with their finding that activists are characterized by warmth, altruism, and social concern, contradicted both popular and academic stereotypes (Bell, 1968), which pictured activists as manipulative and self-serving.

An exceptionally important aspect of activism research has been the investigation of the effects of parent-child relationships and socialization more generally. We will consider this research, along with other developmental variables, in ending this chapter.

We have remarked how studies of extremism as a response style, or of ERS, can be grouped into those which reveal either "desirable" or "undesirable" characteristics. Undesirable characteristics for extreme responders included abnormality (Hamilton, 1968); pathology, rapid closure, and lack of verbal skill (Damarin and Messick, 1965); a concrete versus abstract cognitive structure (White and Harvey, 1965); and rigid personality (Brengelmann, 1960). Desirable characteristics for extremism included Tajfel and Wilkes' (1964) finding that as an object gains importance, judgments of it become more extreme; O'Donovan's (1965) conclusion that responses to meaningful stimuli tend toward the extreme; Moscovici and Zavalloni's (1969) conclusion that the customary equation of extremism and polarizing with "badness," and moderation and consensus with "goodness," was obscuring social reality; and Alker's (1971) summary of the work of the Sorbonne group, which found that in ambiguous settings people with extreme views are seen as being more able and decisive—that is, they are perceived as offering those qualities desired in leadership.

Three important theoretical views of ERS (Hamilton, 1968) relate extremism to the other variables of our concern. Findings that hospital patients, high-anxiety subjects, and members of "unusual" segments of society such as "novice nuns, actors, and actresses" were high ERS scorers led Zuckerman, Oppenheimer, and Gershowitz (1965) to propose that ERS may be a "manifestation of a general behavioral deviancy." The deviancy theory suggests that extremism should correlate with alienation, risk taking, and norm violating among our peripheral and framework variables.

A second theory is that of Brim and Hoff (1957), who see ERS as an effort to "achieve a greater degree of structure in the environment, thus reducing ambiguity." This theorized need to reduce ambiguity or uncertainty suggested the possibility of a correlation between extremism and Machiavellianism, with the rationale that the Machiavellian drive to manipulate others may be seen as a facet of the need to control one's social environment.

A third theory is that of O'Donovan (1965), who proposes that meaningfulness of stimuli encourages the extremism response. Here the developmental variable we will identify as "parental interest in issues" seems relevant. A strong relationship has been found between the parents' interest in social-political issues and the child's degree of activism (Lewis and Kraut, 1972). As interest conveys meaningfulness, it seemed probable that parental interest in issues should relate to extremism as well as activism in the child.

Peripheral Variables

Surrounding the hypothetical core variables is an area that might be termed ideology's active periphery. This includes variables that have received considerable experimental study in social and clinical psychology, but little attention has been directed to their possible relationships to ideology, or their relationship to ideology is cloudy and ambiguous. Thus, we found that investigations in risk taking (Kogan and Wallach, 1964), locus of control (Rotter, 1966), alienation (Keniston, 1965), anomie (McClosky and Schaar, 1965) had resulted in points of interaction with the conceptual area of ideology which provide additional hypotheses for testing.

Risk Taking. Difficulties in linking risk taking to constants of personality in previous research limited hopes for significant correlations of this variable with LC or other variables in this study. Wallach and Kogan (1961) found that older subjects were significantly more conservative in risk taking than college students. Kogan and Wallach (1964) also found that among women, independence significantly related to higher risk taking and rigidity to lower risk taking. This finding suggested the possibility that independence could be equated with activism, and rigidity with either conservatism (Adorno, 1950) or extremism (Rokeach, 1960). However, these possibilities were too slight to support a hypothesis. A more compelling reason for investigating risk taking as a peripheral ideological variable came from the fact that it has been extensively investigated as a component in leadership decision-making processes, as measured by the Choice Dilemma Questionnaire.

The Alker-Kogan (1968) study of the effects of group discussion of normative choice items on risk taking, earlier described, suggested that risk taking would relate to norm violating as a testable hypothesis. Coupling the Tomkins (1963) and Wilson (1973) theories of ideology with these findings then suggested that risk taking and norm violating would both relate to LC, with the liberals (Tomkins' humanistic type) being higher risk takers and norm violators than conservatives. Tomkins' historical study of the development of abolitionism as an expansion of risk taking (Tomkins and Izard, 1965) also suggested that activists would show greater risk taking than inactivists.

As for the relationship of risk taking to ideology in terms of our framework, logic suggested that risk taking would relate more to norm violating than to norm maintaining.

Machiavellianism. Machiavellianism, or the need to manipulate others, has been found by Christie and Geis (1970), as well as other investigators, to correlate with many variables. It was included in our study partly because of the prevalence of research using Christie's (1970) excellent measure of this variable. Earlier we noted the finding by Lewis and Kraut (1972) that the activists of their study were, contrary to expectation, less rather than more Machiavellian than the inactivists. A comparable finding by Christie and Geis (1970, p. 354) is that Machiavellians avoid extremism.

Most relevant to our inclusion of Machiavellianism as a variable, however, is its operation through ideological personality in history and current affairs. Machiavelli's own historical importance as the "father" of political psychology and the manipulative activities of an American president and associates that led to the Watergate disaster mandated its inclusion. It was of further interest that, though intuitively relevant, it was impossible to hypothesize any clear relationship for Machiavellianism to our theoretical framework.

Alienation-Anomie. Of the so-called peripheral variables, alienation is probably the most complex and of widest interest. At one point or another, it seems to relate to all of the variables being investigated. Studies by Keniston (1965, 1968), Flacks (1967), and Abcarian (1971) have found alienated youth to be characterized by both activism and inactivism, by norm violating, by both Machiavellianism and idealism. The well-publicized bombings and defiance of the obviously alienated New Left during the late 1960s indicated high risk taking for this group. Clinical aspects of alienation are explored in developmental studies of parent-child interactions (Bettelheim, 1967; Erikson, 1968), and the concept had its earliest meaning within classical psychiatry. Rather than to a therapist, the alienated mentally ill went to an "alienist."

Repeatedly, this concept, as it is now conceived and measured within both psychology and sociology, has shown a high correlation with left ideology (Ray and Sutton, 1972; Lewis and Kraut, 1972). At present, however, alienation is conceptually such a woeful muddle that the question rises whether there may be forms of alienation peculiar to the right and to the conservative. The possibility has received some attention in terms of the contemporary scene (Hamden-Turner, 1970; Schweitzer and Elden, 1971), but an understanding of the historical context within which this concept emerged is crucial if the issue is to be clarified.

Alienation was first a philosophical concept of Hegel's which Marx extended into the social context in the early 1800s (Fromm, 1961). At the core of the original concept lay a historical situation, which gave a cohesion to the concept that has since been lost through overgeneralizing. The term was originally used by a definitely leftist social philosopher, Karl Marx, to convey the unhappiness of many with the dominant social systems of his time, to lay the base for protest against these systems, and to serve as a rallying concept for the revolutionary attempt to change these systems—by violence if necessary. Most vitally, in terms of our interest in developing a theoretical framework of wide-ranging usefulness, it was a concept used to express *unhappiness with present norm constraints* and a desire for *violating them to create norms expressive of a better future.*

Keniston's early studies of the alienated youth of the 1960s indicate that this original meaning persists (Keniston, 1965), yet a curious fact is that the bulk of formal measures used by psychologists to test for alienation do not tap this "protest" meaning. The fourteen leading measures grouped under the alienation category in the Institute for Social Research (ISR) collection of measures of social psychological attitudes tap dimensions labeled powerlessness, helplessness, meaninglessness, normlessness, social isolation, emotional distance, and anomy (Robinson and Shaver, 1969). All of these concepts, through the passage of time and the cumulation of empirical study, have come to mean "alienation." But to find its original meaning—which might be called, a sense of norm constriction and the need for protest—one must look elsewhere. The best source we found was the Christie, Friedman, and Ross (1969) New Left Scale, compiled from rancorous statements of opinion by student protestors and other youths clearly alienated from establishment society and all its norms.

If it were possible to define such a form of left or liberal alienation with a scale of "protest" items, using present measures, what might then be used to determine whether there is a counter form of right or conservative alienation? Again the historical context is instructive. Following Marx's establishment of alienation as a concept in the early 1800s, the next most forceful term relating to this general area of social unhappiness was proposed by Durkheim, in the late 1800s, with his concept of anomie (Durkheim, 1951). Over the years it has come to mean "a sense of normlessness," but again, only the originating historical context adequately conveys what this may mean in terms of both personality and social behavior. Whereas Marx was earlier concerned with liberal and leftist needs for inducing social change, Durkheim—who came to manhood much later, following a major social disaster for France, a defeat by Germany—was concerned with the conservative function of strengthening society through institutions, and with processes for gaining or preserving social stability. Anomie, then, was used by Durkheim in his classical analysis of suicide to describe the socially-induced dismay of the conservative side to our nature with any situation that shatters the norms. It was a concept to express the emotional state of feeling adrift within a situation of social ambiguity so characteristic not only of Durkheim's time, but of the worldwide mood of the 1970s following the protests and aspirations of the 1960s. To place the matter again within the framework we seek to erect—and here a relevance to the question of political and managerial leadership becomes evident—where the Marx-alienation concern was with the constraint of norms and their violation and replacement, the Durkheim-anomie concern was with the loss of norms and regaining and maintaining them.

Ironically, whereas the classical meaning for alienation has faded from formal alienation measures, the basically conservative construct of anomie has become one of their chief components. Within the social-psychological context, it has been renamed anomy (McClosky and Schaar, 1965) and anomia (Srole, 1956). It is viewed as the sense of normlessness, which was central to the concept for Durkheim, but it has also taken on other, blurring meanings within psychology. The McClosky and Schaar (1965) measure of anomy, which deals with the concept as a separate entity rather than as part of an alienation measure, has shown both face and construct validity (Robinson and Shaver, 1969). McClosky's validation studies for this anomy measure also show appreciable correlations with conservatism as measured by cognitive functioning, psychological inflexibility, aggression, extreme beliefs, and misanthropy—including low faith in people, high elitism, and high ethnocentrism (Robinson and Shaver, 1969, p. 170).

It seemed worthwhile, then, to see whether the prevailing entanglement of alienation and anomie could be pulled apart into something much more generally useful by proving "new" alignments to the norm-relational framework we posit. Our hypothesis was that anomie items selected from the McClosky measure would relate to conservatism and to the norm-maintaining response on the Stouffer-Toby measure, and that alienation items selected from Christie's New Left measure would relate to liberalism and to the norm-violating response on the Stouffer-Toby measure.

Locus of Control. The concept of locus of control seemed of exceptional interest, not only theoretically but for its implications in therapy and educational policy. Whereas our other variables may be visualized as relating to norm-maintaining versus norm-violating patterns, locus of control relates to the question of where the norm to be maintained or departed from is perceived to be. Is it internalized and serving as a personal governor from "within"? Or is it perceived as existing outside oneself?

Both Adorno (1950) and Tomkins (Tomkins and Izard, 1965) clearly identify conservatism with an orientation similar to what Rotter (1966) defines as *externalization* of locus of control, whereas *internalization* is identified with the liberal. In a section of the Adorno work specifically titled "Externalization vs. Internalization," Frenkel-Brunswik characterizes the F scale high-scoring conservative as controlled by "the external world to which the feared qualities of the unconscious are ascribed." The F scale low-scoring liberal places "the blame for mishaps too much upon himself" and struggles to establish "inner harmony and self-actualization, whereas the high scorer is concentrated on an effort to adjust to the outside world" (Adorno, 1950, pp. 474, 475).

Tomkins states these alignments even more sharply. He characterizes the liberal's internality as defined by the question "Is man the measure, an end in himself?" By contrast, the externality of the conservative is characterized by the view that "man must realize himself . . . through . . . conformity to a norm" (Tomkins and Izard, 1965, p. 79).

Both of these conclusions, however, although based on sizeable empirical studies, are contradicted by research using the familiar Rotter I-E (internalization-externalization) scale of locus of control. In his basic monograph on I-E, Rotter (1966) reports studies of 114 Republicans, Democrats, and Independents, and of Nixon versus Kennedy supporters in 1961 that showed no significant differences in I-E response. More recently, in a study of the parents and children of 60 liberal and conservative families, Thomas (1970) found that conservatives had significantly higher internality scores than liberals, a finding that Abramowitz (1973) tends to support.

There is a similar conflict between I-E theory and research bearing on activism. Based on Rotter's social-learning theory, Rotter, Seeman, and Liverant (1962) hypothesized that "individuals with a high belief in the external control of reinforcement might be relatively passive in any attempt to change the world" (p. 475) and that the "real innovator" would be "relatively high in generalized belief in internal control of reinforcement" (p. 476). Gore and Rotter (1963) and Strickland (1965) apparently confirmed the hypothesis with findings of higher internality among black civil-rights activists. But further studies with other student populations (Rotter, 1966; Hamsher, Geller, and Rotter, 1968; and Abramowitz, 1973) have failed to find any significant relationship between I-E scores and activism.

Developmental Variables

The influence of parent-child relations on the development of the ideological personality is of major interest to this study.

There is, first, the fact that no adult personality can be adequately understood without knowledge of its history, which includes the key formative interaction of the developing human being with its seemingly all-powerful, all-knowledgeable parents. Secondly, if we are to understand how ideology may act to shape our future, we must grasp something of the nature of the ongoing process—existing since the time of the very first being on earth—by which the action (or inaction) of parent upon child has shaped the child's ideology. Because of the historical dominance of the male in political and economic leadership, we are particularly concerned with the effects of fathers and mothers upon sons.

In psychological research, this process has been studied within familiar paradigms of socialization for both psychoanalytic and conditioning theory (Dollard and Miller, 1950), which Tomkins (Tomkins and Izard, 1965) has directly related to the development of ideology. Through modeling processes and by direct edict the parent establishes the child's earliest norm structures. It may be inferred that the parent also indicates the degree to which these norm structures may be enlarged, changed, or even directly violated. Thus, we speak of strict versus permissive child-raising practices. As Tomkins has characterized these relationships, the "permissive" liberal parent, delighting in his child, "bestows on the child the feeling that he is an end in himself and that shared human interaction is a deeply satisfying experience" in a world of "endless opportunities for . . . varied positive affects" (Tomkins and Izard, 1965, p. 87). By contrast, the "strict" conservative parent is more concerned with his "obligation to mold the child to some norm." He must "convey to the child that what he wants to do is of no consequence when it is in opposition to the norm" (p. 87).

Such differences in child-raising styles have been found to relate to liberalism and conservatism in adults. In case studies of individuals, Lasswell (1948) concluded that "it is not too far-fetched to say that everyone is born a politician" (p. 160). Through family interrelationships he saw the infant as a born politician trying to gain power over his environment, tending to be shaped either into what Lasswell termed a "compulsive character" or a "dramatizer." These types could be identified as conservative and liberal since Lasswell states that the "hallmark of the former" is "the imposition of uniformity, while the latter tolerates diversity and excels in nuance" (p. 62). Frenkel-Bruns-wik also found that this "strict" versus "permissive" parent-to-child patterning of relationships seemed to lie behind the polar opposites of authoritarian versus humanitarian personalities (Adorno, 1950).

More recently, these developmental aspects of ideology have been explored by those investigating activism and extrem-ism. As noted previously, one aspect of this study centers about the socialization or "continuity" hypothesis and the genera-tional conflict or "discontinuity" hypothesis. The first hypothe-sis assumes a modeling of child after parent and a continuity in kind and degree of political belief—liberal parents producing liberal children, conservative parents producing conservatives, activists producing activists, extremists producing extremists. Studies by Greenstein (1965), Flacks (1967), and Keniston (1968) support this position. However, there is also consider-able evidence (Feuer, 1969; Dunlap, 1970) of the "generational gap" conflict which pits the conservative, moderate, or in-activist parent against the more liberal, extreme, or activist child. This evidence is cited to support a discontinuity hypothe-sis. In a longitudinal study designed to answer the questions of this controversy, Lewis and Kraut (1972) and Kraut, Lewis, and Pepitone (1973) have found support for both positions.

Various interpretations of the discrepancies between the findings and the continuity versus discontinuity hypotheses have been offered (see Rosenhan, 1969, and Tomkins and Izard, 1965). In a study of the motivation of civil rights workers, Rosenhan found two clearly different types of liberal activists, which he identified as the Fully Committed and the Partially Committed. The Fully Committed had worked for a year or more in various civil rights activities, were close to their parents, and seemed to hold beliefs modeled upon those of liberal-activist parents. This Fully Committed typology was also studied in historical depth by Tomkins (Tomkins and Izard, 1965), who found the same type of modeling patterns and a continuity of the parent-child relationship in the early child-hood of famous abolitionists. By contrast, the Partially Committed civil rights activists that were identified by Rosenhan had only participated in one or two freedom rides and were negative toward their parents—many, in fact, reported a "crisis of hypocrisy" over their feeling that the parents did not practice what they preached.

In terms of the variables of this study, such findings suggest that children whose beliefs are similar to those of the parents (reflecting a cross-generational continuity) may also show a continuity of activism and of parent-child harmony. By contrast, the dissimilarity of parent-child beliefs could relate to parent-child conflict and to discontinuity of activism.

The Lewis and Kraut (1972) and Kraut, Lewis, and Pepitone (1973) studies also offer other hypotheses which could be tested in our study. These investigators found that extreme liberals reported markedly greater personal conflict with their parents than did extreme conservatives. They also found that the conservatives tended to report a greater similarity and liberals less similarity to the political orientations of their parents. Liberals also reported more disagreement with parental political views than did conservatives. Particularly striking was their finding of a significant correlation between parental interest and involvement in social and political issues and the activist orientation for both liberals and conservatives.

Summary of Hypothetical Relationships

As the preceding account indicates, many possible relationships could be explored among the variables of this study. The problem was how to confine our investigation to a few salient relationships. Our approach was to group the questions we have raised into the categories of personality suggested by our three "core" dimensions: liberalism-conservatism, activism-inactivism, and extremism-moderation. We will examine these variables as they are customarily viewed both in research and everyday life—in terms of how belief and behavior may differ for liberals in contrast to conservatives, for activists in contrast to inactivists, and for extremists in contrast to moderates. We will then raise questions of possible antecedents (for example, how parent-child relations may affect ideological development) and "consequences" (for example, to what extent certain kinds of alienation "follow" from being a liberal rather than a conservative).

Figures 13-15 provide a visual summary of this approach in a loosely path-analytical format. Investigators whose findings suggest the hypotheses are indicated. The reader may compare these visual statements of hypotheses with our later discussion of results, which show the correlations that were found for all projected relationships (Figures 16-18).

Figure 13

Hypothetical Relationships of LC Ideology and Other Study Variables.

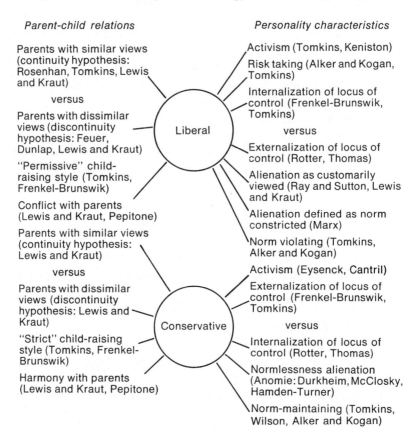

Parent-child relations

Parents with similar views (continuity hypothesis: Rosenhan, Tomkins, Lewis and Kraut)

versus

Parents with dissimilar views (discontinuity hypothesis: Feuer, Dunlap, Lewis and Kraut)

"Permissive" child-raising style (Tomkins, Frenkel-Brunswik)

Conflict with parents (Lewis and Kraut, Pepitone)

Parents with similar views (continuity hypothesis: Lewis and Kraut)

versus

Parents with dissimilar views (discontinuity hypothesis: Lewis and Kraut)

"Strict" child-raising style (Tomkins, Frenkel-Brunswik)

Harmony with parents (Lewis and Kraut, Pepitone)

Liberal

Conservative

Personality characteristics

Activism (Tomkins, Keniston)

Risk taking (Alker and Kogan, Tomkins)

Internalization of locus of control (Frenkel-Brunswik, Tomkins)

versus

Externalization of locus of control (Rotter, Thomas)

Alienation as customarily viewed (Ray and Sutton, Lewis and Kraut)

Alienation defined as norm constricted (Marx)

Norm violating (Tomkins, Alker and Kogan)

Activism (Eysenck, Cantril)

Externalization of locus of control (Frenkel-Brunswik, Tomkins)

versus

Internalization of locus of control (Rotter, Thomas)

Normlessness alienation (Anomie: Durkheim, McClosky, Hamden-Turner)

Norm-maintaining (Tomkins, Wilson, Alker and Kogan)

Figure 14

Hypothetical Relationships of Activism to Other Study Variables

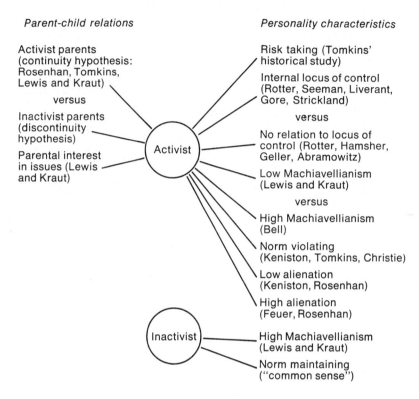

By this means and with the analysis of variance (ANOVA) statistical model in mind, we should be able to first clarify relationships in the "main effect" terms in which they are customarily viewed (for example, liberals, activists, and extremists, being viewed as different types of orientations with differing styles of belief and behavior). However, the ANOVA model also suggests a potentially more important level of analysis. Secondly, we will examine the *interactions* of the three core dimensions and peripheral variable clusterings in an attempt to gain a clear picture of underlying structural relationships.

Table 4 is a crude and open-ended summary of some of the questions we raised at the beginning of our search for a useful new theoretical structure for the investigation of ideological

Figure 15

Hypothetical Relationships
of Extremism to Other Study Variables

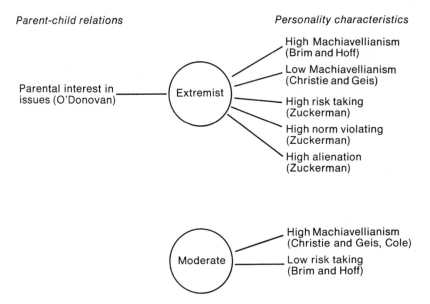

Parent-child relations   *Personality characteristics*

High Machiavellianism
(Brim and Hoff)

Low Machiavellianism
(Christie and Geis)

Parental interest in _____ Extremist
issues (O'Donovan)

High risk taking
(Zuckerman)

High norm violating
(Zuckerman)

High alienation
(Zuckerman)

Moderate

High Machiavellianism
(Christie and Geis, Cole)

Low risk taking
(Brim and Hoff)

meaning. The relationships it very loosely seeks to define are
later reviewed, in terms of the findings and given a tighter perspective.

Table 4

An Exploratory Grouping of Norming Process Relationships

Concern with Processes and States of Social Stability or Norm Maintaining	Concern with Processes and States of Social Change or Norm Violating
Conservatives?	Liberals?
Inactivists?	Activists?
Moderates?	Extremists?
Low-risk takers?	High-risk takers?
External locus of control?	Internal locus of control?
Normlessness alienation or anomie?	Norm-constricted alienation?
Parent-child harmony?	Parent-child conflict?
Parent-child belief similarity?	Parent-child belief dissimilarity?
Conservative ideology for parents?	Liberal ideology for parents?
"Strict" child-raising style?	"Permissive" child raising style?

8

Methods of Investigation

Methods, like test validations, although fascinating to the devotee, are boring to the nontechnical reader. And yet they must be stated, and with great precision, so we may know to what extent the investigator took pains to guarantee that the possibility of error was avoided and his findings are solid. Fortunately, this chapter is short and can be scanned in seconds by those whose eyes glaze on encountering the terms *varimax rotation* or *analysis of variance*.

During the spring of 1972 we administered a battery of liberalism-conservatism measures to eighty-four members of the four Princeton-campus political groups described in Chapters Five and Six. Our purpose was to compare and validate results for the Adorno, Tomkins, self-report, and original measures of liberalism-conservatism. The results of this testing were used to select the sample, the measures, and the methods of questionnaire administration for the study reported here, which took place during the spring of 1973. Participants were all white, male, and below twenty-five years of age. This exclusion of blacks, females, and those over twenty-five was not racist, sexist, nor age chauvinistic, of course. It was a necessary move to control the variance within a relatively small sample; evidence from other studies shows serious confounding of the variables we selected by race, sex, and age factors. Demographic data was not collected for each participant because of lack of funds and time. The comparable Lewis and Kraut (1972) study of students at Yale University found relative socioeconomic homogeneity and no significant correlations of LC, activism, or extremism, with any demographic factors. Because of the great similarity of student populations for these two eastern, Ivy League colleges, the Lewis and Kraut findings suggest that a comparable homogeneity and lack of demographic significance probably existed for this Princeton group. Total N for the sample in this study was 163.

Measures

Two of three LC measures chosen for use included six items from the Adorno Politico-Economic Conservatism (PEC) Scale (identified hereafter as variable LCA); and six items from our adaptation of the Tomkins scale to a Likert scale format (variable LCT). The rationale for pairing the Adorno and Tomkins items was that the original Adorno measures have furnished a majority of items for later measures purporting to measure LC, and they tap what might be termed the social-issue "face" to LC. By contrast, the Tomkins measure derives from a philosophical and clinical concern with ideology in depth personalistic terms. The pairing was to hypothetically tap both outer-social and inner-personal aspects to liberalism-conservatism.

The third measure was a simple self-report scale with six response choices ranging from radical left through the more moderate ideological positions to radical right (variable LCSR). This selection was based on the high correlation ($r = .70$, $p < .001$) between self-report and other measures of LC found both by Lewis and Kraut (1972) and by the spring 1972 testing for this project.

Measures selected for other variables were as follows:

1. *Activism*
    a. *Degree* (variable AD)—self-report ratings of the degree of activism for both high school and college were obtained. A total rating of activism was then obtained by assigning 1 to inactivism in both high school and college, 2 to activism in either high school or college, and 3 to activism in both high school and college.
    b. *Continuity* (variable AC)—the self-report responses were rated 1 for activism in both high school and college, and 0 if the subject reported inactivity at either level.
    c. *Activism degree, college only* (variable ADCO)—for the analysis of variance, self-report responses for college only were used, with a rating of 1 for activism, 0 for inactivism.
2. *Extremism*
    All three measures of LC provided means of obtaining the extremism versus moderation separation. The method and criteria used are explained in the description of the analysis of variance.
3. *Norm violating*
    The Stouffer-Toby measure used originally in the Parsons-Shils (1952) *Theory of Action* work and again by Alker and Kogan (1968). Six items provided belief (NVB) versus action (NVA) options for a total of twelve responses per subject.
4. *Risk taking* (RT)
    The twelve-item Choice Dilemma Questionnaire developed by Kogan and Wallach (1964). The customary scoring of the higher numbers of the 0-6 range for low risk taking was reversed to provide positive correlations in keeping with the general pattern for hypotheses and for clarity in the intercorrelation matrix.
5. *Locus of control* (I-E)
    The twenty-nine-item I-E scale (Rotter, 1966). In keeping with the general practice, responses for the twenty-

three I-E items were scored for externality. The six filler items noted above were also assigned 0-1 response values to test a hypothesis of ideological bias, the value of 0 being assigned to filler items that on inspection appeared to have conservative appeal and 1 being assigned to items that appeared to have liberal appeal.

6. *Alienation* (ANL, AAN, AO)

Three different sets of alienation items were compiled. In keeping with the hypotheses of liberal alienation and conservative anomie, a set of (1) items that seemed to maximize "social-constriction alienation" and to minimize patent New Left identity was selected from items of the New Left Scale (Christie, 1969). This was identified as the ANL set. A set of (2) ten anomie-relevant "normlessness" items was selected from McClosky and Schaar (1965) and other sources. This was identified as the AAN set. For contrast, a set of (3) alienation items was selected on a theoretical basis from a collection of other items in the alienation literature. This set was identified as AO, for "alienation other." Twelve items were selected for ANL, ten for AAN, and eight for AO, for a total of thirty alienation items. A persisting problem with measures of this type has been the exclusive or near-exclusive use of the positively weighted response, leading to the questionability of results due to possible "yea-saying" response bias (Robinson and Shaver, 1969). With this in mind, all alienation sets were balanced with an equal number of positively and negatively worded items.

7. *Machiavellianism* (MAC)

Fourteen items were selected from among the items of the Machiavellianism Scale (Christie and Geis, 1970) that showed the highest-item to total-score intercorrelations.

8. *Parental interest in issues* (PII)

A self-report scale offering four options (very inactive, 1, to very active, 4) for response to the question asking to what extent the subject's parents were interested in social-political issues.

9. *Parent-child belief similarity* (PCB)

A self-report scale offering four options (very different, 1, to very much alike, 4) for response to the question of how similar the subjects' own social-political beliefs were to those of their parents.

10. *Parent-child conflict* (PCC)

A self-report scale offering four options (very harmonious, 1, to very conflictful, 4) for response to the question asking how the subjects would characterize their relation with their parents during recent years.

Administration and Analysis

Items for the above measures were assembled in a questionnaire, which was administered to our 163 study participants. By checking self-report LC and activism scales as questionnaires came in, an effort was made to obtain a sample reasonably balanced for liberalism versus conservatism, activism versus inactivism, and extremism versus moderation. The reason for this expedient was that my previous experience with these students convinced me that without special efforts to encourage their participation, both conservatives and inactivists would tend not to fill out or return our questionnaires. The result would then almost certainly be a distribution badly skewed in the liberal and activist direction. Most studies (for example, Lewis and Kraut, 1972) tend to use whatever responses are received to a mailing of questionnaires and then assign categories by quartiling the frequency distributions. Our experience with both spring 1972 and spring 1973 studies of the Princeton group indicated this procedure will invariably result in the serious underrepresentation in such samples of "real" conservatives and inactivists ("real" in the sense of known group activity or other behavioral criteria, as opposed to determination of ideology only by the statistical artifact of quartiling a frequency distribution).

To discover the nature of the variable relationships, intercorrelations for the sixteen variables of the study were computed. Then, the correlation matrix was factored using Principal

Components Analysis, and the five factors with roots greater than 1.0 were rotated to orthogonal simple structure using customary Varimax and Quartimax methods (Harman, 1967). To determine the differential effects of liberalism-conservatism, activism-inactivism, and extremism-moderation upon all other variables, a three-way analysis of variance for all variables was computed using procedures (Edwards, 1958; Snedecor and Cochran, 1967) as implemented by the ANOVA II and III computer programs of the Educational Testing Service in Princeton.

The eight subgroups compared by ANOVA were: liberal extreme activists (N = 28); liberal extreme inactivists (N = 7); liberal moderate activists (N = 28); liberal moderate inactivists (N = 22); conservative extreme activists (N = 24); conservative extreme inactivists (N = 17); conservative moderate activists (N = 16); conservative moderate inactivists (N = 21).

To determine criteria for these subgroups, a frequency distribution of scores for the LCA (six Adorno items) measure of ideology was used. Liberals were separated from conservatives at the mean of 23 for the sample. Points for separating extremes from moderates of both ideological wings were determined by score values nearest to the quartile points. By this means, with an LCA score range of 6-36, extreme conservatives were those with the score range 6-18, moderate conservatives were scores 19-22, moderate liberals were scores 23-27, and extreme liberals were scores 28-36. Activism criteria for the ANOVA were based on self-report for activism or inactivism during college only.

To answer specific questions of item bias and to determine more generally to what extent the measures of the study were ideologically biased, correlations of items with total scores for one measure of ideology were obtained for all items using all measures. The measure of ideology selected for this comparison was the six-item set from the Adorno PEC (variable LCA). Of the alternatives, the six-item set from the Tomkins' Polarity Scale (variable LCT) showed less power for differentiating liberals from conservatives and the self-report item was questionable for use as a single measure.

9

Defining Results

Our purpose in this chapter is to explore and tentatively establish the nature of findings in terms primarily meaningful to personality, social, and measurement psychologists. In the following chapter we will examine their more generally meaningful implications and state our conclusions. In both chapters, as an aid to the reader, a few key findings will be italicized.

We will examine results in the following order. First, all variables will be viewed in terms of intercorrelations (Table 5), a factor analysis (Table 6), and an item analysis (Table 7). Next, we will regroup these findings into individual profiles for the liberals, conservatives, activists, inactivists, extremists, and moderates of our study viewed as distinctly different personality types. Figures 16, 17, and 18 will summarize these findings. Then we will examine the interactions of the three "core" dimensions with the "peripheral" variables to discover evidence of larger structures affecting ideology revealed by analysis of variance. Table 8 summarizes these intricate but exceptionally useful findings.

Table 5

Correlation Matrix of Variables

	LCA	LCT	LCSR	AD	AC	NVB	NVA	RT	IE	ANL	AAN	AO	MAC	PII	PCB	PCC
LCA		46**	67**	07	03	-01	11	-06	23**	71**	41**	34**	-02	-06	-30**	14
LCT			45	09	08	10	11	14	17*	40**	23**	05	-31**	-01	-18*	09
LCSR				27**	22**	09	08	05	15	57**	40**	21**	-09	-04	-31**	18*
AD					90**	15	03	18*	07	06	09	-00	02	28**	03	07
AC						19*	06	17*	02	04	08	-01	01	25**	07	03
NVB							47**	01	14	-03	-01	-01	10	05	-07	09
NVA								05	16*	01	04	05	10	-08	01	08
RT									-11	-01	-02	-07	-08	-12	03	16*
IE										30**	40**	35**	20*	-12	-13	13
ANL											52**	55**	07	-10	-43**	25**
AAN												43**	27**	-15	-33**	27**
AO													25**	-13	-28**	13
MAC														-07	-07	19*
PII															29**	-27**
PCB																-37**
PCC																

For 163 df, correlations of .16 and .21 are significant at the .05 (*) and .01 (**) levels, respectively.

LCA=Liberalism-conservatism as measured by Adorno items. LCT=Liberalism-conservatism as measured by Tomkins items. LCSR=Liberalism-conservatism as measured by self-report. AD=Degree of activism. AC=Continuity of activism. NVB=Norm-violating belief. NVA=Norm-violating action. RT=Risk taking. IE=Internal-external locus of control. ANL=Alienation items from the New Left measure. AAN=Alienation items from the anomie measure. AO=Alienation items from other sources. MAC=Machiavellianism scale items. PII=Parental interest in issues. PCB=Parent-child belief similarity. PCC=Parent-child conflict.

Correlational Findings

Table 5 is an intercorrelation matrix for all sixteen variables. The coding for all variables, as well as the directions for scoring, is shown beneath the table.

Table 6 gives the results of the Quartimax rotation of a Principal Components Analysis of the data (there were only small differences between the Varimax and Quartimax rotations). This analysis identified five factors with roots greater than 1.0, which accounted for 66 percent of the variance. Loadings equal to or greater than .30 on the largest factor, which accounted for 24 percent of the variance, indicated this can be characterized as the "left-right" factor. These high loadings included all three LC measures, two alienation variables, Machiavellianism, and the PCB variable. The pattern of loadings for

Table 6

Quartimax Rotation: Roots Greater than Unity, Values of Roots, and Commonalities

	1	2	3	4	5	h^2
LCA	81*	28	−02	−00	−00	74
LCT	77*	−20	01	04	17	66
LCSR	78*	13	22	12	03	68
AD	10	04	94*	−01	05	90
AC	07	01	93*	−03	09	88
NVB	01	05	15	03	83*	71
NVA	07	06	−03	04	84*	72
RT	04	−36*	32	46*	01	45
IE	19	60*	−01	−04	25	46
ANL	73*	46*	−00	16	−12	78
AAN	40*	62*	08	23	−07	60
AO	25	70*	−05	07	−08	57
MAC	−38*	68*	08	18	09	65
PII	−01	−11	42*	−57*	−05	52
PCB	−35*	−24	13	−56*	04	51
PCC	08	17	08	78*	07	66
Roots	2.93	2.27	2.14	1.59	1.54	

*Loadings equal to or greater than .35. Decimal points omitted.

Loadings suggest the following identification for factors: 1, ideology; 2, alienation; 3, activism; 4, parent-child relations; 5, norm violating.

the other four factors in Table 6 can be characterized as follows: high loadings for risk taking, I-E, alienation, and Machiavellianism suggest an "alienation" designation for factor 2; loadings for risk taking, activism, and parental interest in issues suggest "activism" for factor 3; loadings for risk taking, parental interest in issues, parent-child belief similarity, and parent-child conflict suggest "parent-child relations" for factor 4; and loadings for both norm-violation variables suggest "norm violation" for factor 5.

Table 7 gives correlations of individual items for all measures with LCA score totals for liberalism-conservatism. By this

Table 7

Item Bias Analysis: Correlations with LCA Total Score for Items of the Tomkins Variant (LCT), Stouffer-Toby Measure (NVB and NVA), Choice Dilemma Questionnaire (RT), Rotter I-E Scale (IE), Norm-Constriction Alienation (ANL), Normlessness Alienation (AAN), Other Alienation (AO), Machiavellianism (MAC), and I-E Filler Items

Variable	Item	Corre-lation	Variable	Item	Corre-lation	Variable	Item	Corre-lation
LCT	1	.17*	IE	2	.11	AAN	1	.05
	2	.23**		3	−.38**		2	.11
	3	.42**		4	.23**		3	.34**
	4	.45**		5	.29**		4	.28**
	5	.08		6	.15		5	−.02
	6	.30**		7	−.03		6	.42**
				9	−.11		7	.24**
NVB	1	.08		10	−.17*		8	−.18*
	2	−.15		11	.09		9	.24**
	3	.04		12	.26**		10	.41**
	4	.14		13	.22**			
	5	−.11		15	.16*	AO	1	.29**
	6	−.00		16	.19*		2	.31**
				17	−.03		3	.03
NVA	1	.17*		18	−.05		4	.13
	2	−.14		20	−.00		5	−.08
	3	.11		21	.12		6	−.10
	4	.27**		22	−.03		7	.42**
	5	−.12		23	.12		8	.21**
	6	.10		25	.15			
				26	.08	MAC	1	−.08
RT	1	−.03		28	.28**		2	−.24**
	2	−.06		29	.04		3	.05
	3	.12					4	.12

Variable	Item	Correlation	Variable	Item	Correlation	Variable	Item	Correlation
RT	4	.02	ANL	1	.48**	MAC	5	.07
(cont'd)	5	−.07		2	.54**	(cont'd)	6	−.02
	6	.02		3	.39**		7	.09
	7	−.12		4	.50**		8	−.05
	8	.08		5	.37**		9	−.21**
	9	−.21**		6	.41**		10	.05
	10	.02		7	.59**		11	−.17*
	11	−.04		8	−.05		12	.12
	12	−.02		9	.24**		13	.05
				10	.42**		14	.03
				11	.40**			
				12	.56**	IE Filler	1	.39**
							8	.09
							14	.26**
							19	.00
							24	.05
							27	.25**

For 163 df, correlations of .16 and .21 are significant at the .05 (*) and .01 (**) levels, respectively.

means, the variability of ideological biasing for these measures may be examined. A significant correlation, for example, indicates an item to which participants' answers were significantly influenced by either liberalism (positive correlations) or conservatism (negative correlations), as well as by the variable ostensibly being measured. Note the prevalence of such items for the Rotter I-E Scale—a critical problem for this scale, to which we will return.

Liberalism-Conservatism. The correlations of the three LC measures with one another (.45, .46, .67) and with other variables reflect an appreciable similarity in patterns of response. Notable is the high correlation (.67) for the self-report with the LCA measure. *However, the lower correlation with LCT indicates how much meanings for this construct are dependent on the measure used.* Had we only used the LCA and LCT measures, we would have found no correlation for liberalism with activism, as appears with the self-report LCSR measure. Had we only used the LCA and LCSR measures, we would have failed to find the correlation of conservatism with Machiavellianism, which appears with the addition of the LCT measure (these and subsequent correlations are all shown in Table 5 unless noted otherwise).

The general pattern of relationships for this variable is best indicated in Table 6, which shows high loadings for two of the three alienation variables, and negative loadings for Machiavellianism and parent-child belief similarity, along with the three LC variables, on the "ideology" factor 1.

Activism-Inactivism. The high correlation (.90) of degree (AD) and continuity (AC) of activism is noteworthy. This could indicate a strong tendency for high school activists to continue to be activists in college. We should note that a reason for including the AC variable was to see if parent-child belief similarity was related to continuity of activism, but no such relationship appears.

Norm Violation or Maintenance. A reasonably high correlation (.47) of norm-violating belief (NVB) with norm-violating action (NVA) indicates the strength of the tendency for those with norm-violating beliefs to also display the norm-violating behavioral readiness, or "action," response. In general these two variables show similar relationships to other variables, but with one potentially important exception. This is the significant correlation (.19) for NVB, but not for NVA, with continuity of activism (AC). As we shall develop with additional evidence, this suggests that although activists may believe in norm violating, they are not motivated to act on these beliefs unless they are also moved by other motivating variables.

Risk Taking. For the main purposes of this study, only the significant correlation of risk taking with activism is of interest. In its subsidiary relationships, however, a marginally significant correlation of .16 between risk taking and parent-child conflict takes on importance when viewed through factor analysis. As Table 6 shows, the high positive loadings for factor 4 are risk taking and parent-child conflict, with high negative loadings for parental interest in issues and parent-child similarity. This would support the view that risk taking increases as conflict with parents increases. In addition, the negative loadings for PII and PCB could suggest that high risk takers who report appreciable parent-child conflict do not feel their parents are interested in social-political issues and do not see themselves as sharing many beliefs with these parents.

Locus of Control. Of the variables investigated, locus of control provided the least satisfactory findings. Positive correlations of I-E with LCA (.23) and LCT (.17) might lead some to conclude that we had resolved a research issue of considerable importance by proving a relation of externality to liberalism and internality to conservatism. But to do so would mean overlooking large questions raised by two clusters of findings. One is the amount of apparent ideological bias for the I-E measure shown by Table 7. The other is the implication of the high correlations for I-E with the alienation scores shown in Table 5 and in Table 6 factor loadings.

Follow-up studies convinced us that the Rotter I-E Scale is so heavily laden with ideologically biased items, and so further confounded by items expressing the powerlessness dimension of alienation, that it cannot be used to reach any conclusions about internality versus externality in this context. In fact, we seriously question whether the findings of hundreds of studies by social psychologists and clinicians who have used this appealing instrument over more than a decade are not, in fact, relatively meaningless.

Alienation-Anomie. Significant positive correlations occurred for all three alienation measures with I-E, and for two of the three measures with Machiavellianism; positive correlations were with parent-child conflict; negative correlations were with parent-child belief similarity. These correlations for alienation measures support the familiar picture of the alienated as feeling powerless to affect their destiny, using Machiavellian coping techniques, holding views at variance with those of their parents, and being in conflict with parents.

Parent-Child Relational Variables. The three parent-child variables display correlations in keeping with expectancies. It is not surprising that parental interest in issues and parent-child belief similarity should show a significant positive correlation (.29), or that both PII and PCB should show significant negative correlations with parent-child conflict (−.72, −.27, and −.37, respectively). A general tendency is for those who feel their parents' views are similar to their own to have parents who are also interested in social-political issues. We may also conclude that those who report conflict with parents tend to have parents who are not interested in social-political issues and who certainly hold differing beliefs from their children. Of further interest are the variables that positively correlate with parent-child conflict: self-reported liberalism (.18), risk taking (.16), alienation (.25 and .27), and Machiavellianism (.19).

Ideological Personality Profiles

The Liberal. Are liberals greater risk takers than conservatives? Our findings say no. All three measures of LC show nonsignificant correlations with risk taking, and, as one might expect, there is also no loading for risk taking on the "ideology" factor 1.

Are liberals more alienated than conservatives? If so, are they alienated in different ways? Here, the answer, with qualifications, is yes. Five out of the six possible correlations between the LC and alienation measures are positively significant. Moreover, the correlations of liberalism with alienation defined as norm constricted (ANL) are considerably greater than with the two other forms of alienation. This is to be expected, as the ANL measure was built of items from the New Left measure as explained previously. Yet the higher correlations for liberalism with ANL than with the other item sets also clearly indicates that this type of alienation, which most ostensible measures of alienation do not tap, is more characteristic of liberals than the other forms we tested. *This finding supports our framework hypothesis that liberals would show more norm-constriction alienation than other forms.*

Are liberals more activist than conservatives? The answer is unclear. On one hand, the evidence from the two indirect measures of LC is negative—correlations for LCA and LCT and activism are practically nonexistent. Nor does activism load on the "ideology" factor. However, scores for the self-report LCSR measure show significant positive correlations with both measures of activism. This contradiction could suggest that whereas liberals perceive and pride themselves on being more activist than conservatives (the self-report results), in fact (the indirect measures) one ideology is not more activist than the other. However, one senses there could be more here than meets the eye.

The locus of control findings for liberalism are reported in Table 5 for their possible value to other investigators, but will receive no comment here for reasons stated earlier.

A relation of norm violating to liberalism was posited as of key importance to our frameworking hypothesis. *At this first, direct, correlational level of analysis, no evidence appears to support this central hypothesis.* Table 5 shows no relation even approaching significance between the LC and norm-violating variables. Table 6 also reveals that on factor analysis, the norm-violating variables heavily load on factor 5 with no appreciable loadings on this factor by any other variables.

In contrast to the ambiguities for personality characteristics, the findings for liberal parent-child relations provide relatively clean-cut answers. Do liberals have parents with similar or dissimilar views? Our findings say their parents have dissimilar views. All three LC measures show significant negative correlations with the self-report measure of similarity of parent and child beliefs. This finding could raise questions about the validity of the continuity hypothesis, which has seemed particularly compelling because of its base in modeling-processes research and theory. These negative correlations suggest that liberals see themselves as definitely having beliefs that differ from their parents, which seems to support the discontinuity hypothesis of liberal activist development. However, findings of no or only marginally significant correlations between liberalism and parent-child conflict, puts the matter in a considerably different light. The two sets of findings, when combined, suggest that, although the liberals of this study may see their views as differing from those of their parents, this difference is really not sufficient to provoke conflict. Thus, it cannot be said these findings confirm or disconfirm either the continuity or the discontinuity hypothesis.

The important hypothesis, deriving from Tomkins and Frenkel-Brunswik, of a relation between permissive child-raising practices and liberalism, is confirmed in a novel way. The third of the six Tomkins' Polarity Scale items used in the LCT measure offers the following choice of options: "Above all, parents should be gentle with children" versus "Above all, parents should be firm with children." Prior use of the Polarity Scale in both its standard, fifty-nine-item form and its shortened, Likert-format variant had convinced me this single item was an exceptionally accurate differentiator between liberals and conservatives. A significantly high correlation of .42 (p < .001) between endorsement of the liberal option and the LCA total score confirms the hypothesized relationship of ideology to child-raising practices. That is, this correlation shows that liberals overwhelmingly endorse the gentle rather than firm, child-raising style.

Further confirmation came from the I-E items. The first (a filler or hypothetically neutral) item for the I-E scale presents the following choice: "Children get into trouble because their parents punish them too much" versus "The trouble with most children nowadays is that their parents are too easy with them." The similarity in meaning and structure of choice to the Tomkins item and to the hypothesis is clear. The correlation with ideology is also similarly high and significant (.38, p < .001). To a substantial degree, then, response to these items supports the hypothesis of a relation between gentle, nonpunitive methods of child-raising and the development of liberals.

One other correlation merits comment. This is the unforeseen finding of a negative correlation between liberalism and Machiavellianism. Scores for the Adorno LCA and the self-report LCSR measures show no such relationship. However, responses to the Tomkins' LCT measure show a significant negative correlation (−.31, p < .001) with Machiavellianism. This clearly indicates that liberals, as defined by the Tomkins items, tend to be low in Machiavellianism.

Figure 16 summarizes the profile for the liberal in the same format that was used earlier for our initiating hypotheses. Our findings thus far suggest the following rather pallid picture

Figure 16

Findings and Relationships of LC Ideology to Other Study Variables

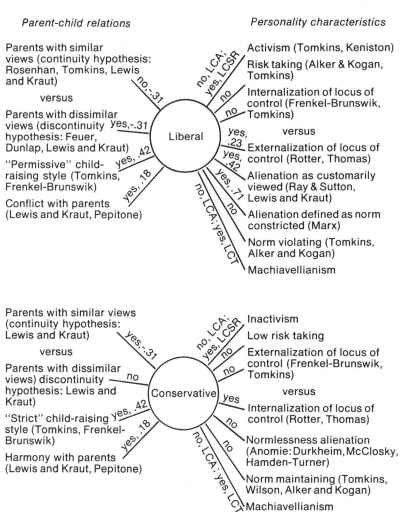

Parent-child relations

Parents with similar views (continuity hypothesis: Rosenhan, Tomkins, Lewis and Kraut)

versus

Parents with dissimilar views (discontinuity hypothesis: Feuer, Dunlap, Lewis and Kraut)

"Permissive" child-raising style (Tomkins, Frenkel-Brunswik)

Conflict with parents (Lewis and Kraut, Pepitone)

Personality characteristics

Activism (Tomkins, Keniston)

Risk taking (Alker & Kogan, Tomkins)

Internalization of locus of control (Frenkel-Brunswik, Tomkins)

versus

Externalization of locus of control (Rotter, Thomas)

Alienation as customarily viewed (Ray & Sutton, Lewis and Kraut)

Alienation defined as norm constricted (Marx)

Norm violating (Tomkins, Alker and Kogan)

Machiavellianism

Parents with similar views (continuity hypothesis: Lewis and Kraut)

versus

Parents with dissimilar views) discontinuity hypothesis: Lewis and Kraut)

"Strict" child-raising style (Tomkins, Frenkel-Brunswik)

Harmony with parents (Lewis and Kraut, Pepitone)

Inactivism

Low risk taking

Externalization of locus of control (Frenkel-Brunswik, Tomkins)

versus

Internalization of locus of control (Rotter, Thomas)

Normlessness alienation (Anomie: Durkheim, McClosky, Hamden-Turner)

Norm maintaining (Tomkins, Wilson, Alker and Kogan)

Machiavellianism

of the "idealized" liberal. Though he may believe in activism and thinks of himself as being one, he is not necessarily an activist in political behavior. Nor is he predictably a risk taker. He has marked tendencies toward norm-constricted but also other forms of alienation, he isn't predictably a norm violator, and he tends not to be Machiavellian. He sees his beliefs as differing from those of his parents, but this difference is not so great as to provoke considerable conflict. He probably enjoyed a gentle, nonpunitive, or "permissive" style of child-raising.

The Conservative. The profile of the conservative, as shown in Figure 16, can be summarized briefly because the same findings are at issue. Positive relations with liberalism necessarily imply negative relations with conservatism and vice versa.

We found no support for the stereotype of the conservative as inactivist. But this holds only for the "indirect" LCA and LCT measures. The implication of the positive correlation (.27) for activism and the self-report LCSR measure is either: (1) as conservatism increases so does inactivism; or (2) because of bad connotations for the word "activism," conservatives perceive, pride, and report themselves as being less activist than liberals, although there could be reason to expect activism from conservatives as from liberals.

The finding of no significant correlation between the three measures of ideology and risk taking indicates that just as we found no support for equating high risk taking with liberals, there is also no support for equating low risk taking with conservatives.

To confirm the hypothesis of anomie as a conservative form of normlessness alienation (as contrasted to norm-constricted alienation for the liberal), the correlation between AAN and the three measures of ideology should be negative. These correlations, however, were significantly positive, indicating a liberal rather than a conservative association for this measure.

As the lack of significant correlations between norm violating and LC indicated no direct relation between norm violating and liberalism, so is its reverse necessarily true: at this level of analysis, no relation between norm maintenance and conservatism can be discerned.

The parent-child relational cluster further differentiates between liberal and conservative. The finding of negative correla-

tions for LC and PCB (Table 5) indicated parent-child belief dissimilarity for liberals. The same finding emphasizes a similarity
of views for the conservative and his parents. This pattern
would support the continuity-modeling hypothesis, and could
suggest that modeling is more important for the conservative
than for the liberal. Also noteworthy is the marginally significant, positive correlation of parent-child conflict with the LCSR
scores. Whereas the correlation previously indicated some conflict with liberals, the implication for conservatives is of parent-
child harmony.

The rationale for the use of the Tomkins and Rotter filler
items to test hypotheses for child-raising style was explained in
our discussion of findings for liberalism. As the significant positive correlations for these items with LCA scores indicated a
relation of the "permissive" style to liberalism, so do both items
support the reverse hypothesis for conservatism; that is the correlations indicate *a relation of the "strict" and punitive parental
style to conservatism.*

We earlier noted the finding of a negative correlation of
Machiavellianism and liberalism as measured by the Tomkins
LCT measure. The reverse situation is a positive relationship between normative conservatism and Machiavellianism, or evidence that Machiavellianism is to some degree a style associated
with those who are concerned with observing the norms or rules
rather than venturing into the unknown.

To summarize: Our findings suggest the following equally
pallid or "hothouse" portrait of the "idealized" conservative.
Though he tends not to think of himself as an activist (a word,
after all, with the bad connotations of "disturber of the
peace"), he is not necessarily an inactivist. He is neither predictably risky nor cautious as a decision maker. He isn't notably
disturbed by a sense of normlessness or any other form of alienation; he isn't predictably a norm maintainer, but he may resort
to Machiavellian tactics if he is notably normative in orientation. He sees his beliefs as being similar to those of his parents
and feels their relationship is harmonious. He probably endured
a "strict" and punitive style of child-raising.

The Activist. Findings for activists and inactivists are of greatest initial interest in how some loose expectations for ideology, which did not materialize in correlations for LC, begin to emerge on this dimension (Figure 17). It was hypothesized there might be a relation between liberalism and risk taking. No such relation was found, but now a significant correlation of risk taking with activism appears (.18), and risk taking is also a significant loading for the "activism" factor 3.

Another variable for which there was a strong, but unconfirmed, expectation of a relationship to liberal ideology was norm violating. Now in the context of activism, the relationship begins to appear. The correlation of .19 is in the predicted direction of an association between activism and norm violating.

In regard to the relation of activism to internal versus external locus of control, our findings support what is becoming a

Figure 17

Findings and Relationships of Activism to Other Study Variables

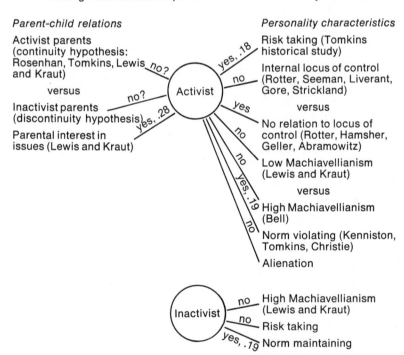

majority position in the literature. No support was found either for the original Rotter, Seeman, and Liverant (1962) theoretical rationale, or the supportive studies by Gore and Rotter (1963) and Strickland (1965), indicating that activists are more internal than external in locus of control. The finding, which confirms studies by Rotter (1966), Hamsher, Geller, and Rotter (1968), and Abramowitz (1973), is of no significant relation between activism and I-E-measured locus of control.

The relation of activism to Machiavellianism was of special interest as another example of contradictory findings in previous studies. Bell (1968) had pictured activists as high Machiavellians, but Lewis and Kraut (1972) found the activists of their study to be low in Machiavellianism. This study finds no correlation between activism and Machiavellianism, and thus no support for either position. We will attempt to reconcile these contradictions in the next chapter.

Turning to parent-child relational variables, we found that neither the continuity nor the discontinuity hypothesis seemed to relate to the development of activists. This conclusion was based on the lack of a relationship between the activism variable and the PCB measure of parent-child belief similarity. However, such a conclusion assumes that if an activist reports a similarity of views to those of his parents, the similarity is of a belief in activism, and if he reports dissimilarity, the parent is thereby inactivist. As parent and child could vigorously disagree on many things and still both be activists, the flaw in this logic is apparent. So at this level of analysis, the findings cannot be used to say anything definite about parent-child modeling or parent-child conflict as they might affect the development of activists.

In comparison to what these findings imply about the activist, the inactivist emerges as a shadowy figure (Figure 17). This seems to be partly a function of the correlational design, whereby inactivism becomes operationally defined as "the other end of" or "a lack of" activism. However, it may also be a function of the concentration on the "figure" to the neglect of the "ground," which has obscured so many relationships in psychology.

The reverse implications of the positive correlations for risk taking and norm violating with activism suggests that as one moves toward inactivism, there is a decline in risk taking and an increase in norm-maintaining tendencies. The finding of no relationship between activism and Machiavellianism also contradicts the Lewis and Kraut (1972) finding of higher Machiavellianism among inactivists than among activists.

To summarize: These findings suggest the following portrait of the activist. As everyday observation would suggest, he is both more open to risk taking and to violating norms than the inactivist. Contrary to what some might expect, he is not predictably more Machiavellian or alienated. He is consistently governed neither by an internal nor an external locus of control. The similarity or difference of his parents' to his own views seems to be of minimal influence, but he definitely tends to have parents who are interested in social-political issues. The more "shadowy" inactivist is less prone to take risks, is more norm maintaining, and, contrary to other published evidence, is not predictably Machiavellian.

The Extremist. Because extremism-moderation relationships were only testable through the analysis of variance, we will have to refer ahead to Table 8, which reports ANOVA findings in the next section. The profiles are summarized in Figure 18.

The theoretical view of extremism as a form of deviancy is supported by two of four possibly relevant findings shown in Table 8 interactions. No relation between extremism and risk taking or norm-violating belief was found. However, extremism interactions for norm-violating action and all three forms of alienation suggest that extremism of political belief may in some way be interpreted as a deviation from the norms of moderation or "middleness."

The theoretical view that extreme political beliefs are a function of the desire to reduce ambiguity and uncertainty receives support, but for *conservatives* only. There are no effects for Machiavellianism as a hypothetical method of social environmental control, nor is there any evidence of low risk taking operating as another method of avoiding uncertainty.

Figure 18

Findings and Relationships of Extremism to Other Study Variables

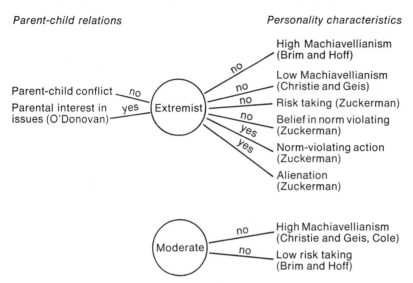

Parent-child relations   *Personality characteristics*

The finding of an extremism interaction for norm-violating action and the pattern for this interaction as shown in Table 8 do suggest, however, that this theory may operate for conservative extremists. That is, the finding is of conservative extremists being motivated to maintain rather than violate norms, and this is clearly in the direction hypothesized.

The theoretical view that meaningfulness of stimuli encourages extremism also seems to receive the support hypothesized. As Table 8 makes evident, parental interest in issues correlates more significantly with extremism than with activism. A still stronger, three-way interaction between LC, activism, and extremism further emphasizes the possible relation of meaningfulness of stimuli, through parental interest in issues, to extremism.

To summarize: The findings suggest the following tentative profile of the extremist. He isn't notably a Machiavellian, a risk taker, nor expressive of beliefs in norm violating. He is, however, alienated and prone to norm-violating action. His behavior

Table 8

Analysis of Variance with "Peripheral" as Dependent, and "Core" as Independent, Variables

Dependent Variable	Liberal				Conservative				Effects	F	P
	Extreme		Moderate		Extreme		Moderate				
	Active N=28	Inactive N=7	Active N=28	Inactive N=22	Active N=24	Inactive N=17	Active N=16	Inactive N=21			
Risk taking (RT)	44.5	43.6	42.8	40.1	45.2	43.0	45.6	41.4	Activism	5.2	.05
Machiavellianism (MAC)	42.0	46.7	45.4	42.9	44.1	43.5	45.3	43.5	none		
Locus of control (IE)	12.3	14.0	12.4	11.7	10.1	9.8	13.1	11.4	Lib-Cons	4.0	.05
									Lib-Cons X Extremism	5.1	.05
Alienation (ANL)	42.7	45.3	36.3	35.0	24.0	28.8	32.1	30.8	Lib-Cons	95.7	.0001
									Lib-Cons X Extremism	37.1	.0001
									Activism X Extremism	5.1	.05
Alienation (AAN)	37.7	35.0	35.1	35.5	31.5	30.5	35.1	33.5	Lib-Cons	13.8	.001
									Lib-Cons X Extremism	6.3	.05
Alienation (AO)	29.9	31.4	28.6	28.1	25.2	27.1	27.1	28.1	Lib-Cons	11.4	.001
									Lib-Cons X Extremism	5.6	.05
Parental interest in issues (PII)	2.6	3.1	3.0	2.1	3.0	2.4	2.6	2.3	Activism	3.7	.07
									Extremism	4.1	.05
									Lib-Cons X Activism X Extremism	8.1	.01

Measure										
Parent-child belief similarity (PCB)	2.3	2.0	2.3	2.2	3.0	2.8	2.4	2.5	Lib-Cons Lib-Cons × Extremism	9.5 .01 3.7 .07
Parent-child conflict (PCC)	1.6	1.7	1.6	1.4	1.4	1.4	1.6	1.3	none	
Norm-violating belief (NVB)	9.4	7.9	9.1	8.4	8.8	8.5	9.6	8.7	Activism	4.2 .05
Norm-violating action (NVA)	11.0	9.3	9.8	9.5	9.3	9.9	10.4	11.1	Lib-Cons × Activism Lib-Cons × Extremism	3.4 .07 3.7 .07

can be understood both as a form of deviancy and as being responsive to meaningfulness of stimuli. *If he is a conservative, his extremism may additionally be motivated by a desire to reduce ambiguity and uncertainty* (supporting Wilson's important theory). He has parents who have shown an interest in social-political issues, with whom he does not tend to be in conflict. As for the moderate, there is insufficient data on which to speculate.

Analysis of Variance and Personality Dynamics

The foregoing analysis of correlational findings provides us with a perspective on ideology as though it operated in reality in terms of one-dimensional personality types. This useful approach to understanding social behavior dates back at least to Plato and Aristotle, has been used to great effect by such perceptive analysts as Balzac and Shakespeare, and is the approach used today in most experimental studies by psychologists. This perspective views ideology as operating through the liberal, the conservative, the activist, the inactivist, and so on, as distinct and separable types of people. However, inevitably this view misses much that lies within the vast meaning space that surrounds and exists between the artifacts of the single-dimensional man, *and thus often fails to grasp ideological reality.* It misses the interaction of variables providing the continuity and structuring for a multidimensional reality. To probe such interactions, we turned to the powerful technique of inferential statistics known as analysis of variance.

By means of analysis of variance we can more closely approximate the following aspects of social-psychological functioning. It gives us a way, first, to examine the interaction effects of LC, activism-inactivism, and extremism-moderation as though these dimensions were *independent* variables forming the motivational "core" we hypothesized for ideological personality. Secondly, it allows us to examine the variables of ideology's "active periphery" to see how they relate as *dependent* variables to this motivational core. Thirdly, rather than examine only crude general differences of liberal versus conservative, within the "cells" of the ANOVA table we may now examine more specific differences, such as between the extreme liberal activist and the extreme conservative activist, or between the inactivist liberal and the conservative moderate, or any other comparable, *multidimensional* subgroups. This analytical capacity is of great interest because there is increasing evidence that many aspects of ideological behavior can only be understood in terms of subtypes, roles, and role-functional relationships.

Risk Taking. As Table 8 shows, there is no significant difference between liberals and conservatives in risk taking—no such "main effect" is listed in the far-right column under the heading of "effects." What does appear is a significant main effect for *activism,* with an F test value of 5.2, which has a probability (p) of significance at the .05 level, or fewer than 5 chances in 100 of occurring by chance. This main effect bears out the earlier correlational finding that activism, rather than liberalism or conservatism alone, accounts for differences in risk taking tendencies among these politically-oriented young men. The lack of extremism-moderation effects further emphasizes a difference related solely to activism.

Table 8 not only shows main or interaction effects, and assigns an F test significance; additionally, both the strength of and the direction for effects is shown by the differences in means within the cells. Thus, we may now see the general finding of a main effect for activism take on the specificity of a risk taking score of 44.5 for the extreme liberal *activist* in comparison to the markedly lower score of 40.1 for the moderate liberal *inactivist.* Similarly, the extreme conservative activist has a risk taking score of 45.2 in comparison with the lower score of 41.4 for the moderate conservative inactivist.

We are left, then, with this important finding with considerable implications for dialectical theory: both liberal and conservative activists show significant tendencies toward risk taking.

Machiavellianism and Locus of Control. The analysis of variance for Machiavellianism shows no significant effects. This would contradict both the Lewis and Kraut (1972) findings of higher Machiavellianism among inactivists than activists and the findings of Christie and Geis (1970) of higher Machiavellianism among moderates than extremes. The measure of liberalism-conservatism used in the analysis of variance was the LCA, however, which does not correlate with Machiavellianism. Had the LCT measure, which does correlate, been used, effects would have been obtained. (This is a further certainty because of the findings of Alker and Poppen, 1973, unknown to me at the time of this study. Using the full Tomkins' Polarity Scale, they obtained significantly positive correlations for Machiavellianism with conservatives, and negative correlations with liberals.) Again, this emphasizes how findings from measures purportedly of the same dimension can vary considerably, and how important it is to thoroughly understand the instruments being used. Because of the difficulties we noted earlier with the I-E scale, we will attempt no analysis of these findings for locus of control (although we might also note that Alker and Poppen, in the study just cited, found no significant correlations for I-E locus of control with either liberalism or conservatism.)

Alienation. As we have seen, correlational analysis failed to support the hypothesis of a conservative "normlessness" alienation (AAN) as a counterpart to a liberal "norm-constriction" alienation (ANL). The analysis of variance, however, shows a vast gap between extreme-active-liberal (42.7) and extreme-active-conservative (24.0) means for the ANL measure, in comparison with a radical diminishing of such differences for the AAN measure. This indicates a definite right-left difference in the direction hypothesized, although the findings are still insufficient to support the right-alienation hypothesis. Also notable is how our ANL-cell means for the activism X extremism interaction seems to confirm Keniston's (1968) finding that liberal inactivists are more alienated (45.3) than activists (42.7). The AAN measure composed of anomie items shows a pattern for the LC X E interaction which further contradicts our hypothesis for right alienation: extreme conservatives are significantly *less* anomic than are the moderate conservatives. The AO measure shows little worth noting.

Parental Interest in Issues. The analysis of parental interest in issues provides a particularly interesting example of the most significant effect deriving from a three-way interaction (LC ✕ activism ✕ extremism). Such effects can only be adequately untangled by resorting to the graphics shown in Figure 19.

Figure 19

The LC-Activism-Extremism Interaction for Parental Interest in Issues

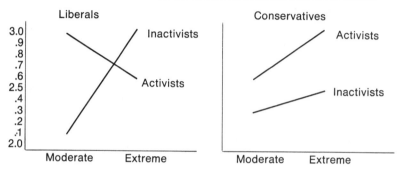

Figure 19 shows that we have peculiarly different patterns of response for liberals versus conservatives. For conservatives there is a parallel response for both activists and inactivists, whereby each reports increasing parental interest in issues as they move from moderate to extreme ideological beliefs. With the liberal, however, a surprising reversal appears. For the liberal *in*activist, there is a trend in the same direction as for the conservatives—increasing parental interest in issues as one moves from moderate to extreme beliefs. But for the liberal activist, this effect is reversed. The activist is *less* rather than more dependent on parental interest as he becomes extreme in his beliefs.

Viewed together, these two patterns suggest possibly important differences between liberal and conservative activism. It must be kept in mind that the findings are the students' opinions of how interested their parents are in social-political issues. The pattern suggests that for conservatives, parental interest in issues is an important factor in encouraging and maintaining their own extreme activist beliefs. The finding also suggests that the conservative activist closely identified his own interest in issues with that of his parents. For the liberal, however, this pattern only holds for the inactivist. The reversal for the liberal activist suggests that as his beliefs in activism move toward the extreme, he sees his parents as being less rather than more interested in social-political issues. This conclusion would seem to conflict with the findings of Tomkins (1965), Keniston (1968), and Rosenhan (1969) of strong cross-generational continuities for liberal activism. However, within the Rosenhan, Feuer (1969), and many other studies are accounts of student extreme activist "types" who were not close to their parents. This finding, then, seems in keeping with the findings of Kraut, Lewis, and Pepitone (1973), of parent-child continuity as well as discontinuity, and of Rosenhan, who found two "types" for liberal student activism. Or, in other words, we seem to be glimpsing from another perspective the recurring evidence of a liberal activism that departs from as well as adheres to the parent.

Parent-Child Belief Similarity. In the case of parent-child belief similarity, we find the expected corroboration of the earlier finding that conservatives see themselves as having beliefs more similar to those of their parents than do liberals. It is also notable that this view of the parent having beliefs similar to one's own is strongest with the extreme conservatives, whereas for the other groups, the differences are minimal.

Parent-Child Conflict. Table 8 shows no significant main or interaction effects for parent-child conflict, as well as no discernible differences across cells. On the face of it, this is very surprising. The lack of effects for LC, activism, and extremism suggests, first, that contrary to expectancies *none* of these personality dimensions relate to parent-child conflict! A literal reading of the findings would be that the parental homes of these liberals, activists, and extremists were as free of parent-child conflict as were the homes of conservatives, inactivists, and moderates. This finding, however, is only the beginning of the mystery. For the lack of interactions and mean differences among the eight subgroups greatly extends the sense of some large contradiction between the findings and social reality.

Part of the mystery is that this study was carried out immediately following the decade of the 1960s. During this period, generational conflict and the so-called generational gap were documented by hundreds of studies (e.g., Feuer, 1969; Rosenhan, 1969); the fabric of society itself was repeatedly shattered by generational conflict exploding in such events as the Kent State massacre and the Columbia and Berkeley riots. Yet this study, conducted during the spring of 1973, of students ranging from right to left and from moderate to extreme, found a unanimity of response as to how they view their relations to their parents—and this response is overwhelmingly on the side of harmony. These students were asked to rate their relations with their parents on a four-point scale, 1 for very harmonious, 2 for somewhat harmonious, 3 for somewhat conflictful, and 4 for very conflictful. Without exception, the means for all the groups in this study fall midway between "very" and "somewhat" harmonious in their rating of relationships to parents. We will venture an explanation in the next chapter.

Norm Violating. We come now to the most important of the ANOVA findings for our framework, the results for norm-violating belief (NVB) and norm-violating action (NVA). As we have seen, correlational analysis failed to show the hypothesized relationship between norm violating and liberalism or extremism. Only the relationship between activism and norm-violating belief proved significant. This relationship is confirmed, as we might expect, by the activism main effect for norm-violating belief. As we might further expect from the correlational analysis, no main effects appear with NVA. However, interaction effects for LC X activism and LC X extremism appear, and what they reveal, when seen in relation to the NVB finding, is of more than usual interest.

Table 9 summarizes the results of the LC X activism interaction in a way designed to make explicit the relationships. We

Table 9

The LC X Activism Interaction for NVA

	Inactivism	*Activism*
Liberal	9.4	10.4
Conservatism	10.5	9.8

see that, as one moves from inactivism toward activism, for the liberals there is an increase, whereas for conservatives there is a decrease in NVA or norm-violating action.

Table 10 shows comparable results for the LC X extremism interaction. As we move from moderation toward the extreme, for the liberals there is an increase, whereas for the conservatives there is a decrease in NVA.

Table 10

The LC X Extremism Interaction for NVA

	Moderate	*Extreme*
Liberal	9.6	10.1
Conservative	10.7	9.6

It is important to keep in mind the basic difference between the two variables: the NVB score is an indicator of what the subject *believes* is the right action to take, and the NVA score is an indicator of the action he thinks he himself might take under the circumstances.

Taken together, then, the NVB and NVA data suggest the following interpretation. The finding of an activism main effect for NVB indicates that belief in a possible need for norm violation exists as a significant behavioral tendency only among activists. But what then impels these activists to go beyond belief to action? And what governs the intensity and the direction for this action? Here the NVA findings offer statistical support for the intuitively logical answer. On the face of it, the LC X activism interaction suggests *that belief in action is impelled to become action in fact by adding a right or left directional motivation to the activist potential.* The LC X extremism interaction then suggests that the amount of norm-violating action that occurs depends on how much extremism is involved. Finally, basic differences of direction for the combined action of these core variables are indicated by the NVA interactions. *We see that in keeping with our frameworking hypothesis, the extreme liberal activist is motivated in the norm-violating direction, but with the extreme conservative, the direction for activism is reversed, toward norm maintenance.*

Bit by bit, we thus see crucial dynamics for the dialectical relationships lying at the heart of ideological functioning—originally discerned by Hegel—beginning to take shape in terms of modern, empirically defined personality variables.

10

Implications and Conclusions

Every feature in this parable, my dear Glaucon, is meant to fit our earlier analysis. The prison dwelling corresponds to the region revealed to us through the sense of sight, and the firelight within it to the power of the Sun. The ascent to see the things in the upper world you may take as standing for the upward journey of the soul into the region of the intelligible; then you will be in possession of what I surmise, since that is what you wish to be told. Heaven knows whether it is true; but this, at any rate, is how it appears to me.

This was how Socrates qualified his theory of man's situation in Plato's classic study of ideology, leadership personality, and social change, *The Republic*. The passage serves well to set the tone for the conclusions of this search for ideological structures over 2,300 years later in the development of man. In this chapter, we will examine implications of our findings for understanding liberals and conservatives, and then consider activism and extremism to see how these three dimensions may interact to form a "core" to ideology. We will also examine the "active periphery" to this core, consider methodological implications, and then briefly venture in two speculative directions—outward toward the social-political reality we experience as a dynamism of subgroups, subtypes, roles, and role interdependencies, and inward to see how our data may further reduce to structural theory.

The Ideological "Core"

Our findings have at least four implications for the understanding of liberal and conservative ideology. The first is that these terms are generally meaningful only if we know whether the liberal or conservative is additionally an activist or an inactivist and an extremist or a moderate. The summaries of liberal and conservative characteristics in the previous chapter indicated certain general differences. The liberal is more governed by norm constriction when alienated. The liberal tends to be less Machiavellian than the conservative by at least one measure. The liberal's beliefs also differ, and by self-report, he is in conflict somewhat more with his parents than is the conservative. Liberal and conservative also are likely to experience "permissive" and "strict" child-raising methods, respectively. But these are only a small part of the differences generally associated with one or the other ideology. The implication of this study is that *most of the qualities that additionally differentiate liberal from conservative in "popular parlance" are furnished by degrees of activism and extremism.*

To elaborate on this point, we have seen that the activist is more the risk taker and norm violator than the inactivist. During the 1960s and earlier historical periods of social reform (the pre-Civil War period of abolitionism in the United States, for example), "liberal" was generally equated with "activist." To many, then, liberal has a risk taking, norm-violating connotation. Yet acquaintance with right-wing activism (for example, the Nazis in Germany or rightist juntos in South America) reveals that, for some, the risk-taking and norm-violating connotation may also be associated with conservatism. It is, however, the combinations of these dimensions of LC, activism, and extremism that seem to more closely approximate the everyday meanings for liberal and conservative and to reveal new facets of their interaction. For now—as documented in our previous chapter—we begin to find that it is the extreme activist, for both liberals and conservatives, who is the greatest risk taker. We find that the extreme inactivist is markedly more alienated than the moderate inactivist. We find that as parental interest in issues increases, conservative activism increases, but liberal activism decreases. We find that the extreme liberal activist is motivated toward norm violation, whereas the extreme conservative activist is motivated toward norm maintenance.

Moreover, the implications of certain extremism findings should be noted in this context. Findings supporting the view of extreme beliefs as forms of deviancy confirm the perspective of the nonideologue, or those either made uncomfortable by extreme beliefs or who maintain a stance of objectivity. From such a perspective, extreme beliefs can be viewed as departures from the prevailing norms of "practicality" and "respectability," or from those norms that generally represent a compromise of extreme and middle positions. From such a perspective, both extreme liberal or conservative views are generally "on trial," that is, they are viewed as suspect, requiring the "proof" of appreciable social support before one should consider giving either orientation a portion of one's time or allegiance. On the other hand, the finding supporting the view of extreme beliefs as a function of meaningfulness confirms the perspective of the ideologue. To extreme liberals or extreme conservatives, theirs is a meaningful commitment, in contrast to what they view as the rudderless wandering of the "middle"; they see their social function as being to influence the moderate and the middle to move in either the right or the left directions they personally feel are desirable on the key issues of the time.

A second implication for understanding liberals and conservatives is that these "loaded" terms gain meaning mainly within a social context. To those accustomed to viewing liberal or conservative as simply a matter of situationally-induced political attitudes not wedded to any deeper personality differences, this may seem no surprising conclusion. The point, however, gains significance as one views liberalism-conservatism from the viewpoint of personality theory—as an individualistic mix of differing cognitive, affective, and conative tendencies that find expression, and become labeled "liberal" or "conservative," according to the demands of the social context. The ways we have sketched above, by which the meanings of liberalism and conservatism take shape as one makes explicit the contribution of activism and extremism, begin to suggest the social contribution. That is, activism as an orientation is meaningless without the social context—one is, by definition, active in regard to taking action on social issues. And extremism, as we have seen, may be closely aligned through liberal or conservative ideology to the social context.

The connection between ideology and social context is supported by the finding of response differences for the LCA and LCT measures. The LCA, it will be recalled, is composed of items from the Adorno social-attitude measurement tradition which are designed to tap attitudes toward political and economic issues. By contrast, the LCT is composed of items from the Henry Murray-Silvan Tomkins tradition of personality investigation (both Murray's TAT and Tomkins' PAT tests lie behind the polarity-scale development). The differences between liberals and conservatives that begin to appear with the LCT personality measure radically intensify with the use of the LCA social-attitude measure. These results confirm what one may repeatedly observe of liberals and conservatives in social contexts —that they may chat amiably and show many interests in common as long as their dialogue does not arouse deep personality and social belief differences. But let political or economic issues come up and the sparks begin to fly.

A third implication of our findings is that to speak with sophistication of a liberal or conservative "ideology," or to speak of the two together as forming a "political ideology," one must be aware of several levels of meaning. This study originally began, in keeping with prevailing usage, by classifying liberal and conservative as "ideology," with activism and extremism being explored as separate dimensions. It could be said we have now reached the point where the study of "ideology" has been expanded into the study of the "ideology-activism-extremism complex." But we cannot leave it there. In general terms, an ideology is any system of highly interconnected beliefs and values, whether it be political, religious, educational, or whatever (Loye and Rokeach, 1976). In this study we have used psychological measurement to better define an ideology conventionally associated with politics, but more generally operative.

Finally, there is the implication that these three dimensions—LC, activism, and extremism—in some sense comprise a "core" to ideology, to which the other variables of this study relate in important but peripheral ways. It could be said that there is a certain amount of circularity in concluding the existence of this core-periphery relation from findings inevitably shaped by the assumption that guided the study design. It could be said that the only clear proof for such a separation of "core" from "periphery" variables would be to give participants like ours a battery of all possible relevant measures and then subject the results to a regression analysis, which would rank order effects for each measure. In theory, this makes sense; however, what this study has revealed of measurement difficulties (for example, with the I-E scale), also indicates the practical pitfalls for such an approach. Such an ordering would be likely to more closely reflect the adequacy of the measures than the structure of reality. We feel justified, then, in using the core-periphery relation proposed as both theory and a useful analytic tool.

Let us now examine this periphery—locus of control, alienation, anomie, risk taking, and parent-child relationships. In particular, we will examine how parent-child relationships may interrelate with norm maintaining and norm changing to form a developmental framework for ideology.

Locus of Control

As we have seen, the question of "inner" versus "outer" self-governance for liberals versus conservatives has interested investigators from the time of the Adorno group. We confront an extremely appealing construct, but it defies measurement—at least with the Rotter I-E Scale.

We could project various alternatives for further work with the I-E itself. One, at least, seems worth mentioning—further development of I-E variants in the Likert format used by White (1965) and Abramowitz (1973) as a means of overcoming some of the problems of the paired choice format. However, it seems advisable to free ourselves from any further concern with the "trees" of the I-E and instead take another look at the inner-outer locational "forest."

It is apparent from the literature and the high factor loadings for I-E with alienation in this study (Table 6), that the externality score is to a large degree measuring the feeling of powerlessness. The tendency is to equate the high externality score with "weakness" and lack of an internal "rudder," and to equate a high internality score with "strength" and a firm sense of inner direction. But careful consideration of at least one fundamental difference known to exist between liberals and conservatives places the situation in a different perspective.

The Adorno (1950), Eysenck (1954), and Eysenck and Coulter (1972) studies found a higher degree of ethnocentrism among conservatives. From these and many other sources (Tomkins, 1965; Hamden-Turner, 1970), we may visualize liberals as resonating both affectively and cognitively to a wider range of concern about their fellow beings and social surroundings than do conservatives. Situational analysis (Lewin, 1951) then suggests that the liberal who by personality is impelled to a wider range of concern may feel relatively small and powerless in relation to the range of his awareness, whereas the conservative will feel relatively more powerful in relation to a more limited range of concern. It is the old difference between the feeling of the proverbial big frog in a small pond and the small frog in a big pond.

We would suggest, then, that before progress can be made in clarifying the locus of control relationship to ideology, the instrumentation must be improved by compiling and testing rationales such as this. As Brewster Smith notes, such advancement is badly needed for locus of control (Smith, 1974). Investigations of internality-externality concepts and instruments that could be examined are those of Witkin (1962), Rorschach (Klopfer, 1962), Jung (Mann, Siegler, and Osmond, 1972), and Eysenck (1957). The Eysenck work is of particular interest. Eysenck's interest in relating tough- versus tendermindedness to the left-right dimension is generally well known, but what has been "lost" is his subfinding of the strong relation of extraversion-introversion to the T dimension. It is conceivable, then, that adding measures of T and introversion-extraversion to a study of this type might begin to reveal the ideology-locus of control relationship.

Alienation-Anomie

In understanding the LC-alienation-anomie relation, it is again essential to keep in mind the basic difference between the ANL and the AAN sets of items. ANL items were selected to express a sense of alienation through feelings of "norm constriction" ("You can never achieve freedom within the framework of contemporary American society"). AAN items were selected to express a sense of anomie through feelings of "normlessness" ("With everything so uncertain these days, it almost seems as though anything can happen").

The assumption that alienation leads to liberal and left activism is the thrust of Marxian theory, as well as New Left activism as a movement during the sixties. Within the context of this study, one would then assume that scores for ANL "norm-constriction" alienation would correlate with activism as well as LC, but, as we have seen, this correlation does not appear. In marked contrast to this theory, it has been assumed by others that alienation leads to withdrawal from society and its issues, or to positions of inactivism. This was Keniston's conclusion (1968), and social isolation, for example, is a familiar alienation dimension for some investigators (Robinson and Shaver, 1969). It would seem then that the more passive "normlessness" AAN scores might show a negative correlation with activism, but such is not the case. Neither measure shows any relation to either liberal or conservative activism until we apply the analysis of variance. We find then, that when measured for the ANL sense of "norm constriction," it is the extreme inactivists who are the most alienated (Table 8). This might indicate support for Keniston's equation of alienation with inactivism, but this difference appears only in a weak interaction for one of three measures of alienation.

We are left, then, with little evidence of a relation between alienation and activism or alienation and inactivism. Yet the literature of alienation and activism indicates something is missing from our study. Our conclusion is that the methodology of this study suppressed relationships that would reveal themselves most meaningfully in the form of subtypologies through participant-observer studies or cluster analysis of larger samples.

Now let us consider a question of no small weight: Was our theoretical rationale for a sharp right-left differentiation of types of alienation in error? In instances such as this, there is always the temptation to bow to empiricism and methodology and write off the clean-cut theoretical construct as merely another of one's own unreliable mental products. In this case, however, the mind balks, and it would be well to ask why. It seemed that although these findings might reflect a true general state of affairs, it was equally likely that they were a reflection of the sample and the methodology. Anomie as a concept was derived from a historical situation of vast social upheaval involving a whole society, and was used to convey a feeling of normlessness, no doubt felt most strongly by middle-aged French financiers, merchants, officials, peasants, and bourgeois intellectuals, such as Durkheim, who resonated to their plight. It is evident that their situation was vastly different from that of the relatively secure, nonthreatened elite, quite young conservatives in this study. This comparison suggested that the findings might be quite different if the same approach were taken with an older population, particularly one with specific norm structures that were being threatened—an Italian or Jewish inner-city population threatened by the black incursion, for example, or government bureaucrats caught in the institutional chaos following an election that had turned out the party in power. Convinced of this possibility, we carried out the replication with an older sample reported in our next chapter.

Risk Taking

The risk taking findings have fascinating implications if viewed as empirical groundings for a speculative leap using the thoughts and findings of several theorists. Within the context of a relation to the liberal or conservative, activist or extremist "core" to ideology, risk taking can be viewed as a first venturing outward from this core of potentiality—as an avenue from person into environment, from being to becoming, as a beginning for the man-nature interaction, or for social action.

The limitations of this study, using the "static" correlational approach, in contrast to the possibilities for studies of personal interaction with the environment, are suggested by one perceptive criticism of the Adorno (1950) work on the authoritarian personality. "One could not diagnose authoritarianism from an inventory of beliefs but only from knowledge of the circumstances that will change belief," Brown (1965) has commented. Although the correlations of risk taking with activism and parent-child conflict are thus only "static" evidence for a behavioral tendency, factor loadings and ANOVA findings suggest a portrait with active flesh-and-blood connotations: the picture of high risk takers who do not feel their parents are interested in social issues, who do not see themselves as sharing many beliefs with the parent, who report parent-child conflict rather than harmony. Psychoanalytic as well as social learning experiments and theory (Dollard and Miller, 1950) have shown the linking of attitudes toward parents and toward society; if one then substitutes "society" for "parent" in our portrait, what emerges is a classic picture of the alienated, young social reformer.

With such a personality type in mind, it is of interest to consider Tomkins' psychohistorical study of the lives of the abolitionists from early childhood into active manhood (Tomkins and Izard, 1965). Tomkins' analysis of "the psychology of commitment," which is based on his ideo-affective theory of personality development, posits a cyclic growth in risk taking. By means of historical analysis, he identified the first slight instance of risk taking by each of the young potential abolitionists on behalf of the antislavery cause. Such incidents he identified as instances of a first violation of the proslavery norms of the southern status quo. Then he showed how, through a sequence of stages over time, each man (James Birney, Wendell Phillips, Theodore Weld, and William Lloyd Garrison) became progressively more committed to the cause of abolitionism. Repeatedly, the sequence was of a series of progressively greater risks being taken in promoting the cause, or an increase in risk taking from a slight beginning to the proportions of major social action, through a series of behavior-building, need-rewarding, person-environment interactions over time.

This type of dialectical and interactionist analysis has been applied to behavior in many contexts and at many levels—to the smallest units of behavior by Miller in his feedback concept of TOTE (Miller, Galanter, and Pribram, 1960), by Myrdal to social analysis in his concepts of cumulation and cycling (Myrdal, 1962), by Riegel (1972) to the relation of individual to social and historical developmental patterns. Within such a frame of reference it is of special interest then to recall the Alker-Kogan (1968) experiment, which suggested initiating directions for this study. This was an experimental study which brought some real people, with real beliefs and behavioral tendencies, together in group discussions over a period of time for the purpose of arriving at behavioral decisions. It was thus an experimental analogue for the group life that repeatedly requires of every one of us action toward one goal or another, all of which involves taking certain risks.

In this Alker-Kogan study something happened that aroused subjects who chose norm violating to also increase their risk-taking response. Conversely, those who chose norm maintenance became more conservative. Thus, it seems not unreasonable to suggest that within the Alker-Kogan study, and within this study—and with Tomkins' historical study and the dialectical-interactionist view of behavior-building in mind—we may discern the possible identifying, and an initial quantifying, of the beginning of social action. We see, motivated by right or left values, the first taking of a very small risk, the first slight stretching of a norm. This action results in some satisfaction, enticing one on. Then, with an escalation of ideological commitment and a cycling of energy and aspiration, the progressively greater risk taking and norm violation of social action unfolds.

Some Methodological Considerations

In several instances our findings contradicted one another, or contradicted earlier findings, or were otherwise loose ended. We feel three factors accounted for these cases: (1) limitations of the sample; (2) overriding situational influences; and (3) subtypological and social role influences.

We have noted the possible influence of *sample restriction* on the alienation-anomie findings, suggesting that the hypothesized "right alienation" would be found in an older noncollegiate population. Sample restriction also seems a likely explanation for the finding by Lewis and Kraut (1972) of low Machiavellian activists, which wasn't supported by this study. It seems to us this difference was a function of the Lewis and Kraut method of sampling through spontaneous response by freshmen to a questionnaire mailing. It seems highly probable that "hardnosed" and Machiavellian ideologues of both extremes did not return their questionnaires and that response was overwhelmingly from the "nice guys"—that is, the low Machiavellian activists. We assume the difference in our findings was that we obtained a more representative sample.

The impact on findings of *overriding situational influences* is a factor to which the social-psychological investigator must be particularly sensitive. In the alienation-anomie case, we noted that the concept of anomie was based on the overriding sociological situation of a norm-shattering national disaster for France, for which there was no analogue in the comfortable and secure situation of the young Princeton conservatives of this study. In this study the most interesting instance of the possible effect of situational influence is the finding of the surprisingly harmonious parent-child relations reported by everyone in this study, even extreme liberal activists. When asked how conflictful or harmonious was their relation with their parents, all groups rated the relationship either "somewhat" or "very" harmonious. The bafflement here is in reconciling this finding with all the evidence of generational conflict which so vividly characterized the 1960s. The conclusion we find most compelling is that during the "liberal" sixties, there were social pressures toward, and it was popular to emphasize, the conflict that exists in all parent-child relations. However by the seventies, the prevailing national sentiment—or *overriding* social situation—had shifted from left to right. Our findings in the "conservative" spring of 1973 seem to fit with the lack of student protest and other overt social evidence of generational conflict; they suggest that by this time it was considered "cool" to report harmony rather than conflict with one's parents. In any case, it seems highly likely that this was an instance of results influenced more by the overriding social climate than by personality variables.

The third major factor influencing our results was likely *subtypology and role dictates*. What is meant by this category is best clarified by noting contradictions in our findings that raise the need for this explanation.

One puzzling finding was the negative correlation with Machiavellianism for liberalism, as measured by the LCT measure, in contrast to no correlation for Machiavellianism with the LCA or LCSR scores. It could be said that this contradiction simply indicates the variability of measures. However, we have indicated how the personal-oriented LCT and the social-attitudinal LCA seem to measure overlapping but different subsets of liberalism-conservatism. Both our findings and the much more decisive findings by Alker and Poppen (1973), which used the full Polarity Scale, indicate a liberal kind of low-Machiavellianism and a conservative kind of high-Machiavellianism. However, we suspect that rather than a general relationship for all contexts, the "truth" lies in *social-functional* subsets of liberals who are low-Machiavellians, and *social-functional* subsets of conservatives who are high-Machiavellians. (For example, it seems to us quite evident that within the vivid drama of the Watergate scandals we saw at work the actors and the action of such a Machiavellian conservative subset. This joint Machiavellianism was shaped not only by personality, but to a much greater extent by the *social-functional* requirements of a particular kind of presidency.)

For the relation of activism to Machiavellianism, we have noted three different findings—of high Machiavellian activists (Bell, 1968), of low Machiavellian activists (Lewis and Kraut, 1972), and of this study's finding of no relationship between activism and Machiavellianism. Unless we try to reconcile these as being differences of social context, again the social-functional subset or subtypological explanation must be considered.

The findings for risk taking also reveal *suggestive* contradictions. Positive loadings for risk taking and parent-child conflict, and negative loadings for parental interest in issues and parent-child belief similarity on factor 4 (Table 6) suggest the following "portrait": of high risk takers who feel their parents are not interested in social issues, whose beliefs differ from their parents, and who report conflict with their parents. The portrait suggests a person who might logically fall within the classification "alienated activist." We do find a positive loading for risk taking on the "activism" factor, but a negative loading for risk taking on the "alienation" factor. Possibly again, this complex of relationships is best reconciled by some method of identifying subsets.

These examples emphasize what the work of Lasswell (1948), Lane (1962), and Block (1971) makes clear beyond question: that one of the most important directions for ongoing research in this area lies in the identification of ideological subsets—and not as the free-floating mysteries of exclusively psychological subtypes, but as subtypes rooted within social-system realities, in terms of roles and social-functional relationships.

A Developmental Framework

As a conceptual structure to interlink hypotheses for the relationships of core, peripheral, and developmental variables to ideology, we posed the theoretical framework outlined in Chapter Seven. This was based on observations, central to psychology, sociology, and history, that the interaction of processes of stability and change is the core dynamic for psychological, sociological, and historical movement. In social psychology this dynamic lies at the heart of norming processes. These processes are generally viewed as being of two types: (1) those by which norms are established and maintained, such as by parental modeling and instruction in childhood, and later in adult life by consensus processes; and (2) those by which they are changed, such as conflict or polarization processes operating in childhood and later life. In this study, we used the Stouffer-Toby questionnaire to tap this conceptual opposition of norm maintaining versus norm violating.

The hypothesized framework related liberalism, activism, extremism, risk taking, "permissive" child-raising styles, parent-child belief dissimilarity, and "norm-constricted" alienation to processes of change, or to norm violating, and it related conservatism, inactivism, moderation, low risking, "strict" child-raising styles, parent-child belief similarity, and "normlessness" alienation (or anomie) to processes of stability, or to norm maintenance. It was further hypothesized that measurement of external versus internal locus of control might reveal where the source of norms to be maintained or violated was perceived to be. It was also hoped that measurement of Machiavellianism might clarify its ambiguous relationships to ideology.

As we have seen, the evidence is still too ambiguous to attempt to relate locus of control or Machiavellianism to such a framework. For alienation and anomie, however, striking relationships to this theoretical structure are beginning to emerge. These are further clarified in the West Coast replication reported in our next chapter and will be integrated into new theoretical models in Chapter Thirteen. Meanwhile, our remaining variables not only cohere forcefully to this framework, but together form a pattern of possibly considerable utility in both theory bearing on and practice in education, therapy, politics, and many other fields. We will attempt a useful integration of findings here, and then in Chapters Twelve and Thirteen will outline possible applications.

Characteristically, what is of most interest about our findings is not apparent when one views them separately. It only emerges if we construct a perspective of how the key variables may relate to one another in a developmental sequence over time. The hypothetical beginning point is the difference in liberal versus conservative child-raising practices, with this study corroborating earlier findings. We may visualize the two situations at the outset of a life posed by Tomkins (1965): one, in which a liberal parent or milieu may permit the child a certain freedom to explore, emphasizing reward; the other, in which a conservative parent or milieu may restrict this movement, emphasizing punishment. From the pioneering work of Durkheim, through Freud, to modern socialization studies (Parsons and Shils, 1965), the establishment through the parent-child interaction of our earliest and most enduring norms for thought, emotion, and behavior has been massively documented. We may visualize, then, the dominantly liberal parent presenting all norms as flexible to a degree and offering rewards for venturing. The dominantly conservative parent, however, creates a normative climate wherein the norms are viewed as sacred, to be maintained at all costs, and wherein venturing risks punishment. (It is evident, of course, that for most parents, child-raising involves the use of both styles, dependent on the situation and the child; we are speaking here of an emphasis weighted toward one style or the other, with parental consistency across situations.)

Now let us move ahead in the hypothetical lives of the developing young liberal and conservative. Studies by Greenstein (1965) have shown that in middle-class samples, ideological orientations to issues, and even political-party identifications, first become evident toward the end of the latency period, quite specifically between the age span of nine to ten. This is the age, Greenstein notes, that Gesell and Ilg characterize as that of "an adult in the making." It is a time of "relative fluidity" with "important cultural implications. It makes the ten-year-old peculiarly receptive to social information, to broadening ideas and to prejudices, good and bad. It is relatively easy to appeal to his reason. He is ready to participate in elementary discussions of social problems" (Gesell and Ilg, 1946, pp. 636-637).

The pattern for parent-child interaction through the high-school years may be visualized as continuing this process of an "adult in the making," and we arrive at the age of our study participants, young men in college. It is then notable that in reporting the degree of interest shown by their own parents in social-political issues, our study participants were expressing what they had experienced during the short, recent, and crucial span of adolescence, during which their political attitudes developed and their first fledgling political behavior occurred. We have seen that our findings, which confirm the earlier findings of Lewis and Kraut (1972), show significant correlations for parental interest in issues with both activism and extremism in liberals and conservatives. We see, then, the evidence for inferring that left norm-violating or right norm-maintaining tendencies established in early childhood may be intensified and given both the behavioral *direction* of activism versus inactivism, and the behavioral *degree* of extremism versus moderation, by parental interest in issues during adolescence. (Depending on the person, other factors may be more dominant, of course. We seek here merely to develop one forceful developmental track.)

We then come to the findings for norm-violating *belief* and norm-violating *action*, which take on new interest within this developmental perspective. We have seen that belief in norm violating (NVB), the *potential* for action, seems to exist only among avowed activists. But to move from belief to action, the LC X extremism and LC X activism interactions for norm-violating action (NVA) suggest that liberal or conservative motivation must be added to provide *direction* for this activism, and the intensity of extremism must be added to provide the *degree* of movement. These NVA interactions further indicate crucial differences in direction of movement for liberal and conservative. We have seen that for the liberal, as moderation moves to extremeness, and as inactivism becomes activism, norm violation increases. For the conservative, this movement is the exact reverse—as moderation becomes extremeness, and as inactivism becomes activism, the movement is toward norm maintenance.

Seen within this perspective, the findings for risk taking add a particularly exciting theoretical aspect to these dynamics. For both liberal and conservative there is an increase in risk taking as one moves from inactivism to activism. As we have seen that the liberal activist is norm violating, and the conservative activist is norm maintaining, we may infer that both will take risks to carry out these different behavioral objectives.

The composite picture suggested by these findings and those of other studies is then as follows: A norm-relational framework that both *determines* and can be useful for *interpreting* ideological behavior is established over time. It seems to begin with the implanting of different attitudes toward norms within the infant liberal and the infant conservative. One is encouraged to view norms as only human and changeable, the other to view them as sacred and fixed. Behavioral directions and degrees for these attitudes are shaped by parental interest in issues (and other factors) during adolescence. By late adolescence these tendencies may become full-blown ideological complexes that operate according to a rather simple pattern: conservative extremists and activists are motivated toward norm maintaining, and liberal extremists and activists are motivated toward norm violating. These children become parents and the pattern then tends to repeat itself. The developmental picture is of social behavioral consistencies that advance through time rooted in replenishing cycles of ideologies, which pass from parent to child to society and thence to parent and child again.

Figure 20 summarizes the basic variable relationships underlying this developmental complex in terms loosely derived from Lewinian visualizations of personality and social behavior (Lewin, 1951). Liberal and conservative are viewed in the figure as separate personality types, each differing in attitude and behavior according to whether they are moderate or extreme and activist or inactivist. These personalities are enclosed within circles representing the ideological core. Our other variables are then viewed as a periphery of vectors indicating the force and direction (or lack of same) for findings summarized in Table 8.

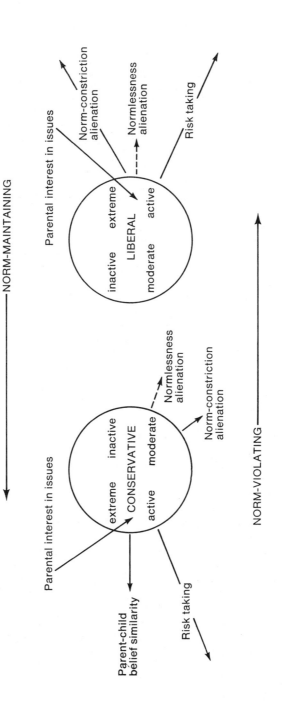

Figure 20

A Comparison of Liberal-Conservative and Other
Variable Relationships on the Personal System Level

11

A West Coast Replication

As we have seen, the findings for the Princeton study seem to greatly extend our understanding of how ideology, or the "leadership passion," operates. The fact that these were findings with a single East Coast sample confined to young male politicos in an elite university setting, however, rightfully raises the question, How general are both findings and the theory they support?

It is important to keep in mind that our theory by no means rests on this study alone, for the Princeton study mainly provided an empirical integration for both the theory and findings of many other investigators in many contexts and over a considerable span of time. However, a replication and extension of this study was desirable, so during the spring of 1976 we carried out such a study with a West Coast sample of 207 Los Angeles residents. This follow-up study (1) updates the 1972 study with 1976 findings; (2) provides West Coast corroboration for East Coast findings; (3) extends a study limited to

young men to both men and women aged twenty to over sev-
enty; (4) extends a study of college students to older married
couples with a wide range of educational backgrounds; and (5)
extends a study exclusively of leadership elites in training to
both leaders and followers in active, working careers.

A questionnaire was assembled and administered by mail
to the study participants; 400 were sent, with 207 returns. The
test battery consisted of new, separate scales for norm maintaining and norm changing; scales for liberalism-conservatism, alienation, anomie, risk taking, and locus of control constructed
from the best items from the Princeton study; and additional
new scales for activism, extremism, and tough- versus tendermindedness. In addition, we obtained information to classify
participants as leaders versus followers, and according to levels
of age, income, and education. We will describe all measures at
the end of this chapter.

Results

The most important question to be answered in this follow-up study was the true extent to which, in keeping with our
frameworking theory, liberalism equates with norm changing
and conservatism with norm maintaining. The correlations in
the Princeton study were significant and in the right direction,
but by themselves were not large enough to support the weight
of our theory. We replaced the Stauffer-Toby measure, which
we felt was inadequate, with two new scales constructed of
items from the Comrey Personality Scale, one scale for norm
changing, the other for norm maintaining. This time our results
provided strong support for the norm-process relational framework we posit.

Table 11 shows three compelling bits of supporting evidence. The high negative correlation (−.63) of norm maintaining with LC in effect says that yes, indeed, conservatives are
powerfully motivated by needs for norm maintaining. The high
positive correlations (.63) of norm changing with LC indicates
that liberals are equally motivated by needs for norm changing.
Thirdly, the high negative correlation (−.70) between scores on

Table 11

Correlations of Key Variables for West Coast Sample (N = 207)

	NM	NC	LC	AI	EM	TT	RT	AL	AN	IE	YO	FI	ED
Norm maintaining (NM)		-.70***	-.63***	-.05	-.21***	-.20***	-.19**	-.42***	.23***	-.14**	.35***	.09	-.10
Norm changing (NC)	-.70***		.63***	.07	.19**	.19*	.09	.49***	-.06	.03	-.19**	-.13*	.08
Liberalism-conservatism (LC)	-.63***	.63***		-.03	.04	.05	.14*	.40***	-.18**	-.02	-.20**	-.18**	.06
Activism-inactivism (AI)	-.05	.07	-.03		.20**	.05	.05	.02	-.22***	.22***	.17**	.17**	.23***
Extremism-moderation (EM)	-.21***	.19**	.04	.20**		-.05	-.04	.30***	.02	.04	.11	-.08	-.07
Tough-tenderminded (TT)	-.20***	.19*	.05	.05	-.05		.12	.03	-.09	.09	-.04	.12	.03
Risk taking (RT)	-.19**	.09	.14*	.05	-.04	.12		-.10	-.14*	.09	-.18**	-.00	.12*
Alienation (AL)	-.42***	.49***	.40***	.02	.30***	.03	-.10		.27***	-.10	-.12*	-.11	-.08
Anomie (AN)	.23***	-.06	-.18**	-.22***	.02	-.09	-.14*	.27***		-.38***	-.00	-.13*	-.17**
Locus of control (IE)	-.14**	.03	-.02	.22***	.04	.09	.09	-.10	-.38***		-.06	.08	.13*
Young-old (YO)	.35***	-.19*	-.20**	.17*	.11	-.04	-.18**	-.12*	-.00	-.06		.13*	-.11
Family income (FI)	.09	-.13*	-.18**	.17**	-.08	.12	-.00	-.11	-.13*	.08	.13*		.21***
Education (ED)	-.10	.08	.06	.23***	-.07	.03	.12*	-.08	-.17**	.13*	-.11	.21***	

*p < .05   **p < .01   ***p < .001

these two new scales for norm changing and norm maintaining shows that these two personality dimensions are strongly related to one another, but in an *opposing direction*. That is, people high on one scale are low on the other.

These correlations were obtained with a liberalism-conservatism scale composed of items with the most discriminating power from the LC scale used in the Princeton study. To further check our findings we crosstabulated norm-changing and norm-maintaining scores with a second LC measure, the participants' own self-report of their ideological identities. The results, shown in Tables 12 and 13, provide still more strongly confirming statistical perspectives on the norm changing to liberal, and norm maintaining to conservative relationships.

Table 12

Distribution of Liberals and Conservatives
According to Levels of Norm Changing

| | Low | | High | | |
	Extremes (12-19)	Moderates (20-26)	Moderates (27-33)	Extremes (34-40)	Total
Liberal	9	45	46	13	113
Conservative	31	38	19	0	88
	40	83	65	13	201

$X^2 = 44$, p $< .02$

Table 13

Distribution of Liberals and Conservatives
According to Levels of Norm Maintaining

| | Low | | High | | |
	Extremes (8-15)	Moderates (16-23)	Moderates (24-31)	Extremes (32-39)	Total
Liberal	9	38	50	16	113
Conservative	0	10	37	41	88
	9	48	87	57	201

$X^2 = 58.8$, p $< .0006$

The second important set of findings to emerge in this follow-up study were those relating alienation and anomie to norm
maintaining and norm changing. In concluding our Princeton
study, we predicted that a retesting with an older, noncollege
population would again confirm our theory that alienation,
based on Marx's thought, may be usefully redefined as a feeling
of norm constraint experienced more by liberals. We also predicted confirmation for the first time of our theory that
anomie, based on Durkheim's thought, may be redefined as feelings of normlessness experienced more by conservatives. Both
aspects of this theory were confirmed by the strong negative
correlation (−.42) of norm-constraint alienation with norm
maintaining, and by the strong positive correlation (.49) with
norm changing and the reasonably strong positive correlation
(.23) of anomie with norm maintaining.

Another finding of considerable interest is of significant
associations between tendermindedness and norm maintaining,
and between toughmindedness and norm changing. This finding
was complicated by the fact we had tough- and tenderminded
scores for only the men (N = 107) in a sample of both men and
women (N = 207), and all correlations for these 107 scores are
with scores for both men and women on all other variables.
However, despite the differences in the composition of the samples, the pattern uncovered suggests a relation of personality to
social change in keeping with expectancies—that is, the courage
to violate norms would logically require toughness, whereas ten-
derness generally seems to equate with norm maintaining.

We will further examine norm-maintainer versus norm-
changer profiles. But first, by making use of the distorting but
handy one-dimensional perspective, let us note the following
characteristics for other aspects of ideology seemingly revealed
by this older West Coast group through significant correlations
of Table 11 variables.

Liberalism-Conservatism. The liberals in this older and
noncollegiate group are greater risk takers than the conservatives. As no difference in risk taking was found in our college
elite group earlier, this suggests that in keeping with expectancies, liberals in the general population do tend to take more

risks. Liberals are also significantly more alienated, less anomic, younger, and have lower incomes. The reverse of this is that the conservatives are more cautious, less alienated, more anomic, older, and have higher incomes.

Activism-Inactivism. Activists in this group tend to hold extreme beliefs, have higher incomes, and have received more education. Inactivists are more moderate, suffer from anomie, are younger, with lower incomes and less education. Of great interest is the finding of a significantly positive correlation for activism with I-E, indicating that at least these activists are internally motivated, in keeping with Rotter's original hypothesis.

Extremism-Moderation. Extremism showed curiously few correlations, possibly as a function of the scale used. Extremes are more active and alienated, moderates more inactive and less alienated.

Risk Taking. The risk taker has significantly less interest in norm maintaining, is more liberal, is not anomic, and is younger and better educated. The cautious tend to be norm maintaining, conservative, suffer anomie, are older and less well educated.

Alienation. The alienated are motivated to change rather than to maintain norms, are liberal rather than conservative, have extreme beliefs, also suffer from anomie, and are younger. The nonalienated prefer norm maintaining to norm changing, are conservative, moderate, not anomic, and older.

Anomie. The anomic are motivated to maintain norms, are conservative, inactive, take fewer risks, are also alienated, and have lower incomes and less education. Those low in anomie tend to be norm changing, liberal, active, risk takers, nonalienated, with higher incomes and more education.

Locus of Control. The chief difference between the I-E scales used in the Princeton and West Coast follow-up studies was that in this study we used a subset of *nonbiased* items from the I-E scale—that is, items that showed none of the correlations with liberalism or conservatism that riddle the full I-E scale. This does not, in our opinion, alter the need for a better measure for the concept of locus of control. But we do believe the portrait that emerges this time for internal versus external motivation is much closer to the "truth." With the biased items removed, we now find *no* correlation with either liberalism or conservatism; this confirms our contention that something else is needed to probe the evident meaningfulness of I-E to ideological development. We found that the "internally governed" is low in the need for norm maintaining, is an activist, is not anomic, and is better educated. The "externally governed" needs to maintain norms, is inactive, anomic, and less well educated. (The significant anomie-externality relation is of special interest. Another problem with the I-E scale is that the externally keyed items so heavily measure feelings of powerlessness, associated with anomie, that powerlessness, anomie, and externality appear hopelessly confounded in the scale.)

Age. As age increases, so does norm-maintaining motivation, conservatism, activism, extremism, internality, and income; risk taking and alienation decrease. The younger tend to be norm changers, more liberal, surprisingly less activist, higher risk takers, more alienated, and have lower incomes.

Income. Higher incomes are associated with norm maintaining, conservatism, activism, less anomie, and increasing age and education. Lower incomes are associated with norm changing, liberalism, inactivism, anomie, youth, and less education.

Education. The highly educated are more active in social-political causes, willing to take more risks, and have higher incomes than the less educated. Of particular interest are the findings that depict the highly educated as being significantly more *internally* motivated and *less* anomic. In general, these findings combine to give us a portrait of the highly educated as having greater confidence in themselves, less fear, more courage, more faith in their ability to control their own destinies to some degree. Many studies in recent years have questioned the value of higher education. Our findings support what seems obvious to many educational practitioners and observers: that education is not only an irreplacable way to gain culture or marketable skills, but also a crucial institution for training leadership.

Norm Changing and Norm Maintaining

Additional evidence for the discriminating power of this basic social and personality polarity is summarized in Table 14,

Table 14

Characteristics of Norm Changers versus Norm Maintainers

Characteristics	Norm Maintainer	Norm Changer
1. Liberal-conservative	−.63*** (more conservative)	.63*** (more liberal)
2. Anomie	.23*** (more anomic)	−.06
3. Alienation	−.42*** (less alienated)	.49*** (more alienated)
4. Locus of control	−.14** (more external)	.03
5. Risk taking	−.19** (less risk taking)	.09
6. Tough- tenderminded	−.20* (more tenderminded)	.19* (more toughminded)
7. Activism-inactivism	−.07	.09
8. Extreme-moderate	−.21*** (more moderate)	.19** (more extreme)
9. Age	.35*** (older)	−.19** (younger)
10. Family income	.09	−.13* (lower income)
11. Education	−.10	.08
12. Leader	54%	55%
13. Follower	56%	44%

Note: Items 1 through 10 are correlations with N=207. Leader-follower figures are based on crosstabulations and percentages of those scoring above the mean for NC and NM in relation to total number of leaders (82) and followers (126), for sample.

*p < .05   **p < .01   ***p < .001

which gathers correlations from Table 11 to show forcefully different personality profiles. The norm changer tends to be significantly more liberal, alienated, toughminded, extremist, and younger, with a lower income. By contrast, the norm maintainer is more conservative, less alienated, more anomic, more externally controlled, less given to risk taking, more tenderminded, moderate, and older. The similarity between these two personality configurations and the "radical man" and the "anomic man" of Hamden-Turner (1970) are striking. The main difference is in how we view them. We see them not as gross abstractions, which we must pledge allegiance to or vilify, but as "ideal types" in the sense Max Weber intended—abstractions of personality tendencies found to repeatedly occur in real life, which cohere into socially meaningful gestalts. The basic social meanings for this typology, we contend, lie in the role-pairing relationships of many variants of these polarities as they operate (1) within us as individual human beings—the conflict within each of us between our norm-changing and norm-maintaining needs; (2) among us as individual human beings—the conflict of

liberal and conservative; and (3) in the relationships of groups—
the conflict of Democrats and Republicans, or communist versus fascist in Italy.

The West Coast study also reveals *leader* versus *follower*
characteristics. Table 11 shows that for our sample, norm
maintainers are more often followers, but the leaders for this
group included almost identical proportions of norm changers
and norm maintainers. Moreover, this balance generally held for
all *types* of leadership. As a whole, our respondent group had a
high proportion of leaders (82) to followers (126). We were able
to identify their dominant leadership activities as social, political, economic, educational and religious, entertainment, or a
combination of these. Only among the latter group (for example, a leader in social as well as political and economic activities)
did there appear to be any significant difference. Here, curiously, there were almost twice as many norm maintainers. This
could suggest that the norm changer, occupied with the difficulties of inducing change, may tend to focus on one area of
intensive interest, whereas the norm maintainer, whose less
demanding task is to maintain the status quo, finds it easier to
spread over several activity areas.

Again, we seem to have isolated polar personalities suggesting role-pairing dialectics that for hundreds, possibly thousands
of years, have underlain the dynamics of social change. This
mechanism seems by now quite apparent to us, whether it be
the role pairing of liberal versus conservative; of son versus
father—the drama of the young power seeking vying with the
older power possessive; or the role-pairing contrast of "leaders"
and "followers" so vital to all leadership systems.

Crosstabulations also revealed the following significant
relationships for other variables of interest. For activism: leaders are activists, followers more inactivist. When activism is measured by reported contributions of money versus volunteering
time to the cause, those with higher incomes tend to contribute
money whereas those with lower incomes contribute time.
There was, however, a strong association between all measures
used for activism: self-reported activities, contributions of
money, and contributions of time. Liberal activists tend to

volunteer time whereas conservative activists tend to contribute money. By contrast, inactivists are more alienated and more governed by internality. A final variable of interest in this context was our participants' reports of having experienced traumatic stress (divorce, job loss, and so forth) or life-enhancing stress (marriage, birth of a child) during the nine months previous to participating in this study. Norm maintainers, conservatives, inactivists reported significantly fewer traumatic events than norm changers, liberals, and activists. However, those low in norm-changing scores also reported they had experienced significantly less life *enhancement* than the high norm changers.

To summarize: We have presented additional evidence which replicates and extends the Princeton study findings with an older, more varied sample. It further substantiates our theory that beneath the shopworn concepts of liberalism-conservatism lies the fundamental, enduring, and theoretically much more useful polarity of norm changing versus norm maintaining. We have additionally substantiated our theory that alienation may be profitably redefined as a feeling of norm constraint by liberally motivated norm changers, and anomie be redefined as a feeling of normlessness experienced by the conservatively motivated norm maintainer. Additionally useful information has been presented on activism, extremism, tough- versus tender-mindedness, risk taking, locus of control, leaders and followers, and age, education, income, and liability to stress.

Notes on Measures

Norm Maintaining and Norm Changing. Our conviction of the inadequacy of the Stauffer-Toby measure used in the Princeton study motivated our search for a better instrument for these key variables. We decided to build two new scales, one for each variable, by the following method. Five independent raters with social-scientific backgrounds, mainly in anthropology, were presented with the idea that there are two kinds of people who are particularly sensitive to the norms which govern social and all other types of human activities: those who are motivated to change norms, and those who are motivated to maintain them. They were then given a standard personality test, the Comrey Personality Scale (Comrey, 1970), composed of items from many previous sources. They were asked to rate all 180 CPS items by selecting those items to which they felt one or the other type of person might be particularly responsive. From items upon which there was either four out of five or total agreement, eight norm-changing and eight norm-maintaining items were selected, for a total of sixteen for this dimension. There was no suggestion made to these judges that the difference was between "liberal" and "conservative." Moreover, political science majors were specifically excluded; anthropologists were selected to obtain judges who would be hypothetically least inclined to stereotyping. These items were put in the standard five-point Likert format.

Norm-Constraint Alienation. From items coded positive and negative for norm-constraint alienation, originally selected for the Princeton study from the Christie New Left Scale (Christie, Friedman, and Ross, 1969), four items were selected, all positively coded. To these were added two more, a positive rewording of a previously negatively oriented item (5, oppressive norms), and a new item based on a line from a poem by William Blake about "mind-forged manacles." All six items were positively coded because of personal convictions that the previous attempt to reverse meanings with negative codings weakened the test through possible confounding.

Normlessness Anomie. Six items were selected from those previously used from McClosky's scale (McClosky and Schaar, 1965). Again all items were positively coded, for reasons given above.

Locus of Control. From Rotter I-E items (Rotter, 1962) previously shown through item analysis of Princeton data to be unbiased toward liberalism or conservatism, five item pairs were selected that seemed least difficult to cognitively process (many Rotter I-E pairs set up a confusing conceptual dissonance rather than pose clear polarities). These items were handled as sequential rather than discrete pairs to provide an unbroken flow to the test taker—that is, each item was given a separate number in sequence, rather than being presented in single, numbered pairs.

Risk Taking. This was a selection of ten of the twelve items in the standard Choice Dilemma Questionnaire (Kogan and Wallach, 1964). The two items discarded were those with which this particular age range could have difficulty identifying. To add interest they were presented as "exercises in choosing futures."

Liberalism-Conservatism. The six Adorno items shown to be the best discriminators in the Princeton study were used, along with two Polarity Scale item pairs that showed the highest correlation with Adorno items in the Princeton study, for a total of ten items. These item-pairs were run in sequential juxtaposition, as with the I-E items, to maintain the ease generated by a continuous numbered format. This scale not only offered a continuum for obtaining correlations with other variables, but also provided a continuum to be recoded for the extreme-moderation rating.

Activism. Three measures were used for activism: (1) amount of reported social-political activities; (2) reported contribution of money to such activities; (3) reported contributions of volunteer effort.

Extremism. Scores for the LC scale described above were processed in two ways: (1) to assign high- and low-quartile scorers to the extremes category, and mid-quartile scorers to the moderates category; and (2) to construct a six-point continuum EM scale for obtaining correlations.

Leader-Follower. Participants were asked to list all posts of leadership held during the previous three years. On this basis, assignments were made to categories of "leader" (reported posts) and "follower" (no reported posts).

Tough- or Tenderminded. Scores for the masculinity-femininity scale for the Comrey Personality Scale were used. This scale is based on previous scales by Eysenck and Cattell of tough- and tendermindedness.

Age, Education, and Income. Standard questionnaire queries.

═══ 12 ═══

*Social Implications
of the
Ideological Personality*

If we date this investigation from the time of Hegel into the 1970s, we have covered a span of approximately 180 years of thought and research directed to the question of how the "leadership passion" operates within us as a motivation and set of values, as armor in a threatening world, and as shaper to the action of our will upon social reality. In our introduction, we outlined why these questions are important not only to the student and established scholar in the social sciences, but also to leaders and managers of political, economic, social, and educational organizations.

Up to this point, we have dealt chiefly with the past. We began the book with the insights, visions, and "grand" theories of giants—Hegel, Marx, Pareto, Weber, Freud. We then tried to pull into an intelligible framework several decades of psychological studies spurred by the smaller insights and microtheories used to define reality empirically. In our final chapters we will leave this past in order to deal increasingly with the question of futures—with the future of social applications in this chapter, of theory in the next, and finally and most speculatively in our last chapter, with the future of our society as it concerns leadership.

Implications of the Periphery

We have made much of the "core" variables in our theorizing. The variables of the "periphery," however, are more generally fascinating and merit further consideration. Our empirical study (Part Four) begins to find a place within the study of ideology for risk taking and redefines the alignment of alienation, anomie, Machiavellianism, locus of control, and parent-child relations. This seems to us an important beginning. Although these variables have been studied and defined by many investigators, for the first time their findings are brought together within a single investigation to explore relationships in terms of a unified and wide-ranging hypothesis. This hypothesis relates most of these peripheral variables to a basic polarity for pre-dialectical theory: our findings that norm maintenance motivates the activated conservative and norm changing motivates the activated liberal. A second potentially significant perspective on the peripheral variables views them as "input" and "output" variables in the development of ideology as a personality system. We will further examine these perspectives in the next chapter. Beyond considerations of theory, however, lies the enticement of everyday reality: the peripheral variables have exceptionally widespread social implications because of the ways they touch so many aspects of our lives.

We will explore findings for peripheral variables with two purposes in mind. One will be to note their implications for both social scientists and social practitioners. As an aid to scanning, we have italicized specialties (for example, *sociologist, educator*) wherever findings may be of special interest to these particular readers. Our other purpose will be to note relationships to our theoretical framework to aid those who wish to test or make heuristic use of it during this early stage of development.

Parent-Child Relations. As our visualizations have indicated (see Figures 13-18), in the periphery-to-core relationships the parent-child interaction is seen as possibly the most important *input* to ideology as a system extending in social and temporal space. The studies we cited in earlier chapters (chief among them, Frenkel-Brunswik's findings and Tomkins' analysis) and our own research indicate the following patterns are probably the most prevalent for ideologically formative parent-child relationships. In the orderly conservative home, the learning of rules and norms for behavior is stressed. These rules and norms are invariant and must be observed. Should they be infringed in any way—and the transgression discovered—punishment will tend to be swift, severe, and likely physical. In religious terms, it is an Old Testament childhood, with father or mother acting as the earthly personification of the jealous, vengeful, and all-powerful Yahweh who leveled Sodom and Gomorrah. This developmental climate helps form the conservative or normative core personality for whom *maintaining the norms and observing the rules of the established order becomes a sacred obligation.*

In the more disorderly liberal home, the learning of rules and norms is pursued in a more arbitrary and haphazard fashion. There is more stress on the delights of discovery, particularly of the capacities of this small, developing being, one's own self. Rather than the rules being invariant, they are often set aside in order to realize the benefits of some interesting ongoing pursuit—the child is allowed to stay up late to see a favorite relative rather than be forced to bed by schedule, for example. Should the rules be infringed, there may or may not be punishment—in any case, it is seldom swift, severe, or physical. In religious terms, it is a New Testament childhood, with father or mother acting as the earthly personification of the God of Jesus, at times gentle, at times fiercely demanding, but generally nurturant, fair, and understanding. This developmental climate helps form the liberal or humanistic personality, who has learned *that violating the norms and changing the rules of the established order are acceptable behaviorally in pursuit of the larger goal of self- and societal-realization.*

An implication of these differences for *parents, educators,* and *therapists*—as well as *sociologists* and *political scientists*—is that in dealing with one or the other type, it is important to keep in mind the high probability of these varying developmental climates. This difference suggests one should provide supportive structures for those to whom the need for rules is paramount, and leeway to those who must have the freedom to explore. However, one must also be sensitive to the possible need to moderate the extremes of one or the other orientation. That is, the overly constricted (or rule-full) must be encouraged to roam, and the overly loose (or rule-less) encouraged to learn self-governance. A general implication for homes, classrooms— and governments—seems to be that giving over entirely to one extreme or the other is unwise. The desirable forms to life seem to embody a mixture of norm-maintenance and norm-changing functions.

The relation of these two developmental climates to our norm-relational theory are as we have indicated and seem rather straightforward. As best articulated in the works of Tomkins, the conservative parent, by stressing rules, lays down the conservative, norm-maintenance motivational base. The liberal parent, by stressing freedom to explore, lays down the liberal, norm-violation motivational base. All of us in reality, of course, are neither one nor the other exclusively. We are generally mixtures weighted more one way than the other, and are open to change through change of circumstance. We should also add that parent-child relationships are by no means the only input variables to the formation of the ideological personality. For some, genetics and history are undoubtedly far more decisive factors, but such considerations are beyond the range of this study.

Risk Taking. If we view norm violating versus norm maintaining as a core dynamic encouraged by parent-child input variables, risk taking may then be seen as an important *output* variable intensifying the social impact of left versus right ideology. Our research modified the stereotype of the conservative as cautious and nonrisking, and the liberal as venturesome and risk taking. As expected, we found that the liberal activist will take risks to violate or change the norms, but unexpectedly we found that conservative activists also risk to *maintain* norms.

These findings should be rigorously examined through further study, for although respectable, the correlations upon which we base this conclusion are not comfortably large. The pursuit of such an investigation should be of special interest to *economists, business and financial leaders,* and *managers.* Within social psychology, many studies of risk taking have been motivated by the investigator's recognition that it is a key variable in all economic and moneymaking activities (see Kogan and Wallach, 1964). Yet because these studies often involve what appear to be children's games played by adults, few economists or business and financial leaders have been motivated to seek anything useful from them. By linking risk taking to the dynamics of liberalism-conservatism, which so obviously affects leadership and management styles, we hope to encourage the social application of previous risk-taking studies as well as to help generate new ones. Moreover, the originating work of Pareto outlined in Chapter Two should alert economists to the relevance of this risk taking ideology complex to the mystery of economic cycles, upon which the fate of both individuals and nations depends throughout much of the world.

On the economic front, these findings suggest to us the utility of knowing to what extent either the leadership of an organization or some portion of the financial community is dominated by liberal or conservative personalities, or by situationally-induced liberal or conservative "moods." Assessments of this type are already regularly made on an intuitive basis by possibly a majority of the world's leading economists. They are undoubtedly included in the designation of a "bull" or a "bear" market. An objective of science, however, is to bolster the intuitions of the brilliant with formulae that can be understood and used by the less-than-brilliant. Hence, it is possible this line of study could lead to an operationalizing of knowledge markedly improving prediction of both individual and market behavior. For example, the normal assumption would be that when conservative personalities or market moods prevail, risk taking will decline and investment will shrink. Although this pattern is generally operative, our research indicates a secondary pattern which the sharp observer of the market may observe: that a significant number of people, conservative by nature, will continue to take large risks. Why is this?

Our research suggests that risk taking persists among *activated* conservatives, or those who through pressures of personality or system simply must be active no matter what happens. But the *direction* of this risking will be toward maintaining what already exists, in terms of property and holdings. For example, they may shift their investments from risky new ventures to equally risky but established concerns, concerns in fact quite shaky behind an old, seemingly reliable facade. By contrast, when liberal personalities or market moods prevail, our research suggests that risks will be taken in new ventures and to enlarge one's holdings. One might then, through systems analysis, extend the predictive possibilities of this ideological risk-taking paradigm to the larger social reality of the expanding or contracting economy.

Risk taking also relates to the serious concerns of *political scientists, sociologists,* and *government leaders* with national defense and foreign relations. For undoubtedly the most horrible problem to which the study of risk taking relates is the possibility of atomic annihilation for millions of us—or short of that eventuality, the resorting of nations to warfare rather than negotiation to resolve conflicts. For this reason, the Advanced Research Program of the United States Defense Department has funded many highly sophisticated studies of risk taking and conflict resolution. Again, by relating risk taking to left-right ideology, our findings open new dimensions for studies relevant to national security. Within most governing regimes in the world there exist both liberal and conservative factions. Gauging which faction is dominant, and what may be the possibly large implications of seemingly small shifts in power from one to the other, now occupies a considerable workforce throughout the world. The American and Russian investment in mutual eyeballing of this sort alone must involve more people than the world's total investment in disarmament specialists. Much research in ideology suggests that when a shift to the left occurs, risks may be taken to advance liberal goals of more equality, brotherhood, peacefulness, and trust among nations. By contrast, when shifts to the right occur, our research suggests that one may look for: (1) policies of caution and low risk, or pulling back to preserve what one already has; *or* (2) high risk policies aimed at defending what the affected nation perceives to be its own endangered territory, trade areas, or other vital areas of influence. This particular high-risk policy is familiar historically as a basic pattern leading to war.

For the *therapist* and *educator*, further investigation of the patterns suggested by these findings may also have import. In Chapter Four, we examined the contribution of the great motivational theorist, Abraham Maslow, to the study of ideology. He related defense and being needs to the conservative side, and growth and becoming needs to the liberal side of personality. It is a commonplace of both clinical observation and theory that to grow, to self-actualize, to realize one's potential through either therapy or education, one must learn to take the psychological risks involved in venturing into the unknown of new emotions, new habits, even in extreme cases, new personalities. This fits with our finding for the risk taking, norm-changing, liberalistic relationship. But the counterpart to this pattern is often overlooked in both education and therapy. The common assumption is that the person who is not responding to therapy or education is refusing to risk, and is regressing to, or refusing to leave old self-defensive, affective, cognitive, and social structures. This is often the case, but our study also indicates support for another option to which educators and therapists may not always be alert. If sufficiently motivated (that is, cast into a situation inducing high anxiety or posing too grave a threat to one's self-esteem), patient or student may take great risks to regain earlier and better-known, affective, cognitive, and social structures. In extreme cases, they may attack the therapist and educator, or burn or vandalize the school; less violently, they may simply withdraw from treatment or drop out of school.

Another implication of risk taking relates to the concerns of *business managers, political scientists, sociologists,* and *historians.* Our findings suggest that when confronted by a violation of the norms or a threat to the established order, the conservative will risk to suppress the violator, to eliminate the threat, or to strengthen the norm and the order. This type of risk taking may be confined to the relatively innocuous experience of the individual. For example, it could take the form of a vociferous public expression of his beliefs by an enraged conservative in a liberal or neutral setting. In this situation, he risks losing potential friends or esteem for the sake of what he perceives to be his endangered beliefs. However, this particular dynamic may also be the basis for mass risking of the type indulged in by the German conservatives, who risked their entire culture on Hitler and his promise of invariant rules and norms and the maintenance of a perfect order.

Alienation and Anomie. Because these concepts have been confounded in theory and method, we suggested a redefinition in relation to one another. Going back to their conceptual roots in Marx and Durkheim, we outlined the case for viewing alienation as primarily a liberal, and anomie as primarily a conservative, affliction, both relating to the norming-process framework. That is, alienation is viewed as the ideoaffective outcome of a situation within which the person feels frustrated, restricted, constrained by the prevailing norms for thought and behavior, or by the prevailing social or organizational order. We reasoned that liberals, motivated by the need to expand and change norms in search of novelty and fresh stimuli, would be more subject to feelings of alienation than would conservatives—and ours as well as much other research bears this out.

In direct opposition, we proposed that anomie be defined as the ideoaffective outcome of a situation within which the person feels *lacking* desired norm constraints—that is, one feels oneself floating in a social sea of uncertainty, within an ambiguous or shattered system of norms and rules, following a disastrous blow to the social order or during its decline. We reasoned that conservatives, motivated by the need to establish and strengthen norms in order to reduce the uncertainty that novel stimuli present, would be more anomic than liberals. As we predicted, and following a failure with the Princeton study, this theory was supported by our West Coast study, bearing on earlier research by McClosky (1965) and theorizing of Hamden-Turner (1970).

The concepts of alienation and anomie are chiefly of interest to *sociologists, political scientists,* and *social and clinical psychologists.* Our hypotheses and findings imply the need for further research to substantiate, refute, or extend them. In this regard, the pioneering work of McClosky with anomie, the thoughts of Hamden-Turner about this complex, the work of Schwartz (1973) in alienation, and a reappraisal of Keniston's studies (1965, 1968) should provide a rich conceptual matrix for anyone interested in further pursuit in this direction. For *therapists, educators, parents,* and *personnel managers,* they have potentially important implications for the nurturance of patients, students, children, and employees. They suggest the desirability, first, of recognizing whether one is dealing with a dominantly liberal or conservative personality. This identification may then determine the right treatment for preventing, modifying, or—at times recognizing the functional necessity for such a state—encouraging alienation or anomie. If alienation is to be decreased, the liberal personality must be given room to explore, to range, to venture, to deviate from and, if necessary, to change the norms. If anomie is to be decreased, on the other hand, the conservative personality must be given a structure of rules and an order to maintain.

Machiavellianism. Originally we were unable to relate Machiavellianism to the left-right, norm-relational hypothesis. We included this variable in our study of the ideological personality because of its interest to *historians, sociologists,* and *political scientists* as a quality and strategy of leadership; to *politicians* and *business managers* as a survival tactic in the modern world of business and statesmanship; and to *social psychologists* as a measurable variable since the development of the excellent Mach scale by Richard Christie in the 1960s.

In our own research, we found evidence—not much, but some—relating Machiavellianism more to conservatives motivated by norm maintenance than to liberals motivated by norm changing. With the full range of research and theory on the subject in mind, however, we are convinced that relationships of the following nature exist. With the appropriate sample and approach, we feel that at least two important and ideologically different kinds of Machiavellians will be identified. One will be the ethically neutral, "pragmatic," character-deficient conservative of the type represented by Richard Nixon and many of those who participated in the Watergate disaster. The other will be a type that flourished in the late 1960s among leftist radicals which could be characterized as "the amoral plotter." We would further predict that both types usually serve staff rather than line management functions, the relationship being that of Iago to Othello, rather than the leader as "plotter" as in the case of Shakespeare's *Richard III* or with Richard Nixon. However, the Uriah Heep pattern for this type will also be discernable—that is, the rise of the left or right Machiavellian to line management power through careful plotting over a period of humble servitude.

Ideological Machiavellianism further seems a quality worth more investigation because of the unique relationship of ideology to social change. If ideology is to induce social change toward either liberal or conservative ends, it must act through mechanisms linking leaders to the social surroundings. One can sense the operation of the Machiavellian as a type of personality, or Machiavellianism as a type of tactic, within such mechanisms. Watergate and innumerable other historical examples (for example, the murder- and intrigue-racked history of the Roman, British, and Russian rulerships) suggests a pattern whereby the ostensibly noble values and goals of left or right are trumpeted by leaders to gain adherents and launch social movements. But once these movements are underway, the pressure mounts to find ignoble means to gain these noble ends, thus creating the functional need for Machiavellianism.

Again, the implications for social scientists are to test these possibilities. For leaders and managers of organizations, who long ago learned to act upon hunch rather than wait for the slow proofs of social science, an implication is that Machiavellianism is inevitable in organizational life. The record of human history repeatedly shows that even the noblest of causes will die aborning unless it offers some kind of base or "gut" appeal;

hence there are social functional needs for those to whom the means are far more important than the ends. What this fact of life seems to impose upon ethical and responsible leadership might be termed the wisdom of Watergate—the need to more carefully monitor, dominate, and when necessary exclude from the system the servant Machiavellian.

Locus of Control. We hypothesized that understanding how the *source* of norms is perceived is of fundamental importance for an adequate psychology of ideology. That is, if our theory is based on a norm-maintenance versus norm-violation paradigm, the question of the grounding for this structure is crucial. We noted the contradiction between the theoretical views of Frenkel-Brunswik and Tomkins and empirical findings with Rotter's ubiquitous I-E Scale for measuring locus of control. On one hand, Frenkel-Brunswik and Tomkins felt that the norm source was perceived as outside oneself by conservatives and inside oneself by liberals. However, most of those using the highly popular Rotter measure, including ourselves, found externality correlating with liberalism and internality with conservatism.

The conclusion from our research was that the Rotter I-E is too flawed in its present form to do much beyond confuse the issue, and that to resolve this important question, other measures (such as those of Witkin and Eysenck) should be additionally employed. Ideally, a new instrument should be developed after intensive thought has been given to questions that have been raised about the relation of locus of control to ideology. In lieu of such research, we will venture some personal hunches and convictions. One difficulty seems to lie in resolving the contradictions posed by two perspectives on the developmental situation of man. Despite the lack of confirming empirical evidence, Tomkins' original rationale is still compelling: the norm-structure is sensed as outside by conservatives and inside by liberals. Visualizing the relation of the norm-receiving child to the norm-giving parent, he reasoned that because the conservative parent discourages self-expression and encourages submission to an external mystery of norms, within the small conservative in social embryo there is implanted a sense of the norm-structure as external to one's self. He reasoned that liberal parents, by more lightly raising the importance of external norms and encouraging self-expression, encourage a sense of the ultimate governor or norm-source as residing within oneself.

When one looks at the situation of liberal and conservative later in life, however, one may detect a difference that merits further research. It is the difference of the adult right versus the adult left perception of one's situation in relation to a social system that has been phenomenologically transformed since childhood. The conservative, by nature a norm maintainer, tends to identify more with whatever social system exists than does the liberal. The conservative now perceives its norms as his own, therefore *internalized.* By contrast, the liberal, by nature a norm changer, is more sensitive to the flaws of the present system and can also more readily visualize alternatives to the system as it exists. Therefore the liberal perceives its norms as not necessarily his own, or *externalized.*

The implications of this "developmental switch" hypothesis for social science is to test it with research that would ideally involve the development of a new instrument based on a thorough evaluation of the Rotter, Witkin, Eysenck, and any other relevant measures. The resolution of this question could be of exceptional importance in sociological and in child and adult developmental theory.

An implication for *therapists, educators,* and *parents,* could be the desirability of making us aware of these internal and external complexities at the right times in our cognitive and affective development. The goal of education, therapy—and of life itself, we believe—is to gain, through knowledge, more control over ourselves, our environments, and our destinies. Certainly it could help self-mastery to gain more awareness of the source for the controls within us, how they were formed, and how they function. It brings to mind the educational philosophy upon which our culture is founded, from which our political, economic, and social systems derive—a philosophy expressed long ago by Socrates in the dictum "Know thyself," or more recently by Freud as "Where id is, there shall ego be."

13

New Models of Ideological Personality

For centuries thinkers have tried to grasp the essence of ideological personality. It has been a particularly frustrating task, for what intuitively seems obvious swiftly dissolves into a wordy mush under the pressure of the need for precise definition. Moreover, there has been a loss of support for this task because of the decline and passing of the metaphor. For Nietzsche, the essential difference was between the balanced Apollonian and the creatively disruptive Dionysian; for Pareto, between the majestic Lions and the clever Foxes; for Freud, between the striving of Eros and the leveling of Thanatos. From these heights one drops a considerable distance to the cold directions of "left" versus "right," or the bland impersonality of "liberal" versus "conservative." Still, these are terms that retain some touch of simple humanity. How is it that we have reached the point at which we can only adequately survey ideology's "hot" core with talk of "dimensions" and many very cold numbers?

"The tigers of wrath are wiser than the horses of instruction," William Blake once opined, in keeping with the above concerns. However, another poet observed that "only Euclid has looked on beauty bare." This is the scientific ideal of beauty unadorned—to strip away surfaces to uncover structures, to define useful truths with spare precision. While still mourning the loss of the old verbal warmth and color, we will forthwith plunge into the cool lake of the scientific perspective to examine implications of our findings for building new models of ideological personality. This examination will be of the core-periphery model: the core as three dimensions, in Osgood's and Winter's terms; the core as four-dimensional; an interrelating of ours and the Rokeach two-value model; and a glimpse at the challenge of developing a fully dialectical theory of ideological personality.

The Core-Periphery Model

In Chapters Three and Four, we examined theoretical models of the functioning of ideology developed by psychologists from the 1940s into the 1970s. We examined the one-dimensional models of the Adorno group and Rokeach's early work, the two-dimensional models of Eysenck and Rokeach's later work, the glimmering of a three-dimensional model in the work of Lewis and Kraut, and the bold statement of a four-dimensional model by Tomkins. It was within such a context that we began our own studies to test, and, if possible, range beyond these earlier models.

In Part Four, we explored in depth the implications and substantiated the nature of a new model of ideology consisting of two elements. One was a view of the operation of ideology along three dimensions: liberalism-conservatism (LC), activism-inactivism (AI), and extremism-moderation (EM). We found that this three-dimensional model helped account for certain types of thought and behavior better than did the customary models using only one, or at most two of these dimensions. We found, moreover, that the introduction of a second element to this model greatly extended its usefulness. This was to view LC, AI, and EM as the "core" dimensions for ideology, which then interact with social reality through a set of "peripheral" variables—the ideologically meaningful variables of parent-child relationships, risk taking, alienation, anomie, Machiavellianism, and locus of control.

This new model could be called the Three-Dimensional Core-Periphery Model of Ideological Functioning. In earlier chapters, we reduced such concepts to visualizations to aid analysis. In keeping with this practice, we could depict this model as shown in Figure 21.

Figure 21

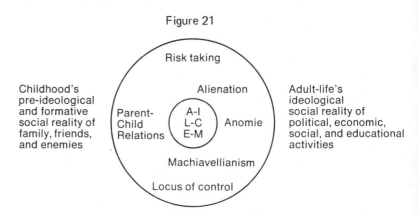

In Chapter Three, we made use of Kurt Lewin's visualization of the person as a circle within the larger surrounding area of his hypothetical life space. Figure 21 is an application of the same approach to the situation of the ideological personality within both life space and life span. At the center of the circle representing the ideological personality, we may visualize the "core" dimensions of liberalism-conservatism, activism-inactivism, and extremism-moderation. Less central to ideology, but still operating within the boundaries of the individual personality, are the variables of the "periphery." These are of two types: "input" governing variables of parent-child relationships and "output" governing variables of risk taking, alienation, anomie, Machiavellianism, and locus of control. Of exceptional importance in our view is the operation of these peripheral variables as ideological personality interface with social reality. As Figure 21 illustrates, we visualize this interface in terms of a life span system. At the input end is childhood's social reality of family, friends *and* enemies, wherein the "seeds" of ideology are implanted and possibly its "roots" take hold. At the output end is adult life's social reality of political, economic, social, and educational activities, into which ideology may thrust itself as a figurative sapling or a mighty (or poison!) oak.

Figure 22 depicts some of the same concepts from another visual perspective. The fundamental difference between Figure 22 and Figure 21 is that in the *empirically* grounded Figure 22, liberalism-conservatism is not viewed as a single entity (as in Figure 21). In Figure 22, it is viewed as two psychosocial "islands," one liberal, one conservative, linked together structurally by norm maintaining-violating dimensions, each enclosing the core variables of EM and AI, each surrounded by peripheral variables.

Figure 22

Structural and Core-Peripheral Model of
Ideological Functioning

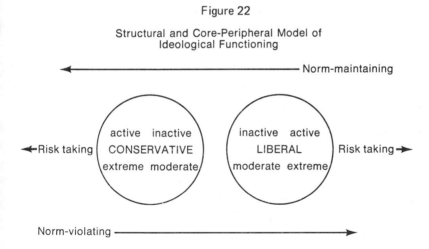

Now the inevitable question at this point is which model or view is correct? The one- or the two-dimensional? The only sensible answers are both—or neither. As many philosophers have articulated (for example, Plato, Kant, Vaihinger), all theories, all models, are only abstractions. They are nothing more (as well as nothing less) than our tiny attempts to bring the immensity of phenomenal experience within our conceptual grasp. As all models are limited, they can only show facets of a larger reality which is immeasurably beyond our known sensory and cognitive capacities. And so two—or many—apparently contradictory models may be needed to approximate experiential reality. We must, in short, be equipped to respect and deal with all models of any sophistication, rather than be blocked by the notion of one *absolute* model, as though it were all a pitching of flawed apples from a barrel with the idea that at the bottom lies one perfect creation.

This brings us to a conceptual juncture in understanding ideology where we must consider having to live comfortably with a contradiction. It seems to us that we must accept what many investigations now tell us—that LC is *both* a continuum and two separate islands, depending on how you look at it. This further seems a contradiction resolvable at a higher level of thought more akin to the Oriental than to the Western mind set. Identified by Maslow (1966) and Riegel (1972), this is the conceptual processing level of both/and rather than either/or relationships.

To many psychologists and sociologists both/and thinking still seems an impossibly alien notion. How can two seemingly contradictory models of reality *both* be true? Prompted by Einstein, physicists long ago learned to swim in this choppy mental sea, along with readers of Lao-Tzu. Moreover, although we think of this both/and orientation as alien, Western social science seems to have been using it unwittingly for many years. The evidence is the increasing proliferation of models we use to try to convey our perceptions of reality to others. Our problem seems to be the intellectual chauvinism that blinds us to the legitimacy of all but our own pet theories.

With this orientation in mind, then, we will proceed to build—and unbuild—theoretical models in this chapter.

Osgood, Winter, and Three-Dimensional Models

Earlier we used the metaphor of a plunge into a cool lake for a transition to the realm of model building. This choice proves apt in relation to work with three-dimensional models, for among its most striking visual products are the three-dimensional "meaning spaces" of Guilford for intellect (1967), Osgood for affect and cognition (1971), and Winter for power (1973), all of which look like ice cubes festooned with names and numbers. By casting our three-dimensional model into this "cube" form, we arrive at the depiction in Figure 23.

Figure 23

Three-Dimensional Semantic
Space of Ideology

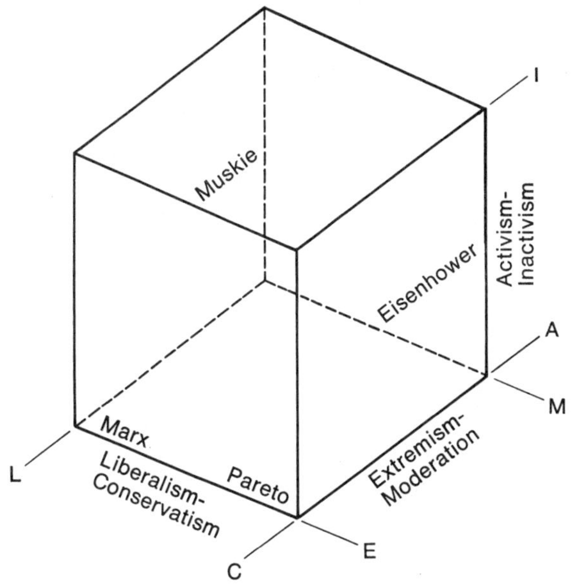

One advantage of this method of visualization is that positions of personality orientation or belief can be precisely pinpointed in relation to a large context of ideological meanings. In Figure 23, for example, we have located within this meaning space both personalities and ideological beliefs in terms of some familiar figures. Karl Marx is positioned at the activist, extreme, liberal "corner" of the cube. Vilfredo Pareto is positioned at the activist, extreme, conservative "corner." President Eisenhower then occupies a position along the conservative "face" at the moderate end, midway between activism and inactivism.

Senator Edmund Muskie, a leading Democratic presidential aspirant in 1972, occupies the counterpart position along the liberal face.

That such "cubes" can have meaning and usefulness far beyond mere classification is shown by the work of Charles Osgood in the measurement of meaning (Osgood, Suci, and Tannenbaum, 1957; Osgood, 1971) and David Winter in the study of the power motive (Winter, 1973). Both Osgood and Winter have visually defined their findings and theories in the form of well-known, similar "cubes" derived from extensive empirical investigations. The Osgood meaning space is enclosed by three dimensions, which he finds account for most of the variance of conceptual meanings for all major world cultures. Despite a wide variety of languages and customs, he finds that people throughout the world assign meanings to all objects primarily in terms of the dimensions of evaluation ("Is it good or bad?"), activity ("Is it fast or slow?"), and potency ("Is it strong or weak?"). Osgood's work is the modern fruition of tridimensional theories articulated by Wilhelm Wundt during the beginning of experimental psychology in the late 19th century. This suggests to us that the three-dimensional core we propose for ideology must be a basic configuration because of its correspondence to the Osgood-Wundt "cube," which has proved serviceable over such a span of time. Our analogue for Osgood's evaluation dimension is liberalism-conservatism ("Is he left or right?"); for activity, activism-inactivism ("Is he an activist or an inactivist?"); and for potency, extremism-moderation ("Is he an extremist or a moderate?").

The same correspondence may be found with Winter's psychometric "cube" for the power motive. Winter visualizes power motivation as the result of drives within the power seeker (O) that are modified or enhanced by the nature of the person or group (P) which the power-seeker wants to influence. Winter's three dimensions are: (1) Status of strength of O and P ("Is there a great difference in strength between me, as the power seeker, and those I would act on, hence increasing my freedom of action? Or are we on a par, requiring more caution and finesse on my part?"). (2) Legitimacy, morality ("To what extent are the means which are available to me to gain my ends traditionally approved or disapproved?"). (3) Resistance of P ("What are the probabilities of resistance to, or compliance with, my attempts at influence?").

As with Osgood, Winter arrived at his "cube" not through armchair theorizing, but as the result of a series of ingenious empirical studies over a number of years. The correspondence for these investigations is roughly as shown in Table 15. A correspondence between Winter's "resistance of P" and "activism-inactivism" for this study, for example, is relatively easy to visualize. No matter how fierce one's activist potential may be, what one *does* is heavily dependent upon the degree of resistance one faces. In the United States and worldwide, for example, there were great numbers of student activists during the 1960s because of the weakening of institutional forces of resistance.

Table 15

Correspondence Between Osgood, Winter, and Loye Dimensions

Osgood	Winter	Loye
Evaluation	Legitimacy of action	Liberalism-conservatism
Activity	Resistance of P	Activism-inactivism
Potency	Status equality of P and O	Extremism-moderation

More difficult to visualize is the correspondence between "status equality of P and O" for Winter and "extremism-moderation" for our model. It is possible to sense an equivalency through the correspondence of the Osgood "potency" dimension to both "status equality-inequality" for Winter and "extremism-moderation" for our model. However, there are conceptual problems if one attempts to go beyond this intuition. For example, if the power seeker is lower in status than those he seeks to influence, he may resort to *either* moderation *or* extremism. This was demonstrated historically by both the moderation advocated by Booker T. Washington and Martin Luther King and the extremism advocated by W. E. B. DuBois and Malcolm X as black advancement strategies against the dominant whites (Loye, 1971). Such contradictions we must leave to others to resolve in order to focus on Winter's third dimension, which may lead, we believe, to a useful advancement in ideological theory.

Prospects for a Four-Dimensional Model

A contradiction is to the theoretician what a trace of yellow metal is to the prospector for gold. It can signal the tiny bonanza of advancement or more "fool's gold." What this will yield, only time will tell; however we immediately encounter an inviting contradiction if we attempt to equate Winter's "legitimacy-illegitimacy" power-motive dimension with "liberalism-conservatism." We are first faced with the problem of aligning two dimensions. Ours consists of liberalism at one end of a continuum and conservatism at the other end. Winter's is a continuum with legitimacy at one end and illegitimacy at the other end. This forces us then to ask, What are the polar matches for the ends of these dimensions? Is liberalism to be aligned with the legitimate or illegitimate end for the power dimension? Is conservatism legitimate or illegitimate?

The absurdity of these questions help force us to answers which may unlock gold from rock. For here, from another perspective, we again come upon the inadequacy of the either/or view of LC as either a continuum or two separate conceptual "islands." It is evident we must shift into both/and thinking and resort again to the view of two "islands," one liberal, one conservative. This then makes it possible to extend the "cube" modular form to pose a four-dimensional model of the type shown in Figure 24.

We have now separated the LC continuum into two components, left versus right. We may visualize each as a separate personality or group orientation, whose "core" (or most characterizing) ideology may be expressed in the form of separate three-dimensional meaning spaces. We are suggesting that theoretically this visualization expands the scope of what we mean by left versus right ideology compared with our previous conceptualization. We now have a theoretical system consisting not

Figure 24

Four-Dimensional Model of Ideology

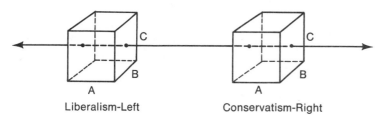

Liberalism-Left   Conservatism-Right

solely of the three dimensions we have examined so far: LC, AI, and EM. We have a four-dimensional system comprised of liberalism-conservatism separated in accordance with both/and thinking, plus dimensions A, B, and C.

From our previous work it is evident that dimension A is activism-inactivism and dimension B is extremism-moderation. But what is dimension C? We are convinced the likeliest candidate is William James' and Hans Eysenck's tough- and tendermindedness. Let us summarize the evidence.

In Chapter Three we described how, through factor analysis, Eysenck isolated T, or toughmindedness versus tendermindedness, as one of two factors accounting for the major part of the variance in political ideology (Eysenck, 1954). His data and conclusions expressed in the 1950s were then severely questioned by Rokeach and Hanley (1956), Christie (1956) and others into the 1960s. Ever since then, within the study of ideology, the T dimension has remained under a cloud. In the early 1970s, the investigator closest to and most heavily influenced by Eysenck, Glenn Wilson, was expressing grave doubts as to the usefulness or importance of T in the study of ideology (Wilson, 1970, 1973). Even Eysenck himself has retreated under this pressure (Wilson, 1973).

There are other sides to the picture, however, which we feel more than counterbalance the arguments cited above. One aspect is the persistence of T as a major factor in the personality measurements of Cattell (1965) and Comrey (1970). If one takes time to understand the data base, the measurement objectives, and the methodology, it seems hard to avoid the conclusion that T remains a dimension of exceptional continuing interest in the study of ideology. Both Cattell and Comrey, measuring *general* not specifically ideological personality, and through factor analysis of a wide range of items from many sources, repeatedly find T emerging as a prime factor, one of sixteen in Cattell's and one of eight in Comrey's personality measures.

A second aspect convincing us that T is the logical fourth dimension of our proposed model is the usefulness of toughversus tendermindedness as a conceptual tool for interpreting social movements within the context of history. Ideology is a concept peculiarly reminiscent of traditional difficulties with the concept of God in religion. It is both immanent and transcendent, or both psychologically emergent and motivational, and socially overarching and pressuring. It is, to put it another way, a compound of the individual and society, a concept linking the two worlds of psychology and social change. In past and contemporary history, there is much evidence of this dimension operating within social movements involving the action of ideological personalities. This theme runs through Feuer's compendium and analysis of the student protest movement throughout the world, *Conflict of Generations* (1969). Repeatedly Feuer finds a tenderminded "initiating" leadership being replaced by a toughminded "implementing" leadership, which drives student movements to disaster and dissolution by provoking an inevitable clash with a powerful and entrenched authority. A particularly ingenious analysis of how tendermindedness escalates to toughmindedness, involving person and society and intergenerational influence, was carried out by Tomkins in his paper on "the psychology of commitment" examining the lives and social impacts of the four best-known American abolitionists (Tomkins and Izard, 1965). In our own work we also found this pattern operating over 350 years of American race-relations history (Loye, 1971). Historical polarities counterpose the tendermindedness of John Woolman and Thomas Jefferson with the toughmindedness of Nat Turner and John Brown. Of particular interest were the developmental sequences by which tendermindedness became transformed to toughmindedness within the same person, as most remarkably expressed in the life of the greatest of the black abolitionists, Frederick Douglass.

Finally, throughout other formal work in psychology, part experimental, part theoretical, there is a strong and enduring interest in this dimension. It began with William James, involved many others whom Eysenck cited in announcing his own work, and persists today in studies such as those of De Fronzo (1972).

The next logical step for the interested investigator is to test this model by administrations of appropriate tests. Although not an overwhelmingly difficult task, this will have to be done with considerable care. Meanwhile, the model may be found heuristically useful by political scientists, sociologists, anthropologists, and historians, as well as social and political psychologists interested in the study of ideology.

Extending the Freedom-Equality Model

We would leave an essential part of our task undone without an attempt to relate the most interesting new theory of ideology, the Rokeach two-value model of political ideology, to the core-periphery and norm-process framework.

As we outlined in Chapter Four, Rokeach suggested that the four major political ideological alignments (communism, socialism, capitalism, and fascism) can be understood in terms of their adherents' ranking of two key end or terminal values: freedom and equality. Socialists care for both of these values, fascists for neither, communists for equality but not freedom, and capitalists for freedom but not equality. Empirical studies using different methods have confirmed this hypothesis in considerable detail (Rokeach, 1973).

Values have been found difficult to relate to the usual motivational concepts without the use of elaborate diagrams and theorizing. Part of this difficulty is that in terms of prevailing drive theory, values appear to serve more as regulators of drives than as drives themselves. However, if one considers the historically activating values of equality and freedom, and if one views motivation in field-theoretical terms as a composite of

many forces acting on the person or society, it is apparent
values also act as motivators. An expedient for relating the
Rokeach values model to our core variables is to make use of
Lewin's field theoretical method of visualizing levels of reality
in relation to levels of "irreality" (Lewin, 1951). As shown in
Figure 25, Lewin viewed reality as being the concrete, complex,
operational level wherein our sensory, perceptual, and cognitive
equipment is actively engaged with the moment-by-moment
reality of our external environment, or the phenomenal world.
This is the level wherein we are governed as organisms by stimulus seeking which alternates with stimulus reducing, or as we
indicate in Figure 25, by the interaction of norm-changing and
norm-maintaining motivation. Simultaneously, however, we are
living in an epiphenomenal world "within the head," wherein lie
the concepts we abstract and the fantasies we create. This second level Lewin called the level of "irreality," noting that much
of what motivates the individual can only be understood by
visualizing interactions between these two levels of our being.

Figure 25

The Rokeach Model as an Irreality-Reality Relationship

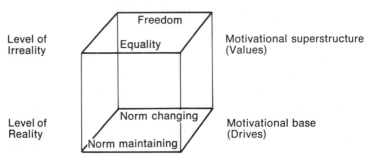

Thus we feel the values of equality and freedom may be
visualized as acting upon the individual's operational level of
reality through the level of irreality. Like the gods of old, they
reside in a mental Valhalla or Mount Olympus, wherefrom they
thunder down into the baffling complexities of our operational
world to warn us of the necessity to act according to the proper
standards for our own particular ideology.

In such terms, the potential relationship of the Rokeach model to our peripheral variables is quite fascinating. We will note three correspondences that may help others to adequately define the connections. We dealt first with questions of the formation of ideology in the individual through a consideration of parent-child "input" peripheral variables. The analogy we used of the Rokeach values acting like the gods of old suggests the obvious connection, both gods and values being abstractions of parental dicta internalized by the child in the ways Freud (1966) articulated in the formation of superego and ego ideal, or others have more recently projected in modeling theoretical terms (for example, Bandura and Walters, 1963). In other words, through parent-child and other relationships on the reality level, during our childhood we gradually abstract the concepts of freedom and equality from our experiences and store these concepts on the irreality level. Acting within us, these concepts then monitor the reality of later childhood and adulthood. We relate each new situation we encounter to this irreality level of abstracted standards, which serves to shape our beliefs, attitudes, and behavior according to its dictates.

Two other possible connections between the Rokeach model and our peripheral variables are more elusive. Figure 26 is a heuristic summary of how, within the ideological world of left (L), liberal (l), conservative (r), and right (R), "freedom" may relate to alienation and anomie, and "equality" to the complexities of internal versus external locus of control.

We have placed "freedom" on the *vertical* axis to depict the striving aspect that the need for freedom engenders. Our guiding thoughts regarding the relation of "freedom" to alienation and anomie are then as shown in the figure. According to the redefinitions we have proposed, anomie may be seen as a normless state of too much (or high) freedom and alienation as a norm-constrained state of not enough (or low) freedom. This hypothesis would apply to both the child's pre-ideological and the adult's ideological worlds. Along the diagonal we have placed the extreme conservative (R) at a point suggesting susceptibility to the strongest feelings of anomie and the strongest fear of too much freedom. At the opposite pole is the extreme liberal (L), whom we have placed at a point suggesting suscepti-

Figure 26

The Rokeach Model Related to
Alienation, Anomie, and Locus of Control

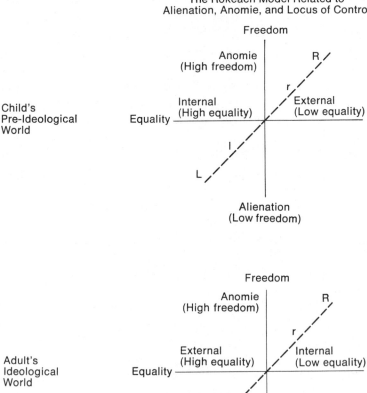

bility to the strongest feelings of alienation and the greatest fear
of too little freedom. This figure does not account for the way
far left joins far right in *de*valuing freedom, but it would
account for the position of liberalism being short of the far extreme.

The relationship of locus of control to "equality" is more
complex. We place "equality" along the *horizontal* axis to

depict a "leveling" that the concept conveys. We then project a use of our hypothesis, outlined in Chapter Twelve, that locus of control undergoes a reverse over the transition from child to adult. Within the child's world, we hypothesize the encouraging of a sense of an *internal* locus of control in the embryonic liberal by parents who exhibit delight in what is already within him, as expressed by his spontaneous behavior of self-discovery. There is also not the gulf between child and parent in this situation, suggesting more of a basic equality in their relationship than in the traditional parent-child hierarchy. In contrast is the placement of the embryonic conservative at the opposite end of the horizontal axis. Repeatedly the child's own diverse impulses are checked, and limiting requirements of *external* standards are forced upon him or her in situations in which the obvious *in*-equalities are emphasized—she is little, they are big; he is weak, they are powerful; she is uncoordinated and inarticulate, they move with incredible ease and communicate in a sophisticated foreign language.

For both "pre-left" and "pre-right" childhoods the moderate positions would be modifications of the rationale developed for the extremes, with placements along the diagonal as indicated. As a whole, it is not an ideal arrangement, but it may be a useful beginning in the right direction.

As the child moves to adulthood, we hypothesize a reversal in locus of control. For the liberal, the locus of control, which, as a child he identified as within himself, seems to have shifted to an externality. For the conservative, the locus of control, which as a child, he identified as exterior to himself, seems to have shifted to an internality. The reasons for this apparent shift remain to be determined; perhaps the equality the adult liberal values relates to externality and the inequality the adult conservative values relates to internality of locus of control.

This much ventured, we seem to face even greater difficulties in relating "equality" and "freedom" to our four-dimensional model of ideological personality. An entry thought is to return to the polarity of the norm changer versus the norm maintainer, which we have articulated at such length. If one applies the norm-changing-maintaining system to our problem, suddenly "freedom" becomes conceptually manageable. For we may now view "freedom" as obviously the leeway needed by us for expanding, changing, and, if necessary, destroying and replacing the prevailing norms in our unending search for new stimuli to sustain life and thought. (It is also our mandate to find new *forms* to regulate ourselves). Certainly this idea is the thrust of the meaning of "freedom" for its most articulate champions—expressed by Socrates' speech to the Athenians during the trial in which he was condemned to death, or by Jefferson's feeling that the "tree of liberty must be refreshed from time to time with the blood of patriots and tyrants."

However, if "freedom" is norm violating in essence, and thereby logically also left in direction, how may we reconcile this with the *conservative* valuing of freedom? A short possible answer is this. Although freedom is norm violating and left-directional in the abstract, in reality it is valued by both the norm changing liberal and norm maintaining conservative because of their functional interdependency in the "mature," "free" social system represented by democracy. That is, although liberal and conservative are attuned to their respective ideologies, *they are also attuned to one another as "shareholders" in an "open" social system dependent on a probing interaction of both norm maintenance and norm violation for its health.* We will return to this theme, which we believe to be exceptionally important, in our last chapter. In contrast, then, with this mutual valuing of freedom by liberals and conservatives, far left and far right do not value freedom because it tends to be dysfunctional in the "immature," "closed" social system represented by dictatorship or autocracy, in which social order must be maintained more by the fiat of the elite than by a fluid consensus of mass and elite.

"Equality" is not quite as open to the direct conjecture. And yet here again it is possible to clarify our thought by viewing this concept as though it were—to convey its fragility within history—a bird on wing within the mountainous perspective of norm-changing and norm-maintaining. Over thousands of years now the world's major religions have agreed upon equality, or the brotherhood of man, as an ideality societies should attempt to realize. Over a few hundred years, the pressuring of governmental process (for example, Civil Rights laws) has also been directed to this end. However, although equality has repeatedly been stated as the ideal, the social reality has always been an inequality that at best is only modified, never eradicated. This hard fact of life then shapes the action of liberal versus conservative on the equality issue. No matter what the individual reality, or social system, or historical period may be, the prevailing norms regulating emotion, thought, and behavior are mainly based on the inequalities of reality rather than the equalities of ideality. Driven by the ideal of equality, the liberal is then motivated to change—and the leftist to violate and if necessary destroy—the prevailing norms in quest of this better world. Conservative and rightist, however, like both the lords and peasants of Pieter Brueghel's alternately mad and sturdy world, are most deeply motivated by the need to maintain the prevailing norms that bind together the existing social order. Thus they are driven to devalue equality because the idea contradicts both their accurate perception of reality and their sense of the norm-maintainer's ideological mission.

Toward a Dialectical Theory

Throughout this book we have referred to dialectics or dialectical theory in ways no doubt baffling to anyone who might assume this indicates some old form of "suspect Marxism." (The truth is, of course, that within psychology speaking of dialectical theory simply indicates that one has decided to extend the sanctified ideas of interactions or transactions into something more usefully complex.) Worse yet are the likely feelings of the dialectical thinker who finds tantalizing bits and scraps here and there, but no attempt to tie them together in his or her terms.

We will not attempt a dialectical theoretical integration for a very practical reason. It cannot be done without an exploration of the psychological meanings of "middleness" at least half again as long as this book. Consequently, we will do this in a companion book to be called *The Psychology of the Middle*.

In dialectical terms, this book defines the right and left polarities—thesis and antithesis, if you will. To do this it has concentrated almost exclusively on the area of psychological studies known as the psychology of personality. The companion book will define the area of the middle—or the synthesis—as well as other options. This will take us beyond the boundaries of the study of personality into the social psychology of small groups and group dynamics, and also initially into the sociology of the relation of right, left and middle to history and social change.

Fortunately, it isn't necessary to have all this done in order to apply what has already been articulated to the ultimate problem of our time. In keeping with questions that initiated this survey, we again ask: What does the future hold for us? Is there anything we can do about it? To these questions, we devote our concluding chapter.

14

Beyond the "End of Ideology"

W_e have examined past and present to define the psychology of ideology. What now of the doubtful future toward which we rush? Let us see where we have been so we may stand on firm conceptual ground in gazing ahead.

We opened this study with a consideration of the insights of Hegel, Marx, and other giants not just to pay the customary obeisance to the past. We returned to their thought because it seemed to us it had strengths that have been lost and which must be regained if, as we move into the unknown future, we are to use our minds as searchlights rather than as flickering candles. Their views of the psychology of ideology included the idea of forces within and immediately surrounding the *person* which we have examined as the "core" and "periphery" to ideological personality. This is the realm of contemporary psychology. But beyond the immediacy of the individual and his nearby environment, Marx, Pareto, and Weber were sensitive to

213

the motivational influence of our larger *situation* in social space
and historical time. This is the realm of contemporary sociology, economics, political science, anthropology, and history.
Additionally, the great "ideologists" were sensitive to the generally overlooked aspect of *task*, or the person and situation-
shaping impact of intervention, will, intentionality, that is, the
passionate thrust of one's physical being linking us to our environment not solely as passive receivers, but as actors, changers,
innovators, or stabilizers. This is the realm of contemporary
leadership and management. Lastly—and most importantly—the
great ideologists understood the psychology of ideology as not
confined to any one of these aspects, but as the embodiment of
all three in the living personality, in each of us, aware of ourselves as caring and holistically meaningful entities existing in a
particular place at a definite point in time.

In our first chapter, we noted that this holistic sense of the
psychology of ideology was not solely the property of the
scholarly founders of social science. Actually it emerged earlier
among such scholarly political leaders and business managers as
Franklin, Jefferson, and Hamilton, who, in forming a government, articulated in action what the founders of social science
were later to write about. We have then in the background to
the future of ideology this past wherein both social scientist and
social practitioner viewed its psychology as Lewin (1935) visualized the operation of personality: as a composite of *person,
situation,* and *task*. We noted the decline of this holism as
through the pressure of bureaucratization and specialization
both the realm of scholarship and the arena for leadership and
management were chopped into ever more isolated and dis-
parate pieces. Specific to our concern was the outcome of a
psychology of ideology divorced not only from the sociology,
economics, and even the political science of ideology, but—of
much greater practical importance—divorced from the science
of leadership and management.

That this phenomenon was only a gust within a more general whirlwind of disintegration is suggested by innumerable
insights. In 1905, historian Henry Adams was predicting that
within this century "explosives would reach cosmic violence" as
part of an accelerating upheaval in which "disintegration would

overcome integration" (Mumford, 1944, p. 392). Weber's dark prophecy of the course bureaucratization was to take is the great sociological development of this theme. Another sensitive to this phenomenon was the Irish poet-politician William Butler Yeats, who perceived that "things fall apart; the center cannot hold." In the 1940s and 1950s these visions of disintegration received their ultimate manifestation in the exploding of atom and hydrogen bombs, which threatened human survival and symbolized the more general problem of an ungovernable technology. It hardly seems coincidental that shortly thereafter, throughout the world scholars were debating the possible end to practically everything meaningful to humanity. Within "proper" and "fringe" religions, the discussions were of the death of God, the impending end to the world, and the coming of Armageddon. Within physical or "hard" science, the ethical question was of responsibility for the possible end of civilization. Within social or "soft" science, the journals reverberated with the conflict over perceptions of an end of ideology.

The Splitting of Psychological and Sociological Man

The "end of ideology" debate is of increasing interest within the context of this study from the perspective of both manifest and latent meanings. As we noted in Chapter One, the designation by Lipset (1959) and Bell (1960) of this as an issue for rational discourse prompted an incredible number of papers, which attempted to define what ideology actually was and produced the odd contention that it was disappearing because society was successfully solving all its problems. The enduring general thrust to "end of" views, however, was that ideology was disappearing because it was no longer an adequate promotional or governing mechanism. Emotion- and value-laden ideologies of fascism, conservatism, liberalism, communism, were being replaced by a nonideological pragmatism forced on leaders and managers by the nature of our political, economic, and social tasks, which ostensibly had been narrowed by historical and technological developments to those that could only be successfully solved by the "pure" rationality of technocrats.

While this manifest face to the issue was engaging many

intellects, it seems to have been only the tip of an iceberg. One aspect latent beneath the surface of the debate was testimony in itself to the persisting power of right-left ideology in man. If one examines the papers of the "end of ideology" debate merely as an exercise in sorting technique, it will be found they fall into stacks expressive of three viewpoints: the ostensibly reluctant conservative (Bell, Lipset), the infuriated and unregenerate liberal (Horowitz, 1968, and Harrington, 1965), and the moderating middle, or those attempting to balance left against right. Aside from the truth or justice of any of the three positions, at the heart of a debate about the end of ideology may be found this evidence of the persistence of both the situational constraints and the basic personality needs that produce heated ideological alignments. ("It was fun while it lasted," the conservatives seem to be saying in these papers, "but ideology—that is, the left—is dead because its goals of equality and freedom are being realized without it." "Not so, not so," the left screams: "How can you be so smug? Open your eyes and look around you.")

While this dissent and uncertainty prevailed in sociology and political science, within psychology both experimentalists and theoretricians were finding increasing support for the persistence of right-left ideology in the individual. Among the core works were those we have examined in this study: the investigations of Adorno, Frenkel-Brunswik, Levinson, Sanford and associates into the nature of the right (Adorno and others, 1950); Rokeach's (1960, 1973) dogmatism and core values of both right and left; Eysenck's (1954, 1972) gradations from right to left, as well as William James' old, closely related dimension of the tough- versus the tenderminded; Tomkins' (1963, 1965) basic division, across all knowledge and affective functioning, of right, left, or middle orientations; Maslow's (1968) internal motivational scheme that moves from rightist "defense" to leftist "growth" needs; Wilson's (1973) cross-cultural generality of the left-right separation on a dimension of conservatism; and our own attempt to integrate these and a wide range of personality, social-psychological, and historical studies within a norm-maintaining-violating theoretical perspective employing core and peripheral functions.

What now seems to be incontrovertible substantiation of a persistence of ideology on one level of psychosocial functioning, however, only adds to the mystery. For if it is true that ideology in man is unabating, why was it thought to be ending? We feel the answer to this question is of importance not only for clarifying the nature of ideological man, but for understanding our place in history and the requirements of the tasks of our time for scholarship and for political, economic, social, and educational leadership.

We have noted evidence for the endurance of ideology in *psychological man.* The observation of the "end of ideology" was made, however, mainly by sociologists and political scientists observing *sociological and political man.* From this quite different perspective they did see, in fact, beyond debate, the particular kind of ending which Bell (1960) so clearly stated as the most pertinent manifest content at the outset. They saw that throughout the last century and into the 1930s, highly articulated and emotionally charged systems expressing right versus left beliefs drove our political, economic, and social world like the pumping pistons of some giant engine. Since the 1930s, however, the power of such overriding or superstructural ideologies has declined. The transformation of the communist ideology in Russia is characteristic. In the historical progression of Marx, Lenin, Trotsky, Stalin, Khrushchev, Brezhnev, we may see the progressive shift from a leadership concern with conceptual (ideological) to operational (seemingly nonideological) realities. Thus we arrive at one answer to an apparent contradiction: Although ideology is declining in the relations among organizations, states, and nations, as perceived by sociologists, ideology in the person as documented by psychologists, still operates unabated within the psychology of the individual.

Beginning to describe this state leads to a much more important question. What can be the meaning of this separation we detect between ideology in social and in psychological man? Earlier we noted how the perspectives of Hegel, Nietzsche, Marx, Pareto, and Weber relate to Lewin's view of personality as a function of *person, situation,* and the nature of the *task* at hand. The overwhelming tendency for psychological study, as we have shown, is to find the ideological *person* as essentially unchanged. But if we raise our gaze from the person to his *situation* today in history, we find so many changes taking place that few can discern the future beyond their own doorstep or plot the course of political, economic, or social leadership beyond the daily agenda. A major reason for this state of uncertainty, we suspect, is that whereas the ideology of personality remains fixed in physiology, culture, and the small-group situation, sociological and political ideology is for the time being adrift because of an epochal change in our larger social situation and the *task* requirements for local, national, and world leadership. It was a sensing of this gap, we feel, that subconsciously motivated all parties to the "end to ideology" debate. For beneath the surface differences, one encounters something transcending the individual, enlisting at times the passionate concern of left, right and "middle." We feel that all parties to the "debate" sensed an inconsistency and a discontinuity of possibly great historical import.

Portents of a "Third Shift" in Ideological Style

That we are in the midst of such a discontinuity has been perceived by numerous sensitive observers, for example, Bell (1967), Kahn (1967), Fuller (1969), Gorney (1972). For our purposes the most relevant observations are those of Lewis Mumford, who, as part of his remarkable multivolume, integrative study of the condition and future of humanity, written over thirty years ago in 1944, noted that the "world crisis that has existed for the lifetime of a whole generation indicates that a radical shift in the direction of social movement has taken place. . . . The external change may be summed up in a brief sentence: an age of expansion is giving place to an age of equilibrium. The achievement of this equilibrium is the task of the next few centuries" (Mumford, 1944, p. 398).

It is only speculation, of course, but the more I examine the past through the works of Mumford and others from the perspective of ideological personality, the more I become convinced of another aspect to this shift: that in deviating from a liberalistic expansion toward a more conservative equilibrium, we have likely embarked on the third fundamental shift in the function and styles of ideology in the history of mankind. As any good summary of history makes apparent (for example, Toynbee, 1947), our early history was dominated by the right ideology—so much so, that for thousands of years the liberal alternative was seen as little more than a strange form of insanity that occasionally seized dirty holy men and misguided rulers. Beginning with such figures as Akhenaton in Egypt, Socrates in Greece, and Jesus in Palestine, the liberal ideals of freedom and equality gained an articulation and a respectability that increased through the Renaissance and Reformation to the leftward triumph of the industrial, American, and French revolutions. But with the Russian and Chinese revolutions in the early years of this century we surmise that a third major shift in direction began, for here the alien left spark was engulfed by cultures with a conservative and authoritarian base. A sharp jolt came with the faltering of the left and the rapid regression of Germany to ultraright barbarism under Hitler. Then during the 1970s came a new cumulation of problems testing the socially free systems' capacity for governance—pollution, corruption, economic disorder, urban decay, crime waves, and the most bitter pill for those industrialized nations spoiled by the historic rewards of the leftward thrust, the first great pinch of worldwide scarcity. Both the scholar and the man in the street have sensed—and among the best of us the anguish is profound—that the youth of our liberality may be coming to an end. However much we may wish to journey on to the New Jerusalem, we seem to have entered a darker time when, with an intensity of pressure that once launched the liberal venturing, the requirements of situation and task seem to call for a new ideology. Let us try to assess what it may be.

Of Passion, Dispassion, and the Future

Our starting point is the assumption of the reality of this split between psychological and sociological man as we have described it. On one hand, there is the structural fixity of a left versus right (growth versus defense, stimulus seeking versus stimulus reduction) motivational system in psychological man. This does not imply we are stereotypically "fixed" for life as liberals or conservatives. Rather, there exists this left-right *system* within each of us, the general thrust of which is subject to modification by a variety of forces over our lives. This system operates more or less within a majority of adults, but particularly within leadership elites. Counterposed to this relative fixity in psychological man, however, is the contemporary *fluidity* of sociological man. While psychological man remains a relatively solid entity within the protective shell of physiology, sociological man is afloat in a turbulent sea of changing norms, customs, values, institutions, philosophies, and technologies, many of which are decaying, some undergoing renewal, all bewilderingly fluid during a time of the vast rip tide of disintegration clashing with the renewing surge of integration.

This split between psychological and sociological man is actually nothing new. An examination of history suggests this must happen at all the great watershed times—the transitional centuries between the Old, Middle, and New Kingdoms of the Egyptian dynasties, or the fourth, eleventh, fifteenth, eighteenth, and now the twentieth century in Western history. An examination of our own personal developmental histories also suggests this split occurs during transitional times such as leaving home for college, leaving college for the world of work, leaving the work world for retirement. What is special about this phenomenon in our time, we feel, is that it underlies and coincides with what may be seen as a "third shift" in ideological style for humanity.

We may then visualize sociological man as searching for settlement, for new terra firma or a safe island of norms and institutions shored up against the turbulence of a transitional time. Correspondingly, we may visualize psychological man as also seeking settlement, in this case the reunion and wholeness of our psychological and sociological sides characteristic of times of a benign balance, such as existed during the earlier years of the Old Kingdom in Egypt, the stable years of the Roman Empire, in pre-white Polynesia, or contemporary Switzerland. This wholeness was conceptualized by Ruth Benedict

(1970) and Maslow (1968) as the self-actualizing alignment of personal and societal goals they termed synergistic.

Such a search for wholeness is not conducted by the useful abstractions of psychological and sociological "man," of course. It must have specific human agents. Although the scholars who perceive and articulate these tasks serve as such agents, of far greater importance is another type of agent who usually is not adept at perceiving or articulating this mission, but who, through intuition derived from his role in society, shapes our future. This agent is the leader and the manager, who, acting as part of and with the support of an elite and at times the mass, either succeeds or fails in shaping the course of the future to his group's advantage. And so we again encounter how crucial to our future is the matter of leadership styles and management philosophies.

It will be apparent that we have opened the doors to some questions too large to answer in these final paragraphs. We can, however, state tentative conclusions. One is that, contrary to the optimistic projections of some of the "end to ideology" theorists, if the "third shift" is to *non*ideological or wholly *dispassionate* leadership styles, we may face the gravest danger yet.

During times of rootlessness and ideological drift, such as we are now experiencing—when both a people and its leaders have lost a clear sense of political, economic, and social ends—there emerges a certain role and style of leadership, which, like a ready-made suit, is filled by a certain kind of person. This is the leadership of unmitigated expediency, whereby leaders become immersed in means and blind to ends. The Nixon-Watergate disaster of the 1970s was prototypical. Both conservatism and liberalism were trumpeted along President Nixon's primrose path to doom, but underneath it all there was no real ideology, only the expediency of a small and fearful man trying to masquerade as a fully functional human being and influencing others to cater to and ape his style. History shows that the good leader need be neither an intellectual giant nor a saint vibrating to the social plight. George Washington, for example, was neither. History does indicate, however, that in addition to possessing the fierce willpower necessary to gain and maintain leadership, our leaders must be reasonably *whole* people, with fully functioning hearts and minds. Tomkins (1965) defines the ideoaffective base to ideology as the resonation of heart and mind to a changing reality. This suggests that whether or not it is liberal, or conservative, or middle, or an amalgam, the good and the great leadership of the future must possess the integrity —or reasonably predictable wholeness—of an ideology.

"The problem of the future is not ideology but technicians," religious historian Martin Marty remarked after pondering the Watergate debacle. He saw it as a symptom of twentieth-century "amorality—a combination of technology, propaganda, and administrative mentality; the kind of danger Kafka and Orwell warned us of." Hitler's industrial commissar, Albert Speer, held conventional political views and was a family man, "but Speer lacked any psychological and spiritual ballast. Our problem now is a general beliefflessness, a nonideological commitment to the system," Marty warned (1973, p. 78). It is, in short, the mind-blowing danger of the technology of the computer, television, and atomic power controlled by the means-immersed and *in*humanist technocrat that threatens in this direction.

If, then, the passions of ideology may not only be desirable, but necessary for the survival of humanism, what is our likely option? What style could we be moving toward if positive developmental trends are to shape the "third shift"? As Darwin made evident, all organisms must adapt to environmental change if they are to survive. Our environment is telling us that disintegration is outrunning integration—that unchecked, planless, and runaway growth piles problems upon humanity that are beyond both our past and present leadership and management capacities. With this grim overriding pressure in mind, it seems that to alleviate our troubles and meet the survival requirements of the times, we are now engaged in a shift from a dominantly expansive, venturing, growth-oriented leftward direction to a new kind of middle direction, composed not simply of an absence, uncertainty, averaging, or compromising of ideology, but of a new synthesis of left and right.

Such a possibility has many implications for leadership

styles. One leadership attribute suggested by such a synthesis of left and right would be a recognition of the need, according to the dictates of time and place, for stimulus seeking as well as stimulus reduction, for norm violation as well as norm maintenance. At its best, this would not be an unpredictably chameleon or protean style of leadership. Rather, it would be based on respect for the integrity of the passionate poles of left and right within the moderating periphery of liberalism and conservatism. Among the attributes of the concomitant management strategy would be a "semipassionate" advancement toward political, economic, and social goals by balancing the requirements for controlling and managing the system with the need to nurture and encourage its capacity for venturing.

Some will say this is an impossible task. They will say the only logical trend is to succumb wholly to the passion of either left or right. They will contend that this inevitable choice determines dominantly right or left management styles. They will further say mankind cannot endure the mush of any "middlistic" compromises. But the styles of a functionally interrelated right and left have been used successfully for thousands of years by heads of households in raising children, by tribal chieftains, by the leaders of religious orders, by management elites in all ages and cultures. Further, this is the leadership style and the management strategy implicit in the founding of the United States. Our documentary evidence includes a Declaration of Independence and a Constitution reflecting the left-right-middle synthesis of the views of Jefferson, Hamilton, Madison, Franklin, Washington, and the rest of that stellar company.

The difference today is that if this style and strategy is to be effective, it must operate in more of both the capitalist- and communist-dominated and the developed and underdeveloped world. Moreover, this must be done in places and during a time no longer open to the fresh adolescent lift of a new venture in social management. Somehow it must come to be through a renewal of vigor and vision out of, worldwide, a scarred and doubtful middle age. Can it be done? It is our own conviction this depends primarily on the extent to which American and world higher education can mobilize itself, not solely for the willy-nilly gathering of a veneer of knowledge, and the casual imparting of a little work competence, but for the *training of responsible and humanistic leadership.*

But even with a rapid expansion and strengthening of the training of such leadership, are not the problems that press in upon us so great that we are still doomed? The story of evolution probably contains as many instances of organisms that failed as succeeded in adapting to the challenge of the environment. It is hard to believe, however, that a creature as ingenious and as young in history as the human being, would, at this still early juncture, fail to adapt. Moreover, within the psychology of ideology there is evidence of something hopeful working within us relevant both to the "third shift" we envisage and the future societies it could lead to beyond this difficult transitional age. This is the existence within human beings of a psychological dynamism driving us toward maturity, which long ago Hegel, Marx, and Freud discerned, and which Maslow has rearticulated in modern times. "It is therefore useful to think of growth or lack of it as the resultant of a dialectic between growth-fostering forces and growth-discouraging forces (regression, fear, pains of growth, ignorance). Growth has both advantages and disadvantages. Nongrowing has not only disadvantages, but also advantages. The future pulls, but so also does the past" (Maslow, 1968, p. 204).

In other words, both left and right styles are necessary if we are to successfully cope with our personal as well as social futures. Within ourselves and our societies, these two sides to human nature can work together, sharing and alternating functions, or they can work against each other, as implacable parties to eternal warfare. And what is the goal toward which this interaction drives us? "At the level of self-actualizing," Maslow ventured, "many dichotomies become resolved, opposites are seen to be unities and the whole dichotomous way of thinking is recognized to be immature" (1968, p. 207). Hegel's vision, cited earlier, was of the self-actualizing society in which "man as man is free."

This ageold prospect tempts us to believe in its social inevitability. But it will not come to be unaided. As in our lives as individuals, what happens to us socially still seems to depend on the quality of our decisions—or upon the kind of leadership we develop within ourselves and support externally.

References

Abcarian, G. "Romantics and Renegades: Political Defection and the Radical Left." *Journal of Social Issues,* 1971, *27,* 123-139.

Abramowitz, S. I. "Internal-External Control and Social-Political Activism: A Test of the Dimensionality of Rotter's Internal-External Scale." *Journal of Consulting and Clinical Psychology,* 1973, *40,* 196-201.

Adorno, T. W., Frenkel-Brunswik, E., Levinson, D. J., and Sanford, R. N. *The Authoritarian Personality.* New York: Harper & Row, 1950.

Alker, H. A. "Social Psychological Explanations for Political Attitude Polarization." A paper presented during the sixty-seventh annual meeting of the American Political Science Association. Chicago, Sept. 7-11, 1971.

Alker, H. A., and Kogan, N. "Effects of Norm-Oriented Group Discussion on Individual Verbal Risk-Taking and Conservatism." *Human Relations,* 1968, *21,* 393-405.

Alker, H. A., and Poppen, P. J. "Personality and Ideology in University Students." *Journal of Personality,* 1973, *41.*

André, J. "Toward a Psychological Theory of Politics." Unpublished manuscript. Department of Psychology, California State University, Sacramento, California, 1976.

Asch, S. E. *Social Psychology*. Englewood Cliffs, N.J.: Prentice-Hall, 1952.

Bandura, A., and Walters, R. H. *Social Learning and Personality Development*. New York: Holt, Rinehart and Winston, 1963.

Barron, F. *Creative Person and Creative Process*. New York: Holt, Rinehart and Winston, 1969.

Bauer, R. "The Obstinate Audience." *American Psychologist*, 1964, *19,* 319-328.

Bell, D. "Columbia and the New Left." *The Public Interest,* 1968, Fall, 52-73.

Bell, D. *The End of Ideology*. New York: Free Press, 1960.

Bell, D. "Notes on the Post-Industrial Society." *Public Interest,* Winter and Spring, 1967.

Benedict, R., Maslow, A., and Honigman, J. "Synergy: Some Notes of Ruth Benedict." *American Anthropologist,* April 1970, 320-333.

Bennis, W. G. Beyond Bureaucracy: *Essays in the Development and Evolution of Human Organization*. New York: McGraw-Hill, 1973.

Bettelheim, B. *The Empty Fortress: Infantile Autism and the Birth of Self*. New York: Free Press, 1967.

Block, J. *Lives Through Time*. New York: Bancroft, 1971.

Boocock, S. S., and Schild, E. O. (Eds.). *Simulation Games in Learning*. Beverly Hills, Calif.: Sage Publications, 1968.

Boulding, K. *Primer on Social Dynamics*. New York: Free Press, 1970.

Brengelmann, J. C. "Extreme Response Set, Drive Level, and Abnormality in Questionnaire Rigidity." *Journal of Mental Science,* 1960, *106,* 171-186.

Brim, O. G., Jr., and Hoff, D. B. "Individual Situational Differences in Desire for Certainty." *Journal of Abnormal and Social Psychology,* 1957, *54,* 225-229.

Brown, R. *Social Psychology*. New York: Free Press, 1965.

Carlson, R., and Levy, N. "Self, Values and Affects: Derivations from Tomkins' Polarity Theory." *Journal of Personality and Social Psychology,* 1970, *16,* 338-345.

Cattell, R. B. *The Scientific Analysis of Personality*. Baltimore, Md.: Penguin, 1965.

Christie, R. "Eysenck's Treatment of the Personality of Communists." *Psychological Bulletin,* 1956, *53,* 411-430.

Christie, R., Friedman, L., and Ross, A. "New Left Scale." In J. P. Robinson and P. R. Shaver (Eds.), *Measures of Social Psychological Attitudes.* Ann Arbor, Mich.: Institute for Social Research, University of Michigan, 1969.

Christie, R., and Geis, F. *Studies in Machiavellianism.* New York: Academic Press, 1970.

Christie, R., and Jahoda, M. *Studies in the Scope and Method of "The Authoritarian Personality."* New York: Free Press, 1954.

Coleman, J. S. "Conflicting Theories of Social Change." *American Behavioral Scientist,* 1971, *14* (5), 633-650.

Comrey, A. L. *EITS Manual for the Comrey Personality Scales.* San Diego, Calif.: Educational and Industrial Testing Service, 1970.

Comrey, A. L., and Newmeyer, J. A. "Measurement of Radicalism-Conservatism." *Journal of Social Psychology,* 1965, *67,* 357-369.

Cowdry, R., Keniston, K., and Cabin, S. "The War and Military Obligations." *Journal of Personality,* 1970, *38,* 525-549.

Cronbach, L. *Essentials of Psychological Testing.* (2nd ed.) New York: Harper & Row, 1970.

Dalkey, N. C. (Ed.). *Studies in the Quality of Life: Delphi and Decision Making.* Lexington, Mass.: Heath, 1972.

Damarin, F., and Messick, S. "Response Styles as Personality Variables: A Theoretical Integration of Multivariate Research." *Research Bulletin,* RB-65-10. Princeton, N.J.: Educational Testing Service, 1965.

De Fronzo, J. "Religion and Humanitarianism in Eysenck's T Dimension and Left-Right Political Orientation." *Journal of Personality and Social Psychology,* 1972, *21,* 265-269.

de Jouvenel, B. *The Art of Conjecture.* New York: Basic Books, 1967.

Deutsch, M., and Collins, M. *Interracial Housing.* Minneapolis: University of Minnesota Press, 1951.

Dollard, J., and Miller, N. *Personality and Psychotherapy.* New York: McGraw-Hill, 1950.

Dunlap, R. "Radical and Conservative Student Activists: A

Comparison of Family Backgrounds." *Pacific Sociological Review,* 1970, *13,* 171-181.

Durkheim, E. *Suicide.* New York: Free Press, 1951.

Eckhardt, W., and Alcock, N. Z. "Ideology and Personality in War/Peace Attitudes." *Journal of Social Psychology,* 1970, *81,* 105-116.

Edwards, A. L. *Statistical Analysis.* New York: Holt, Rinehart and Winston, 1958.

Erikson, E. *Identity: Youth and Crisis.* New York: Norton, 1968.

Etzioni, A. *The Active Society.* New York: Free Press, 1968.

Eysenck, H. *The Dynamics of Anxiety and Hysteria.* London: Routledge and Kegan Paul, 1957.

Eysenck, H. *The Psychology of Politics.* London: Routledge and Kegan Paul, 1954.

Eysenck, H., and Coulter, T. "The Personality and Attitudes of Working Class British Communists and Fascists." *Journal of Social Psychology,* 1972, *87,* 59-73.

Feuer, L. *Conflict of Generations.* New York: Basic Books, 1969.

Finer, S. E. (Ed.). *Pareto's Sociological Writings.* New York: Praeger, 1966.

Flacks, R. "The Liberated Generation: An Exploration of the Roots of Student Protest." *Journal of Social Issues,* 1967, *23,* 52-75.

Fladeland, B. *James Gillespie Birney: Slaveholder and Abolitionist.* Ithaca, N.Y.: Cornell University Press, 1955.

Franklin, B. Letter to David Hartley, 1783. In *Life and Letters of Benjamin Franklin.* Eau Claire, Wis.: E. M. Hale, n.d.

Freud, S. *Civilization and Its Discontents.* London: Hogarth Press, 1946.

Freud, S. *Complete Introductory Lectures in Psychoanalysis.* New York: Norton, 1966.

Freund, J. *The Sociology of Max Weber.* New York: Random House, 1969.

Fromm, E. *Marx's Concept of Man.* New York: Ungar, 1961.

Fuller, B. *Utopia or Oblivion: The Prospects for Humanity.* New York: Bantam Books, 1969.

Gallup, G. *The Miracle Ahead.* New York: Harper & Row, 1966.

Gesell, A., and Ilg, F. L. *The Child from Five to Ten.* New York: Harper & Row, 1946.

Goffman, E. *The Presentation of Self in Everyday Life.* Garden City, N.Y.: Doubleday, 1959.

Gore, P. M., and Rotter, J. B. "A Personality Correlate of Social Action." *Journal of Personality,* 1963, *31,* 58-69.

Gorney, R. *The Human Agenda.* New York: Simon & Schuster, 1972.

Greenstein, F. I. *Children and Politics.* New Haven, Conn.: Yale University Press, 1965.

Greenstein, F. I., and Tarrow, S. *Political Orientations of Children: The Use of a Semi-Projective Technique in Three Nations.* Beverly Hills, Calif.: Sage Publications, 1970.

Guilford, J. P. *The Nature of Human Intelligence.* New York: McGraw-Hill, 1967.

Gurvitch, G. *Social Frameworks of Knowledge.* New York: Harper & Row, 1972.

Hageman, J. *History of Princeton and Its Institutions.* (2 vols.) Philadelphia: Lippincott, 1879.

Hamden-Turner, C. *Radical Man.* Cambridge, Mass.: Schenkman, 1970.

Hamilton, D. L. "Personality Attributes Associated with Extreme Response Style." *Psychological Bulletin,* 1968, *69* (3), 192-203.

Hamsher, J. H., Geller, J. D., and Rotter, J. B. "Interpersonal Trust, Internal-External Control, and the Warren Commission Report." *Journal of Personality and Social Psychology,* 1968, *9,* 210-215.

Harman, H. H. *Modern Factor Analysis.* (2nd ed.) Chicago: University of Chicago Press, 1967.

Harrington, M. *The Accidental Century.* New York: Macmillan, 1965.

Hays, W. L. *Statistics.* New York: Holt, Rinehart and Winston, 1963.

Helmer, O. *Social Technology.* New York: Basic Books, 1966.

Hicks, J. M., and Wright, J. H. "Convergent-Discriminant Validation and Factor Analysis of Five Scales of Liberalism-Conservatism." *Journal of Personality and Social Psychology,* 1970, *14,* 114-120.

Horowitz, I. L. "Another View from Our Left." In Waxman (Ed.), *The End of Ideology Debate.* New York: Crowell, 1968.

Hughes, T. L. "Why Kissinger Must Choose Between Nixon and the Country." *New York Times Magazine,* Dec. 30, 1973, p. 9.

Huxley, A. *Island.* New York: Harper & Row, 1962.

Jay, M. *The Dialectical Imagination: A History of the Frankfurt School and the Institute of Social Research.* Boston: Little, Brown, 1973.

Jones, E. "City Limits." In D. Shoemaker (Ed.), *With All Deliberate Speed.* New York: Harper & Row, 1957.

Kahn, H., and Wiener, H. J. *The Year 2000.* New York: Macmillan, 1967.

Kaufman, W. *Hegel: A Reinterpretation.* Garden City, N.Y.: Doubleday, 1965.

Kelman, H. "The Induction of Action and Attitude Change." In C. W. Backman and P. F. Secord (Eds.), *Problems in Social Psychology.* New York: McGraw-Hill, 1966.

Keniston, K. *The Uncommitted: Alienated Youth in American Society.* New York: Harcourt Brace Jovanovich, 1965.

Keniston, K. *Young Radicals.* New York: Harcourt Brace Jovanovich, 1968.

Kerlinger, F. H. "Progressivism and Traditionalism: Basic Factors of Educational Attitudes." *Journal of Social Psychology,* 1958, *48,* 111-135.

Klopfer, B., and Davidson, H. H. *Rorschach Technique: An Introductory Manual.* New York: Harcourt Brace Jovanovich, 1962.

Knutson, J. (Ed.) *The Handbook of Political Psychology.* San Francisco: Jossey-Bass, 1973.

Knutson, J. *The Human Basis of the Polity: A Study of the Psychology of Political Men.* Chicago: Aldine, 1972.

Kogan, N., and Wallach, M. A. *Risk Taking: A Study in Cognition and Personality.* New York: Holt, Rinehart and Winston, 1964.

Kogan, N., and Wallach, M. A. "Risk Taking as a Function of the Situation, the Person, and the Group." In *New Directions in Psychology III.* New York: Holt, Rinehart and Winston, 1967.

Kraut, R. E., Lewis, S. H., and Pepitone, A. "Generational Conflict and Continuity in Students' Political Ideologies." A paper in draft available from the senior investigator, University of Pennsylvania, 1973.

Kuhn, T. *The Structure of Scientific Revolutions.* Chicago: University of Chicago Press, 1962.

Lane, R. E. *Political Ideology.* New York: Free Press, 1962.

Lane, R. E., and Sears, D. O. *Public Opinion.* Englewood Cliffs, N.J.: Prentice-Hall, 1964.

Lasswell, H. D. *Power and Personality.* New York: Norton, 1948.

Lasswell, H. D. "The Selective Effect of Personality on Political Participation." In R. Christie and M. Jahoda (Eds.), *Studies in the Scope and Method of "The Authoritarian Personality."* New York: Free Press, 1954.

Lewin, K. *A Dynamic Theory of Personality.* New York: McGraw-Hill, 1935.

Lewin, K. *Field Theory in Social Science.* New York: Harper & Row, 1951.

Lewin, K. *Resolving Social Conflicts.* New York: Harper & Row, 1948.

Lewis, S. H., and Kraut, R. E. "Correlates of Student Political Activism and Ideology." *Journal of Social Issues,* 1972, *28,* 131-149.

Lipset, S. M. *Political Man: Essays on the Sociology of Democracy.* Garden City, N.Y.: Doubleday, 1959.

Lipset, S. M., and Schflander, G. M. *Passion and Politics: Student Activism in America.* Boston: Little, Brown, 1971.

Loëwith, K. *From Hegel to Nietzsche: The Revolution in 19th-Century Thought.* Garden City, N.Y.: Doubleday, 1967.

Loye, D. "Correlates and Dimensions of Political Ideology." Doctoral dissertation for the New School for Social Research. *Dissertation Abstracts International,* 1974, *35* (4). Available from Xerox University Microfilms, Ann Arbor, Michigan.

Loye, D. *The Healing of a Nation.* New York: Norton, 1971.

Loye, D. (Ed.) *Research at ETS.* Princeton, N.J.: Educational Testing Service, 1970.

Loye, D., and Rokeach, M. "Ideology, Belief Systems, Values, and Attitudes." In Wolman, B. (Ed.), *International Encyclopedia of Neurology, Psychiatry, Psychoanalysis, and Psychology.* New York: Van Nostrand Reinhold, in press.

Mann, H., Siegler, M., and Osmond, H. "The Psychotypology of Time." In H. Yakis, H. Osmond, and F. Cheek (Eds.), *The Future of Time.* Garden City, N.Y.: Doubleday, 1972.

Marty, M. "God and Watergate." *Time,* Dec. 17, 1973, p. 78.

Marx, K. "Thesis on Feuerbach." In R. Tucker (Ed.), *The Marx-Engels Reader.* New York: Norton, 1972.

Marx, K., and Engels, F. "The Communist Manifesto." In R. Tucker (Ed.), *The Marx-Engels Reader.* New York: Norton, 1972.

Maslow, A. "The Authoritarian Character Structure." *Journal of Social Psychology,* 1943, *18,* 401-411.

Maslow, A. *The Psychology of Science: A Reconnaissance.* New York: Harper & Row, 1966.

Maslow, A. *Toward a Psychology of Being.* (2nd ed.) New York: Van Nostrand Reinhold, 1968.

McClosky, H., and Schaar, J. H. "Psychological Dimensions of Anomy." *American Sociological Review,* 1965, *30,* 14-40.

McGregor, D. *The Human Side of Enterprise.* New York: McGraw-Hill, 1960.

McGuire, W. J. "Inducing Resistance to Persuasion." In L. Berkowitz (Ed.), *Advances in Experimental Social Psychology,* Vol. 1. New York: Academic Press, 1964.

McGuire, W. J. "The Nature of Attitudes and Attitude Change." In G. Lindzay and E. Aronson (Eds.), *The Handbook of Social Psychology,* Vol. 3. Reading, Mass.: Addison-Wesley, 1969.

Milgram, S. *Obedience to Authority: An Experimental View.* New York: Harper & Row, 1974.

Miller, G. A., Galanter, E., and Pribram, K. H. *Plans and the Structure of Behavior.* New York: Holt, Rinehart and Winston, 1960.

Miller, J. G. "Living Systems: The Organization." *Behavioral Science,* Jan. 1972, *17* (1).

Minard, R. "Race Relationships in the Pocahontas Coal Field." *Journal of Social Issues,* 1952, *8* (1).

Mogar, R. E. "Three Versions of the F Scale and Performance on the Semantic Differential." *Journal of Abnormal and Social Psychology,* 1960, *60,* 262-265.

Montagu, A. *The Direction of Human Development.* (rev. ed.) New York: Hawthorn, 1970.

Moscovici, S., and Zavalloni, M. "The Group as a Polarizer of Attitudes." *Journal of Personality and Social Psychology,* 1969, *12* (2), 125-135.

Mumford, L. *The Condition of Man.* New York: Harcourt Brace Jovanovich, 1944.

Mumford, L. *Interpretations and Forecasts: 1922-1972.* New York: Harcourt Brace Jovanovich, 1973.

Myrdal, G. *An American Dilemma.* New York: Harper & Row, 1962.

Nettler, G. "A Measure of Alienation." *American Sociological Review,* 1957, *22,* 670-677.

Newcomb, T. M., and others. *Persistence and Change: A College and Its Students after 25 Years.* New York: Wiley, 1967.

Nietzsche, F. "The Birth of Tragedy." In *The Complete Works of Friedrich Nietzsche,* Vol. 1. New York: Russell and Russell, 1964.

O'Donovan, D. "Rating Extremity: Pathology or Meaningfulness." *Psychological Review,* 1965, *72,* 358-372.

Orwell, G. *1984.* New York: New American Library, 1971.

Osgood, C. E. "Explorations in Semantic Space: A Personal Diary." *Journal of Social Issues,* 1971, *27,* 5-65.

Osgood, C. E., Suci, G. J., and Tannebaum, P. H. *The Measurement of Meaning.* Urbana: University of Illinois Press, 1957.

Packard, V. *The Status Seekers.* New York: McKay, 1959.

Parsons, T., and Shils, E. (Eds.). *Toward a General Theory of Action.* Cambridge, Mass.: Harvard University Press, 1952.

Parsons, T., Shils, E., Naegele, K. D., and Pitts, J. R. (Eds.). *Theories of Society.* New York: Free Press, 1965.

Peterson, R. E. *The Scope of Organized Student Protest in*

1967-1968. Princeton, N.J.: Educational Testing Service, 1968.

Pettigrew, T. F. "Personality and Sociocultural Factors in Intergroup Attitudes: A Cross-National Comparison." *Journal of Conflict Resolution,* 1958, *2,* 29-42.

Powdermaker, H. *Stranger and Friend: The Way of an Anthropologist.* New York: Norton, 1966.

Ray, J. J., and Sutton, A. J. "Alienation in an Australian University." *Journal of Social Psychology,* 1972, *86,* 319-320.

Reich, W. *Mass Psychology of Fascism.* New York: Farrar, Straus & Giroux, 1970.

Riegel, K. F. "From Traits and Equilibrium Toward Developmental Dialectics." In W. J. Arnold and J. K. Cole (Eds.), *1974-75 Nebraska Symposium on Motivation.* Lincoln: University of Nebraska Press, 1975.

Riegel, K. F. "Time and Change in the Development of the Individual and Society." In J. Gewirtz (Ed.), *Advances in Child Development and Behavior.* (vol. 7) New York: Academic Press, 1972.

Riesman, D., Glazer, N., and Denny, R. *The Lonely Crowd: A Study of the Changing American Character and Politics.* New Haven, Conn.: Yale University Press, 1952.

Robinson, J. P., Rusk, J. G., and Head, K. B. (Eds.). *Measures of Political Attitudes.* Ann Arbor, Mich.: Institute for Social Research, 1968.

Robinson, J. P., and Shaver, P. R. (Eds.). *Measures of Social Psychological Attitudes.* Ann Arbor, Mich.: Institute for Social Research, 1969.

Rokeach, M. "Long-Range Experimental Modification of Values, Attitudes and Behavior." *American Psychologist,* 1971, *26,* 453-459.

Rokeach, M. *The Nature of Human Values.* New York: Free Press, 1973.

Rokeach, M. *The Open and Closed Mind.* New York: Basic Books, 1960.

Rokeach, M., and Hanley, C. "Eysenck's Tender-Mindedness Dimension: A Critique." *Psychological Bulletin,* 1956, *53,* 169-176.

Rosenhan, D. "The Natural Socialization of Altruistic Autonomy." In J. Macoulay and L. Berkowitz (Eds.), *Altruism and Helping*. New York: Academic Press, 1969.

Rotter, J. B. "Generalized Expectancies for Internal Versus External Control of Reinforcement." *Psychological Monographs*, 1966, *80* (609), 1-28.

Rotter, J. B., Seeman, M., and Liverant, S. "Internal Versus External Control of Reinforcement: A Major Variable in Behavior Theory." In N. E. Washburne (Ed.), *Decisions, Values and Groups*. Elmsford, N.Y.: Pergamon Press, 1962.

Scammon, R., and Wattenburg, B. *The Real Majority*. New York: Coward-McCann, 1970.

Schlesinger, A., Sr. "The Tides of Politics." In *Paths to the Present*. Boston: Houghton Mifflin, 1964.

Schwartz, D. C. *Political Alienation and Political Behavior*. Chicago: Aldine, 1973.

Schweitzer, D. R., and Elden, J. M. "New Left as Right: Convergent Themes of Political Discontent." *Journal of Social Issues*, 1971, *27*, 141-166.

Selltiz, C., Jahoda, M., and Cook, W. *Research Methods in Social Relations*. (rev. ed.) New York: Holt, Rinehart and Winston, 1959.

Sherif, M. "On the Relevance of Social Psychology." *The American Psychologist*, 1970, *25*, 144-156.

Sherif, M. *Psychology of Social Norms*. New York: Octagon, 1965.

Silvern, L., and Nakamura, C. "Powerlessness, Social-Political Action, Social-Political Views: Their Interrelations Among College Students." *Journal of Social Issues*, 1971, *27*, 137-198.

Simon, H. A. *New Science of Management Decision*. New York: Harper & Row, 1960a.

Simon, H. A. *Sciences of the Artificial*. Cambridge, Mass.: M.I.T. Press, 1960b.

Smith, M. B. *Humanizing Social Psychology*. San Francisco: Jossey-Bass, 1974.

Snedecor, G. W., and Cochran, W. G. *Statistical Methods*. (6th ed.) Ames: Iowa State University Press, 1967.

Sorokin, P. *Sociological Theories of Today*. New York: Harper & Row, 1966.

Srole, L. "Social Integration and Certain Corollaries." *American Sociological Review,* 1956, *21,* 709-716.

Stagner, R. "Fascist Attitudes: Their Determining Conditions." *The Journal of Social Psychology*, 1936, *7,* 438-454.

Stouffer, S. A., Suchman, E. A., DeVinney, L. C., Star, S. A., and Williams, R. M., Jr. *The American Soldier: Adjustment During Army Life.* Princeton, N.J.: Princeton University Press, 1949.

Stouffer, S. A., and Toby, J. "Role Conflict and Personality." In T. Parsons and E. A. Shils (Eds.), *Toward a General Theory of Action.* Cambridge, Mass.: Harvard University Press, 1952.

Strickland, B. R. "The Prediction of Social Action from a Dimension of Internal-External Control." *Journal of Social Psychology,* 1965, *66,* 353-358.

Tajfel, H., and Wilkes, A. L. "Salience of Attributes and Commitment to Extreme Judgments in the Perception of People." *British Journal of Social and Clinical Psychology,* 1964, *3,* 40-49.

Theobald, R. *An Alternative Future for America.* Chicago: Swallow, 1968.

Thomas, L. E. "The I-E Scale, Ideological Bias, and Political Participation." *Journal of Personality,* 1970, *38,* 273-286.

Tomkins, S. S. "Affect and the Psychology of Knowledge." In S. S. Tomkins and C. Izard (Eds.), *Affect, Cognition and Personality.* New York: Springer, 1965.

Tomkins, S. S. "Left and Right: A Basic Dimension of Ideology and Personality." In R. W. White (Ed.), *The Study of Lives.* New York: Atherton Press, 1963a.

Tomkins, S. S. *The Negative Affects.* New York: Springer, 1963b.

Tomkins, S. S. *The Polarity Scale.* New York: Springer, 1966.

Tomkins, S. S. *The Positive Affects.* New York: Springer, 1962.

Tomkins, S. S., and Izard, C. (Eds.) *Affect, Cognition and Personality.* New York: Springer, 1965.

Toynbee, A. J. *A Study of History.* New York: Oxford University Press, 1947.

Triandis, H. C., and Triandis, L. M. "A Cross-Cultural Study of Social Distance." *Psychological Monographs,* 1962, *76* (21 whole no. 540).

Vasquez, J. "The Face and Ideology." Unpublished doctoral dissertation. Rutgers University, New Jersey, 1975.

Verba, A. *Small Groups and Political Behavior.* Princeton, N.J.: Princeton University Press, 1961.

Wallach, M. A., and Kogan, N. "Aspects of Judgment and Decision-Making: Interrelationships and Change with Age." *Behavioral Science,* 1961, *6,* 23-26.

Watts, W., and Free, L. A. *State of the Nation.* New York: Universe Books, 1973.

Waxman, C. I. (Ed.). *The End of Ideology Debate.* New York: Crowell, 1968.

Wells, H. G. *A Modern Utopia.* Lincoln: University of Nebraska Press, 1967.

Wheeler, H. *Democracy in a Revolutionary Era.* New York: Praeger, 1968.

White, B. J., and Harvey, O. J. "Effects of Personality and Own Stand on Judgment and Production of Statements About a Central Issue." *Journal of Experimental Psychology,* 1965, *1,* 334-347.

Wills, G. *Nixon Agonistes.* Boston: Houghton Mifflin, 1969.

Wilson, G. D. "Is There a General Factor in Social Attitudes?" *British Journal of Social and Clinical Psychology,* 1970, *9,* 101-107.

Wilson, G. D. (Ed.). *The Psychology of Conservatism.* New York: Academic Press, 1973.

Winter, D. G. *The Power Motive.* New York: Free Press, 1973.

Witkin, H. A., Dyk, R. B., Faterson, H. F., Goodenough, D. R., and Karp, S. A. *Psychological Differentiation.* New York: Wiley, 1962.

Zuckerman, N., Norton, J., and Sprague, D. S. "Acquiescence and Extreme Sets and Their Role in Tests of Authoritarianism and Parental Attitudes." *Psychiatric Research Reports,* 1958, *10,* 28-45.

Zuckerman, N., Oppenheimer, C., and Gershowitz, D. "Acquiescence and Extreme Sets of Actors and Teachers." *Psychological Reports,* 1965, *16,* 168-170.

Index